BANGKOK

after Dark

BANGKOK

after Dark

MAURICE ROCCO, TRANSNATIONAL

NIGHTLIFE, AND THE MAKING OF

COLD WAR INTIMACIES

Benjamin Tausig

Duke University Press   *Durham and London*   2025

Project Editor: Livia Tenzer
Cover designed by Matthew Tauch
Typeset in Garamond Premier Pro by Westchester Publishing Services

Library of Congress Cataloging-in-Publication Data
Names: Tausig, Ben, author.
Title: Bangkok after dark : Maurice Rocco, transnational nightlife, and
the making of cold war intimacies / Benjamin Tausig.
Description: Durham : Duke University Press, 2025. | Includes biblio-
graphical references and index.
Identifiers: LCCN 2024029873 (print)
LCCN 2024029874 (ebook)
ISBN 9781478031703 (paperback)
ISBN 9781478028475 (hardcover)
ISBN 9781478060680 (ebook)
Subjects: LCSH: Rocco, Maurice. | Pianists—Biography. | African
American jazz musicians—Biography. | Jazz musicians—United
States—Biography. | Expatriate musicians—Thailand. | Musicians—
United States. | African American gay people—Thailand—Bangkok. |
Nightlife—Thailand—Bangkok—History—20th century.
Classification: LCC ML417.R674T38 2025 (print) | LCC ML417.r674
(ebook) | DDC 786.2/165092 [B]—dc23/eng/20250211
LC record available at https://lccn.loc.gov/2024029873
LC ebook record available at https://lccn.loc.gov/2024029874

Cover art: Maurice Rocco in performance at the Oriental Hotel, Bangkok.
Courtesy of the Mandarin Oriental, Bangkok.

For Serena, Julius, and Mae, my family,
whose support and love I acknowledge

always

Contents

Note on Transliteration and Style

Thai names are Anglicized using a person's own preference, where known. Thai words are Anglicized using common convention whenever possible, regardless of transliteration system (such as *mor lam* for หมอลำ). In cases where there is no clear preference or convention for a name or word, I use a modified version of the Mary Haas transliteration system, with the primary aim of accommodating nonspecialist readers. Thai characters are included for titles, quotes, or individual words in cases where the original sense may be particularly helpful to have available.

I follow Viet Thanh Nguyen in using the term *American war in Vietnam* rather than the more common *Vietnam War* in order to identify this conflict with its primary aggressor, the United States.

The book uses endnotes for most citations, except for a handful of in-text acknowledgments, which appear as footnotes marked ACKNOWLEDGMENT.

Unless otherwise noted, all translations in this book are by the author.

INTRODUCTION
Acknowledgments

The only known recording of American jazz pianist Maurice Rocco playing in Bangkok was made on a Saturday night: January 30, 1965.[a] That evening,

---

a ACKNOWLEDGMENT: My thanks to the three anonymous readers of *Bangkok after Dark*. All provided rigorous, engaged comments that have improved the book immeasurably. Thanks as well to Duke University Press editor Ken Wissoker, who has been a tremendous reader and source of feedback and support, as well as to assistant editor Ryan Kendall, project editor Livia Tenzer, and copyeditor Iza Wojciechowska. Special thank you to James Cui, a developmental editor who guided late-stage revisions with genuine care and remarkable insight. Thanks also to the many friends and colleagues who offered expert advice on aspects of the research or manuscript (or simply listened to me ramble) over many years: Ray Anderson, Brooke Belisle, Jonathan Bollen, Matthew David Brounley, Chiranuch Premchaiporn, Lawrence Chua, Kameron Austin Collins, Alexandra Dalferro, Martin Daughtry, Kyle DeCoste, Peter Doolan, Duangkamon Wattanasak, Valerie Elliott, Fai Lamubon, Benjamin Foley, Danielle Fosler-Lussier, David French, Kaleb

Rocco led a small band at the Bamboo Bar, a venue inside the Oriental Hotel, which sits palatially along the river, on the eve of war in nearby Vietnam. But there is no hint of conflict or even tension on the tape, only joy and abundance. Rocco is backed by a drummer, Nonda "Peter" Buranasomphob, who in other moments played in a combo with the king of Thailand. Rocco banters with the crowd, then eases into a slow, soulful version of "Don't Worry 'bout Me," a jazz standard popularized by Cab Calloway and Billie Holiday in the 1930s. He follows with Duke Ellington's "Take the 'A' Train," written in 1939. Later comes "Darktown Strutter's Ball," Rocco's showpiece from the 1945 Hollywood film *Incendiary Blonde*. The scene on the tape seems borrowed from another time, if not another world. The looming war is nowhere.

The entire set features music from Rocco's long-ago commercial peak in the United States, by then almost twenty years past. Even in 1965 he never wavers from the dated styles of swing and boogie-woogie. Conjuring the nightclubs of postwar New York nine thousand miles away and two decades earlier, Rocco wields old-fashioned charm, imitating Satchmo's genial rasp, greeting the crowd in simple Thai, improvising jokes and lyrics, giving propers to Peter, switching tempos. He clicks his shoes in rhythm. "In 1940 my style was called 'boogie-woogie,'" Rocco told a Hong Kong reporter later in the year. "And basically, I haven't changed much since then."[1]

Throughout the tape the crowd thrums with the warmth of inebriation. The space of the Bamboo Bar was intimate, about twenty teak tables plus the bar, as Mongkorn Pikaew, another Thai drummer who played with Rocco in the 1970s, described the scene to me. There, Rocco played in a bubble where the heyday of the American nightclub could still be staged, however anachronistically: "His favorite song was 'As Time Goes By,'" a 1931 jazz standard, Mongkorn said. "He would come and play 100 percent standing. That was showmanship. They had a spotlight. He would stand in it and sing."[2]

Goldschmitt, Jesse Grayman, Denise Grollmus, Tyrell Haberkorn, Matías Hermosilla, Anthony Irwin, Peter Jackson, Kanjana Thepboriruk, Sohl Lee, Siv Lie, Katie Linden, Wyna Liu, Tamara Loos, Maureen Mahon, Wayne Marshall, Craig Mazin, Ryan Minor, Rachel Mundy, Nattapol Wisuttipat, David Novak, Keith O'Hara, Bob Orlowsky, Pahole Sook-kasikon, Parkorn Wangpaiboonkit, Robin Preiss, Maurice Restrepo, Thomas Lee Roberts, Serena Roth, Matt Sakakeeny, Shyam Sharma, Davindar Singh, Ryan Skinner, Norman Smith, Maria Sonevytsky, Emiko Stock, Sudina Paungpetch, Kelly Szott, Eng Kiong Tan, Lee Veeraraghavan, Yun Emily Wang, Yodh Warong, Ben Zimmer, and Eric Zolov. Many others are acknowledged throughout.

Mongkorn saw Rocco as he shined in Bangkok, not as he had in America earlier in the century. But the world in 1965 was no longer what it had been twenty years before, and Bangkok's Thanon Charoen Krung was very far from New York's 52nd Street. The symbols of Black queer performance that had signified so profoundly for Rocco in the 1940s meant something else to his listeners here. Such meetings of distant temporalities, aesthetics, bodies, and language typified Cold War nightlife in Thailand. These meetings became the grounds for new cosmopolitan worlds. This book is a study of those worlds. Rocco is a figure who might help us understand their shape, their history, and their stakes.

On that January night at the Bamboo Bar, Rocco and the crowd stared through their revelry toward a dark horizon, a decade-long quagmire in Vietnam that would claim countless lives and unsettle countless others. Rocco made Southeast Asia his home just as American troop arrivals in the region were set to begin. His career, abruptly uprooted from the United States, would soon be revived in Bangkok, where he would prosper. By the time Rocco came to Asia as an expatriate in 1964, the once-famous nightclub and film star had been almost completely forgotten in the United States, where he remains mostly forgotten today. Yet despite the vintage of the songs he played in Bangkok in 1965, Rocco's Bamboo Bar performance was no mere nostalgia tour. In fact, he was arguably as successful in Thailand as he had ever been in the United States, albeit on different terms.

To this point, consider that Rocco's Bamboo Bar tapes are now housed in the Doris Duke Audiovisual Collection, at Duke University, because the billionaire tobacco heiress personally recorded them. Doris Duke at that time was one of the richest people in the world. She was also a self-styled connoisseur of both jazz and Southeast Asia, where she actively traveled and collected art. In the early months of 1965 she visited Thailand with her boyfriend, the white American bebop pianist Joe Castro. Castro, Duke, and Duke Ellington had recently cofounded a small jazz label called Clover Records. Although their label would soon fold, at that moment the owners were busy scouting prospective artists. An archived receipt shows that during Duke's four-day stay at the Oriental Hotel, she rented a reel-to-reel tape machine, the very one she would use to record Rocco. The two had likely first met in 1943, near the height of Rocco's American fame, when he played a concert at the Duke family's opulent New Jersey farmstead. Duke was also a friend of former Oriental Hotel owner and silk magnate Jim Thompson. In short, Doris Duke was drawn to the bar that night by deep social ties. For someone so wealthy and connected, Bangkok was a premier city in the mid-1960s, and the Bamboo Bar was among its most distinguished social settings. Marlon Brando, Dinah Washington, Mick Jagger, Louis Armstrong, and many others would follow her to the same teak tables in the coming years. The bar had been built speculatively in the 1940s to host cosmopolitan encounters in a rapidly globalizing Thailand. By the time of Rocco's gig, the designers' vision had been fully realized. On that Saturday night in Thailand's cool season, Duke sat with a tape recorder, gripped like everyone around her by Rocco. A faded star in America, a specter of the past there, he had returned to high society elsewhere: in a Southeast Asian boomtown postmodernized by war.

How did the Thai capital develop this way, and so rapidly? And how can one make sense of the central position of non-Thais, including a Black American expatriate, in the country's dramatic transformation? How might Rocco's individual story of displacement from the United States, and his arrival in Thai nightlife, help illuminate the dynamics of greater geopolitical shifts that entangled Southeast Asia and the West during the Cold War?

The Oriental Hotel often advertised Rocco's performances with the word *modern*. Gazing at the Chao Phraya River over a gin glass, a customer could forget that jazz had taken a different turn elsewhere, that rock and roll had long since displaced jazz as the most popular and timely music in the United States. At the Bamboo Bar Rocco's music could still be heard as essentially modern, with no nostalgic caveats. For Rocco Thailand was, at last, after nearly fifteen years of wandering, *somewhere else*, a place that would validate and sustain him. Here his erstwhile identity came into intimate contact with Thailand under American neocolonialism. This contact opened toward something like a parallel universe of modernity. As a work of history, this book is set along the paths to and through this Cold War nightlife dreamworld along which Rocco and many others traveled. It is equally and irreducibly about *both* Rocco and Thailand, two entities that I would argue are, in the lens of history, deeply interlinked. The primary argument of this book is that American and Thai cultural frameworks were synthesized in deep and consequential ways over the course of the war in Vietnam, and that much of this happened within the intimate crucible of nightlife. *Bangkok after Dark* traces and analyzes this synthesis, for which Rocco was one protagonist.

Spirits and Souls

Maurice Rocco is today almost entirely absent from North American jazz historiography. No academic books or articles have ever been written about him, and he is barely known even among devoted jazz fans. But he was, and to some degree remains, a source of fascination to writers and intellectuals. Algerian French philosopher Albert Camus, on a visit to New York in 1945, wrote in his diary that "Rocco . . . is the best [pianist] I've heard in years. He plays standing in front of a rolling piano that he pushes in front of him. The rhythm, the force, the precision of his playing, the way he puts his whole self into it, jumping, dancing, throwing head and hair left and right."[3] Jack Kerouac writes briefly about Rocco in his novel *Visions of Cody*. Rocco has been often recognized by those who regard performance as an art form.

Rocco is also still remembered in Thailand. One recent fictional representation of him appears in Pitchaya Sudbanthad's highly regarded 2019 novel *Bangkok Wakes to Rain*, a collection of vignettes loosely centered on a single plot of land in Bangkok. Early in the novel, a trader builds a house on the land during missionary times. Generations live and die inside. In the 1990s, developers raze the ancient wooden structure to make room for a more modern apartment tower. Worlds emerge, then diffuse into the next, then the next. In an imaginary future set soon after our own time, the same land is flooded by the rising tides of the Chao Phraya River. Bygone worlds persist.

Throughout the novel, spirits good and ill visit the plot of land, as spirits in Thailand do. One vignette is set in the mid-1960s, when a rich Thai socialite hires an American jazz musician named Clyde Alston (a character based on Rocco) to play piano for a group of ghosts who haunt a wooden pillar in her sun-room. The ghosts have been disrupting the socialite's sleep because they suspect her of selling the house—their house. The socialite thus calls on a spirit medium, who tells her that the ghosts want to hear live music. So she hires Alston to give them a private concert.

Shaken, he obliges. It's a gig. With a piano in an empty room, Alston tries to pacify spirits he can neither see nor understand.

Pitchaya's story about a jazz musician playing for animist ghosts is fictional, but nearly every other detail about Alston is true to Rocco's biography. Like Rocco, Alston is a gay Black American who left the United States when his career collapsed, playing in Europe for several years before settling in Thailand, a place of opportunity. Distance from the United States defines Alston as a character, just as it came to define Rocco in reality. He plays in the shadow of the American war in Vietnam, for "young white officers on their five-day leave."[4] These officers are his countrymen, but he is otherwise nothing like them. Meanwhile the windfall he earns for playing in Asia depends perversely on an imperial world order. He plays United Service Organizations (USO) shows in Indochina and at military bases in Europe, wherever young soldiers need distraction from death. Night after night he stands at the piano—his signature gesture—despite aged, aching knees. He misses his boyfriend, seeking community in the muted corners of queer Thai nightlife. He shares a concert bill with a Chinese woman singer likewise uprooted. They connect. He is hired for jobs that did not exist a decade earlier. In Bangkok, a city hastily globalized, he makes his way. He himself becomes something of a medium, channeling not only spirits but spiritualities, realms of inner life, which resist translation.

Rocco lived all of this, and his story and its context are at the heart of Pitchaya's novel. For Pitchaya and many other Thai people now, the era of the war in Vietnam was politically formative, especially because of the lasting cosmopolitan intimacies that it brought about. Rocco is a remarkably evocative figure in Thai history. Intimate Cold War nightlife in Thailand, where souls resonated together, was the setting for his career revival. Playing boogie-woogie for an audience of animist spirits is an apt parable for a postmodern age. Like Alston, Rocco spent twelve years playing to the ineffable in Thailand, where he lived until his murder in 1976. But was this ineffable object soul or *winyaan* (soul)? Or was it a resonant dialogue *among* spirits, *among* souls, between music and place, like jazz in a haunted sun-room? For Rocco, the transmigration of soul was no fictional parable but a daily routine.

Pitchaya's novel distills much of what *Bangkok after Dark* is about—meetings of ideas and identities, dialectics of people and aesthetics, all of which have only ever tenuously resolved in Thailand if they have resolved at all. Rocco spent more than a decade at the center of this upheaval. The Cold War was of course far more than a bilateral conflict. Every place touched by it had a unique experience that must be historicized on its own terms and from a distinct vantage.[5] Thailand is among the many countries that were remapped by imperial encounters in the mid-twentieth century. Faithful to its object of analysis, this book is therefore intentionally and literally all over the map, just as Rocco was throughout his sixty years on earth. The knots of Thai Cold War history have yielded a dense present that wants both explanation and reflection.

What follows is therefore not quite a biography of Maurice Rocco, although at times it resembles that genre. Rocco's life story will be conveyed more or less chronologically. But perhaps this book is ultimately more like a Thai funeral volume (หนังสืออนุสรณ์งานศพ), a type of commemorative book given out at cremation ceremonies. Funeral books are partly biographical, but they also include loosely related ephemera—photographs, recipes, legal documents, and fiction, among other things. Historian Grant Olson describes one funeral book made up of three discrete essays: "'Cancer can be cured,' 'The dangers of electricity,' and 'How to grow sour tamarind.'"[6] In other words, funeral books can be tangential, even though they center one honoree. Like human lives, they are tangled and impure. These volumes call to mind Donna Haraway's notion of *compost*—collections of incongruous things that end up, in the slowly decaying aftermath of their heyday, interdependent.[7] This book makes compost from some unlikely interdependencies, including those that remain in the aftermath of the transnational encounters that the Cold War staged in Thailand. The reader should therefore not expect too clean a narrative, or too narrow a disciplinary focus; neatness would not do this story justice. The book does ultimately aspire to be explanatory, but please expect (and, if you are inclined, embrace) a messy, tangential path to that explanation.

Bangkok after Dark follows Rocco's life from birth to a point beyond death. But his story is told only partly for its own sake. Beyond Rocco's story, this is a book about nightlife intimacies between Thailand and the United States, from a period soon after World War II until the American military withdrawal from Thailand in 1976. That period was thick with nightlife encounters between people of many identities and positions: soldiers; Thai, American, European, Korean, Chinese, and Filipino musicians; sex workers; expatriates; spies; diplomats; developers; and many others. But the main character in the book is Rocco. After twelve years of apparent thriving in his adopted country, Rocco was killed in his own apartment by two hired sexual partners. Throughout his time in Bangkok, the last act of his life, Rocco became emblematic of the ways that Thais and westerners encountered one another in scenes of music and nightlife during a cosmopolitan moment. His late life and career show not only Thailand's growing worldliness during the American war in Vietnam but also the ways in which a variety of cosmopolitanisms emanating from different places resonated intimately together during that era, often following disjunct historical rhythms, as for example we can now hear on Doris Duke's tape of one bacchanalian evening.

As the book's author, I also place myself within these histories. This book draws connecting lines from the war era to the present, where I stand invested, implicated, and obligated, as well as ethically constrained. The authorial challenge of writing about lost figures, especially those very different from oneself, is summarized lucidly by Daphne Brooks, who reflects on another milieu of long-forgotten musicians: "Be all the time mindful that any quest to know, to touch, to inhabit is not only impossible but perhaps the wrong way to honor the questions that hover around and shroud the lost, the dispossessed, the disavowed. Expect to fail and then write yourself through the failure, write about it and draw truths from the conundrums."[8] Guided by Brooks and other theorists of archival practice, I not only situate myself within the histories at hand but aim to be humble about my limits as well as my inevitable failures.

As in the novel *Bangkok Wakes to Rain*, this book's narrative will move through history, listening for ghosts that remain unappeased. The secrets of Rocco's time, the specters that passed through the Bamboo Bar that January night, still stalk our present, waiting impatiently for acknowledgment. This book seeks to offer it.

Acknowledging Intimacy

The margins of the American war in Vietnam, where Rocco spent more than a decade, were sites of commodified intimacy and pleasure. In Thailand especially, the presence of American soldiers and other foreign visitors generated new economies that relied heavily on music and nightlife as engines of consumption. But nightlife was not only economically important. Within scenes of after-dark encounters, people heard and misheard one another, bartering for entertainment, physical protection, opportunity, sexual pleasure, and worldly knowledge on asymmetrical terms each evening. Through the 1960s and 1970s, strips of bars and clubs sprang up in Bangkok and provincial Thai cities to suit every international taste—indeed, every desire. American soldiers were drawn to these strips by the myriad prospects for release. But their demand prompted more than red-light districts. In the presence of so many wealthy and worldly visitors, rich new musical cultures emerged as well.

The success of the Thai hospitality industry, including its music, was of course underwritten by violence in neighboring countries, chiefly Vietnam, Laos, and Cambodia. But in Thailand violence was comparatively rare. There, western foreigners, locally referred to as *farang*, chased pleasure just beyond death's reach. Soldiers' whims and deep pockets spawned vast new sectors. In short order, Thailand built a profitable hospitality sector whose fundamental shape has survived into the twenty-first century. This industry still promises to fulfill any desire, material or spiritual. Penny Van Esterik observes with only the barest of hyperbole that "you can buy anything in Bangkok."[9] Or in any case, *farang* can. Amid the apparently boundless capitalist abundance that Thailand began offering in the mid-twentieth century, new musical worlds proliferated. Music, which played a pivotal role in fostering wartime intimacy and pleasure throughout Southeast Asia, therefore serves as a powerful analytic for understanding how Thailand was reshaped during what Benedict Anderson has called the nation's "American era." For the money that it generated, as well as its paramount symbolic meaning to Thais and non-Thais alike, music is thus a key lens through which to examine this period of intimate encounter in Thai history.[10]

Thailand was relatively peaceful and intensely capitalistic. Music thrived in such a ferment.

Among the rich *farang* circulating in Thailand throughout the Cold War were Americans working for the government, diplomatic entities, educational organizations, and international businesses. They were joined by scores of European and Asian foreign nationals, ranging from monied Japanese and German entrepreneurs to poor migrant laborers from Korea and the Philippines. Of course, there were also American soldiers, who generally flew in from fighting in Vietnam for five days of rest and recuperation (R&R), a coveted reprieve. At the peak of the R&R program in the late 1960s and early 1970s, as many as 44,000 US troops were on the ground at any given time in Thailand.[11] From 1965 forward, Bangkok was in fact considered the "main R&R center for American troops stationed in Vietnam."[12] From a menu of about ten international cities, Bangkok, with its reputation for hedonism, was reliably the most popular option. Soldiers on R&R were temporary visitors, but other military personnel remained stationed in Thailand for years afterward. Quite a few of them still live there today. In the 1960s and 1970s they were mostly young men. Many only ever knew Thailand for its nightlife, but they knew that nightlife intimately.

The concept of *intimacy*, central to this book, has often been used by scholars to examine transnational encounters. Intimacy can help explain how people develop self-identity, closeness with others, shared affinities, and mutual affection. It is an especially useful concept here. Lisa Lowe uses intimacy as a heuristic for understanding how "global processes and colonial connections" are brought to bear on individuals and their subjectivity.[13] Michael Herzfeld meanwhile theorizes intimacy as a mode of individual self-recognition within frames of intersecting national identity. Thus, the mundane habits that make one feel German, Thai, or American form a bridge between abstract national identities and everyday experience.[14] Of course intimacy can also be fragile. Lauren Berlant notes that intimacies are often unstable, potentially resulting in messy endings.[15] And under capitalism, intimacy can be captured by markets. Global intimacies have been readily commodified, including in spaces of tourism, a topic explored ethnographically in 1990s Thailand by Ara Wilson in her book *The Intimate Economies of Bangkok*, which I draw on substantially.[16] All these dimensions of intimacy—articulations of individual and national identity, messy instability, and touristic commodification—were amply present in relationships between Thais and foreign visitors in the 1960s and 1970s.

My decision to study this period from the vantage of intimacy relates to existing literature on Thailand's American era in a couple of ways. On one hand, intimacy is already a common theme in scholarship on Thai-US relations. Studies of geopolitics between the two countries during the Cold War are dominated by tropes of intimacy, especially in the fields of history and political science. The terminology is revealing. Daniel Fineman's *A Special Relationship: The United States and Military Government in Thailand, 1947–1958* details a history of increasing US-Thai entanglements during the middle twentieth century. In his title and throughout the book, Fineman calls these entanglements a "special relationship."[17] Meanwhile, Anderson describes Thai prime minister Sarit Thanarat as having launched an era of "unprecedented intimacy" with the United States from 1959 onward.[18] Joshua Kurlantzick observes that America became Thailand's "new friend" during the Cold War.[19] In short, intimacy and its metaphors pervade the literature. Scholars usually use words like *intimacy* or *friendship* to signal shared policy objectives, mirroring the diplomatic language that was in fact common at that time. As in a personal friendship, relations between the United States and Thailand were marked by mutual exchange and the close alignment of resources and priorities for at least two decades. The United States was of course vastly more powerful than its nominal friend, so it mostly dictated the terms of the relationship. The inequality between the two nations strains the metaphor. But Thailand and the United States were, to be sure, mutually reliant throughout the Cold War.

On the other hand, scholarship that relies on a figure of friendship usually centers intimacies between states, not individuals. This is despite the fact that, as Christina Klein argues, the individual or cultural sphere was of great importance in the United States' approach to Cold War policy.[20] Methodologically, I will not dispense altogether with analysis of state engagements. Rather, I regard individual relationships, such as those involving Maurice Rocco, as linked to geopolitical intimacies, both as consequences of those intimacies and sometimes as their catalysts.[21] The intimacies in this book should thus be understood as flowing in multiple directions. The everyday has often intertwined with national politics, and the book's analysis therefore shifts between broader and narrower scales. One American former soldier who was stationed in Thailand made the point well: "[Thais] always made us feel comfortable, made us feel at home. I think Thailand at that time and the United States had a very good relationship between the two countries and this manifested itself. I felt very comfortable."[22]

National politics affected the bar and the bedroom, just as the reverse was often true. Intimate individual relationships generated macrolevel effects: hybridized language, social archetypes, and economic sectors, for example.

Thailand is well known for its highly visible sex work industry, and this industry is considered in several sections of the book, as it was a form of intimacy that certainly drove macrolevel effects. But I also consider marriage, musical genres, nightlife, fashion, street vending, construction, transportation, and hospitality, all of which were disrupted and refigured even as they contributed to a broader transnational synthesis. To date, only a handful of book-length works in English have discussed the history of individual intimacies between Thais and foreign visitors during the American era in depth.[23] I suggest that the intimacies of the American era ushered in new forms of commodification that persisted long after most American soldiers and government officials left.

Intimacies ultimately remade Thailand. Over the course of the 1950s, the United States came to recognize its friend as an indispensable ally, and Thailand in turn came to depend on the United States in a way that quickly turned from windfall to tragedy. The United States began materially supporting the Thai military at a substantial level in the early 1950s, just a few years into the Cold War. By the time the war in Vietnam became a near certainty, American support had snowballed. Thailand was bloated not only with military investment but with developmental resources of all kinds, earmarked for everything from roads to education and issuing from both government and private sources. The West sent spies and entrepreneurs, then military brass and private contractors, and finally soldiers and tourists, with the last pair in particular proving hard to distinguish. From nightlife worlds that once seemed spontaneous came enduring intimacies—marriages, alliances, bands. In short order, whole cities as well as sectors of the Thai economy were developed in mind of hospitality and a global gaze. Cosmopolitan communions, unplanned and libidinous, later hardened into a set of perceptions about Thailand's value as a place to do business, find love (defined in chapter 4), have sex, and conduct politics. Soldiers on leave or stationed in the country knew these perceptions well. Today the same perceptions largely account for Thailand's international reputation as a sort of libertine paradise. Yet the origins of this reputation, cultivated in the very spaces where Maurice Rocco spent twelve years reviving his career as an elite Black *farang* performer, are not often acknowledged. There is work to be done bringing light to the shadows where intimacies burgeoned.

Thailand in the 1950s, 1960s, and 1970s was a bustling, exploitative world of transnational power brokering, often conducted in the veiled, intimate spaces of nightlife. This transnational "contact zone" created a wealth of neocolonial effects that this book seeks to draw out of their recesses of secrecy and to acknowledge.[24]

Maurice Rocco and the Limits of Acknowledgment

There is, however, a crucial caveat to the project of acknowledging intimacy. Namely, not everyone owes the world transparency, and no one does all the time.[b] At Veterans of Foreign Wars (VFW) Post 2813 in Woodside, Queens, where I conducted fieldwork in spring 2019, two US Army veterans named Dan and Mike were regulars. Both gave generously of their time and memories, but they did not always want to acknowledge what they saw or did while serving in Vietnam or during R&R stints. Dan and Mike's friend Sandy, the widow of another veteran, frequented the bar as well, and Sandy often brokered my attempts to ask the men sensitive questions. But even a single military tour, now over fifty years ago, was more than enough for people like Mike (a white man who served in infantry) and Dan (a Black former medic) to remain vulnerable to traumatic triggers for the rest of their lives. Both were deployed in 1968 and could still recall their service vividly in 2019. War molded them, and the VFW serves as an intimate space for those sustained by the company of comrades. From the wall-mounted television, Judge Judy bathed the room in imperative barbs, a somatic ambience somehow. Behind the bar, Mike drew on his cigar with peaceful focus, as pearls of condensation sweated down our beer bottles. It would have been wrong to interrupt this sacred state by pressing on memories of violence, fear, and loss forever raw. Leisure was often just as taboo a topic as war. As Dan once told me, R&R was a "what happens there stays there" experience for soldiers who had no choice but to assume they would soon die. Nightlife was not only cathartic but, in its way, holy. People's experiences of service, from terror to pleasure to tedium, are not always for others to know. It is important in moments like this to be aware of the limits of acknowledgment and to think carefully about where these limits fall not only for the story at hand but for the researcher as well.

Selective withholding in fact appears routinely in the human annals of war. By hanging out at the VFW, researching in archives, and interviewing older Thai people, I have observed that gaps in acknowledgment—in admitting, sharing, or showing the past—lie at the heart of wartime narratives. Invoking methodologies in both history and anthropology, I contend that these gaps are not always voids but often deeply meaningful things.[25] Some who spent time in Southeast Asia in the 1950s, 1960s, or 1970s have left old identities behind for-

---

b ACKNOWLEDGMENT: SUNY Stony Brook music graduate students Elizabeth Lawrensen and Christine Pash helped to develop ideas about "thinking with silences" in a spring 2022 seminar on the history of ethnomusicology.

ever. Others reserve certain details. Regardless, personal omissions are very different from the denials and redactions of governments. In individual cases, archival gaps may indicate not the whitewashing of events by the powerful, or the erasure of the lives of the weak, or historiographic lacunae, but simply a wish for privacy or closure. Scholarly acknowledgments in such cases are not always an ethical good or a salutary goal of narrating the past. Sometimes archival absence is not a lack but rather evidence of a quietude that was in full force when history transpired. Sometimes there was nothing to say. Sometimes shutting up was indicated, nullity nourishing. "Sometimes a desire to be gone is simply a desire to be gone," observes author Hanif Abdurraqib, like Maurice Rocco a child of Ohio.[26] History is not so transparent anyway, even when it speaks. For these reasons, I will not try to suture every gap in the evidence. It will be my aim not to relentlessly fill in every difficult silence but instead to regard silence sometimes merely as what happened—and what continues to happen. It is our task as researchers to decide thoughtfully how to work with, rather than against, silences. As Brooks notes, the ethical goal of writing history may not always be to "shine a light on that which eludes us" but instead to "honor the silences and make poetry in the corners of [people's] histories."[27] With notable exceptions, people have the right to remain quiet about moments when fear ignited the dry tinder of their youth. Rocco leaves archival gaps like that. I approach such gaps with humility, especially as they are not always mine to bridge. I have developed my research and writing in the long shadow of historians or theorists of history like Brooks, Saidiya Hartman, and Édouard Glissant, as well as ethnographers like Audra Simpson and Michael Herzfeld, all of whom have worked at the limits of transparency, where one might find empirical data missing, untranslatable, or else compromising to someone. These authors think with the fact that certain things cannot, or perhaps should not, be translated or known at all. Their work thus provides a methodological reservoir for this book. Understanding Rocco's place in Thai history, an encounter from which I seek to generate historical explanations, nevertheless requires skepticism toward the chimera of total knowledge.

I did not intend to focus on Rocco when my research for this project began; indeed, I had not heard of him. Despite significant national fame in the 1940s, few people now know his name, including most jazz historians. Aptly, I found Rocco in the margins, precisely where he had chosen to be. Examining peripheries can at times illuminate how power is structured at the center. Studying people like Rocco, whom institutions struggle to accommodate, can reveal what those institutions define themselves against. Certain others play an important role as capital-*O* Others. Rocco's gaps are therefore evidentiary—he was in many ways an exemplary Other, whose absence illuminates normative social structures and their exclusions. But in this book I move beyond an analysis of institutional power by also looking to Rocco's own agentic silences, not only the moments when he was excluded but also the moments when he deliberately withdrew. In this way Rocco offers a powerful case study for understanding how Thailand in the 1960s and '70s was a place of extraordinary refuge as well as financial opportunity for people who had things to run from, fairly or unfairly, or who had reasons to cultivate secrecy. Apart from a series of acts of alleged domestic violence in the United States in the 1940s, I read Rocco's archival gaps more or less as they lie, working *with* them as gaps rather than valorizing exposure. I rein in the sorts of "hungry" impulses that might lead us to seek answers to every conceivable question about a musical life.[28]

I first learned about Rocco when I found one of his regular gigs listed in a bawdy 1968 booklet marketed to American soldiers in Bangkok. The booklet was called *Bangkok After Dark!!!!*, with the first letters of the title words enlarged to spell "BAD," in a conspicuous nod to mischief.[c] The listing read:

Windsor Coffee House (285 Silom Road)
Under new management. Spacious but cozy with modern
decor. An inviting selection of food and drinks are
offered at reasonable prices. The inimitable Maurice
Rocco entertains on piano nightly.
วินด์เซอร์ กาแฟเอ้าส์ ถนนสีลม[29]

The listing was in small print, buried among ads for dart boards, a revolving restaurant, and "huge, tasty pizza." Rocco played a notable role in twentieth-century popular music, including being the most decorated American musician living in Thailand at the time, but a *Bangkok After Dark!!!!* reader would not likely have known this. In the booklet his nightly shows were instead nestled quietly in the margins.

Rocco lived in Bangkok under many layers of secrecy. He had long since become estranged from his previous life in the United States, including from most of his family members and friends. His erstwhile fans, jazz audiences old enough to remember his stardom in America in the 1940s, had no idea where he'd gone by the mid-1950s and certainly by the 1960s. He did not navigate the wake of the Cold War as a soldier or, no less, as the archetypical white

c ACKNOWLEDGMENT: I thank archivist Sheon Montgomery of the Vietnam Center and Archive at Texas Tech University, who assisted me in locating materials from within the archive's vast collection.

heterosexual man that both the US military and Thai tourist economy were then assertively courting. Nor was he a diplomat. Rather, he was a Black gay musician who relocated, along the prevailing currents of wartime deracination, the uproot that conflict so often brings, to seek opportunity and refuge in a place of relative anonymity. Such privacy had become newly possible in the cosmopolitan pockets of music and nightlife that the Cold War opened in places like West Berlin, Paris, South Korea, Tokyo, Panama, and Bangkok. Cosmopolitan Bangkok granted him privacy.

Rocco was not closeted in the contemporary sense of the term. But throughout his life he spoke about his sexuality selectively, even among friends. Each of the different worlds where he spent his early years, including southern Ohio, New York City, Chicago, the film industry, and the US nightclub circuit, presented its own homophobic affronts. But in Thailand Rocco was not compelled to answer for his sexuality. There, whatever visibility he experienced was more of a novelty than a mortal vulnerability. Although sexuality would figure importantly in his life, career, and death, and while this book devotes significant attention to queer histories—indeed, Rocco was present during the very genesis of modern gay identity in Thailand (see chapter 5)—there is little trace of his own perspective on these matters. If indeed Rocco lived in Bangkok in part to escape the hypervisibility and vulnerability of his race and sexuality in the United States, then the archival absences that resulted are part of the history of his experience in Thailand. These absences should be treated as evidentiary.

Rocco chose to live in an archival gap; this is a fact of his life. That gap is now a fact of the same life observed through a historical lens. Queer studies has in recent years grappled with the historiographic implications of working among gaps. Historian of transness Scott Larson argues that "gender-variant subjects have been overexamined" in historical writing, at times redoubling the violent exposures to which trans people were subjected by law, medicine, or religious authorities during their lifetimes.[30] This point might equally be applied to histories of cisgender queer people like Rocco, who routinely navigated life- or career-threatening exposures of his sexuality. Kara Keeling suggests that "a critical apparatus predicated on making visible hidden images, sociocultural formations, ideas, concepts, and other things always drags what interests it into the terrain of power and the struggle for hegemony. On this terrain, the benefits of visibility are unevenly distributed."[31] A project devoted primarily to exposing that which was invisible in Rocco's lifetime would risk reproducing such an uneven distribution of benefits (as well as harms). Rather than relentless detail-gathering in narrating the history of a person like Rocco, Larson therefore calls for a method of "critical *trans-attendance*, which shifts the scene of inquiry to attend to alternate frameworks and articulations of power that surround the subject of examination."[32] I often work in such shifted scenes of inquiry, a choice that accounts for a number of this book's tangents and experiments. Most of the details about Rocco's life that are missing remain so because of Rocco's own actions and concealments. I do not withhold information so much as commit critical time and attention to the places where direct evidence is conspicuously absent, writing poetry in the corners, as Brooks suggests. Among other things, sites of absence allow reflection on how opacity figures into some still-powerful political arrangements.

Still, the significance of Rocco's anonymity in Bangkok cannot be fully explained by examining his years as an expatriate. The book therefore begins chronologically with his youth in Ohio, continuing to the early and middle periods of his career in different parts of the United States. Chapters 1 and 3 situate his family, art, career, performative craft, and identity in the United States and elsewhere, before he moved to Thailand. Rocco was a significant musician whose contributions to jazz and rock and roll merit more attention than they have received (effectively none), but this early history is also important because of how it contrasts with and connects to the worlds he would later traverse in Thailand. Rocco's early life describes vital aspects of the American contexts that fused intimately with Thailand during the war in Vietnam.

It is a subplot to the early chapters that Rocco was an important hinge in the shift from boogie-woogie and other blues-based styles to rock and roll in the early 1950s. His is an important story about queer Black contributions to popular music. Later chapters trace how these facets of identity took on different meanings in Thailand, where the category of gayness in the 1960s was still developing. Rocco took cover in a fog of unsettled sexual identities. He also used global valuations of American Blackness to his strategic advantage as an expatriate artist. In telling both his story and that of the path along which he traveled, this book takes up radical historical juxtapositions (for example, from chapter 1 to chapter 2) between the United States and Thailand, which structurally mirror the dramatic shifts in Rocco's own life. He moved from a world governed by the gravitas of Duke Ellington, white Hollywood, his family, and local Black newspapers to one shaped by the Thai military, voracious imperialism, an increasingly powerful Thai monarchy, and globe-trotting Cold War entrepreneurs. The contrasts that emerge from this relocation might tell us something about how race, sexuality, and music were each transformed in global circulation during the middle of the twentieth century, including when nestled in the neocolonial intimacies between the

United States and Thailand. Rocco's odyssey through starkly different worlds is a story about the disruptions, intimacies, and ultimately persistent effects of the Cold War.

The span of time that Rocco spent in Thailand (1964–76) nearly dovetails with the most active phase of the long American war in Vietnam (1959–76). Neither the beginning nor the end of that span was coincidental. The late 1950s saw the advent of an anti-communist military network across Southeast Asia, as well as an explicitly pro-American commercial and developmental infrastructure in so-called free nations like Thailand. Rocco took savvy advantage of this infrastructure. By 1960, Thailand had become a financially rewarding place for international musicians (as chapter 4 will discuss). The rewards were doubly rich for Rocco, for whom the trials of being gay and Black as well as an aging popular musician had piled intolerably high in the United States in the 1950s. On the other side of the world, things were different, at least for a while. In Thailand, the phenotypical Blackness of an African American was a matter of curiosity more than stigma within the local matrix of skin-tone politics. And in 1960, gayness was not yet an identity category in Thailand at all. The end of Rocco's years abroad, marked tragically by his murder in 1976, preceded the final withdrawal of US troops from Thailand by just a few months, occurring amid near-daily political violence. Rocco's murder was an indirect consequence of the collapse of a political stability—and the end of an invisibility—that had by then granted him anonymity, work, and safety in Bangkok for more than a decade.

Given the intersections of his identity, Rocco was not merely an American in Thailand. This is part of what makes him fascinating. The term *farang*, though a significant marker of identity in its own right, in fact has many subtypes. Rocco's unique position given his race and sexuality show the limits of the privilege that *farang* held in Thailand. Although he enjoyed such privilege for a while, the progression of the war and its impact on Thailand left him exposed in the end, under conditions of homophobia and racial hierarchy that in certain ways came to resemble those of Thailand's patron, the United States. Rocco's years in Thailand thus describe a line around *farang* privilege precisely by showing where (and for whom) this privilege never fully applied. Rocco could enjoy some but not all the status of being *farang*, and his murder shows the vulnerabilities of queer and nonwhite western foreigners in Thailand. I study Rocco not as a scholar of Black studies or queer of color critique, as these are not where I am primarily trained, but rather because his is likely the richest life story within the scope of this research project. Work from these intellectual ferments, cited throughout the book, provides necessary explanatory tools for doing justice to parts of Rocco's biography. I place these literatures in conversation with work in anthropology, Thai political history, and music and sound studies to derive an analytical apparatus suited to the story at hand. The unruliness of this disciplinary apparatus intentionally mirrors the messiness of the history under investigation.

Acknowledging *Farang*

There are many secrets in the stories that follow. This is unsurprising, because Thailand was (and remains) a place where non-Thais could readily hide. Its policing and legal system give wide berth to foreigners, especially those with money, political connections, and light skin. These people, as mentioned earlier in the introduction, have generally been called *farang*. Millions of foreign nationals visited or lived in Thailand during the American war in Vietnam, transforming the kingdom and creating new categories of privileged identity, including modern *farang*ness. These transformations continue to be felt, though their roots in a secretive war and its neocolonial sphere of influence are in many ways now concealed. *Farang* today generally do not know why their experience of Thailand is so easy.

As it turns out, Thailand's $70 billion annual tourism industry grew directly from Cold War contact zones. A national tourist program, inaugurated by the creation of the Tourism Organization of Thailand in 1959, dates to the exact years when the United States was beating the drums of war in Southeast Asia. In late 1964, on the brink of invasion, with Maurice Rocco installed in his new nightly gig at the Bamboo Bar, the *New Yorker* reported that the number of tourists arriving in Thailand had tripled in the past five years. War and tourism were moving in lockstep. *Bangkok after Dark* is a history of encounters that took place in and around this remarkable moment. It is moreover a history of America's role in how that moment occurred, what it displaced, and what it has wrought ever since. The book is therefore also a reflection on how the past has shaped the myths and hierarchies of the twenty-first century. Substantial parts of the research are set in the present, in the memories of living people, in spaces of tourism and commemoration, and within the forms of family, economy, and aesthetics that first appeared during the war.

The war in Vietnam dramatically altered Thailand's relationship with the United States and other countries outside of Southeast Asia. Beginning in the 1950s, this era concretized Thailand's role as a friendly site for global capitalism. Historian Sudina Paungpetch argues that the American war in Vietnam, though a failure militarily, pushed Thailand sharply toward a US-friendly form of capitalism.[d] She concludes that in Thailand, "the U.S. won the cultural front of the Cold War using as weapons its own popular culture and democratic ideals."[33] Although this cultural victory was overshadowed by the mire of war in other parts of Southeast Asia, in Thailand America arguably succeeded in tightening its grip on global power.

One consequence of these "cultural front" victories is that in the twenty-first century, creating knowledge about Thailand as a *farang* means traveling along tracks first laid during America's and Europe's colonial and neocolonial incursions into Southeast Asia. These tracks remain open to *farang* now as paths of opportunity for doing just about anything, from research to pleasure-seeking. Just as many *farang* can "buy anything" in Bangkok, so too do they enjoy unusual levels of research access. Wilson observes that in Thailand, "Europeans' economic and political power intertwined with national and racial identities and established an enduring high status to whiteness that informs the experience of white tourists and scholars today."[34] This status might be called "*farang* privilege," after the more familiar (and not unrelated) concept of white privilege. The term *farang privilege* has even been used occasionally in passing, including by Yuping Mao and Rukhsana Ahmed, as well as Kristen Hill Maher and Megan Lafferty, but has never to my knowledge been theorized as a specific strain of global white privilege.[35] And yet to some degree this privilege shapes not only tourist experiences but all claims made by *farang* working in journalism, history, political science, or ethnography in Thailand, no matter how reflexive, informed, or well intentioned an individual researcher may be. Intellectual work performed by *farang* in Thailand is never separate from tourism's apparatus of privilege. I have routine access to this privilege, and I strive to identify where it shapes this book's authority, audience, and limits. Though I acknowledge many people, this book is ultimately my work, and I am solely responsible for its claims. I have worked on and frequently in Thailand for fifteen years, and I bring particular perspectives and informed opinions to my analyses. Still, *farang* privilege is an inescapable outgrowth of recent neocolonial histories, and for *farang*-identified people there is no space entirely outside of it. "Colonial watermarks," Ann Stoler reminds us, "cannot be erased."[36] *Farang* privilege has endured within a still intact, Cold War–era "infrastructure of America's . . . global dominance."[37]

d ACKNOWLEDGMENT: This book has been deeply informed by Sudina, who has guided me toward sources and interview subjects regularly since 2018, in addition to being a great friend.

This infrastructure should be acknowledged, because it shapes global power relations, including everyday ones, still today. While writing *Bangkok after Dark*, I've experienced bumps, but the tracks along which this book runs have mostly been smooth. These tracks were laid long before my research began. Thailand and the United States have been allies for decades, and their relationship scales from the level of the state to intimate contact between people. *Farang* scholars and journalists working in Thailand, especially those identified as cis men, benefit from assumptions of power and status. *Bangkok after Dark* is reflexive in that it asks what relationships, nodes of access, institutional and social hierarchies, and existing systems of favors have made its own insights possible. This book acknowledges the networks that have led to its own stories of musical, sonic, and nightlife intimacies between Thais and foreigners in Thailand. The need to do so arises directly from the subject matter. The book reveals its own circuits of knowledge, examining how conditions of privilege have come into being. It is a reflexive exercise less at the level of authorship (although that too is considered) than at the level of identity categories writ large. If there is power in keeping the advantages of *farang* privilege a secret, then surely the better alternative is acknowledgment.

Acknowledgment is all the more vital a framework because the facts of the American war in Vietnam have been so thoroughly obscured by the US government. The US military and CIA led major secret operations in Laos and Cambodia, with American citizens unaware that they were funding the mass killings of Hmong, Lao, Thai, and Cambodian people. The cost of these operations in dollars and lives was brazenly hidden. People in Laos and Cambodia even today navigate the deadly threat of unexploded ordnance, not to mention the traumas of past secret wars.[38] The history of the American war in Vietnam, much like the milieu where Maurice Rocco played his final act, remains a black box. The project of studying intimacies in Thailand during the war, and their consequences in the present, is thus a labor of acknowledgment. This is the warrant for writing a book of acknowledgments, especially as a *farang*.

Prolegomena to the Project

This book takes an unconventional approach, which I will explain before outlining its chapters. *Bangkok after Dark* is, at its core, about intimate Thai-American relationships during the Cold War. It takes both sides of that relationship seriously, interpreting the entangled relationship between them as a kind of synthesis. That is the book's intended primary contribution. However, whereas most book-length scholarship is streamlined, if not singular, in methodology, I have applied different approaches to the US-focused parts (especially chapters 1 and 3) and to the Thailand-focused parts (especially chapter 2). Chapters 4 and 5 as well as the conclusion, which describe the synthesis of a global relationship, are interdisciplinary in their own ways. The juxtaposition of different research methods and disciplines is atypical but intended to enact interdisciplinarity in a way that mirrors the real historical paths that the United States and Thailand traveled in the course of their intimate relationship.

In the first three chapters, the story shifts between Thailand and the United States (among other places), between Thai and non-Thai stories, and between Thai and non-Thai archives. These shifts complicate certain binaries, including the distinct national categories of the United States and Thailand. The reader may feel unsteady from the narrative motion between Thai political history and American popular music—not just different places but different intellectual frames. But as Kuan-Hsing Chen notes, "If attempts to engage [questions of imperialism, colonialism, and the Cold War] are locked within national boundaries, we will never break out of the imposed nation-state structure."[39] This book is organized by the idea that anti-colonial scholarship should bring putatively separate frames together, even if the results might feel like an adulteration of different historical knowledge areas. Every part of the book, from biographical discussion of Rocco's years in Ohio to the history of the electrification of traditional instruments in Northeast Thailand, is oriented toward examining Thai-American intercultural encounters.

This same point about bringing separate knowledge areas together also applies to disciplinary boundaries. As Lowe observes, "The modern division of knowledge into academic disciplines" makes disciplinary cohabitation unusual in scholarship, even though most of us are aware that the world is chaotic and interconnected and that few things can be explained by any one kind of analysis alone. This book thus heeds the call for interdisciplinarity as well as border-crossing historical thought. It insists, for example, that Black and queer studies have quite a bit to say to Southeast Asian history, because in fact histories of Blackness and queerness have long been part of Southeast Asian history. So you are invited, as a reader, to think *with* any feeling of unsteadiness you might experience in the pages to come and to consider (perhaps even feel!) how epistemological nausea must have been a routine part of an itinerant musical life during the Cold War. Sometimes the book's theoretical resources and primary sources draw on studies of American popular music, only to shift or combine in subsequent pages with material from Thai historiography. During the Cold War, disparate worlds were intimately entangled in precisely these ways. "[World War II] drew Thailand deeper into a complex international politics involving

Japan, China, and the Western powers, especially the US," writes Janit Feangfu. "Any attempts to define the Thai nation, to control the Thai state and to assert political decisions in Thailand became inextricable from the country's entanglement in the Cold War."[40] This book stays with messy junctures rather than pulling historical threads apart forensically.

The life story of Maurice Rocco is a device for understanding, at a granular level, how American and Thai contexts converged. He is, of course, only one person, whose life was moreover not always well documented. His biography cannot bear the full weight of the Thai-American relationship on its own. But his story does at times allow us to see into dense phenomena like cosmopolitan aesthetics; global formations of race, sex, and gender identity; and the military basis of tourism. His story also shows the extent as well as the complexities of *farang* identity and privilege in ways that I hope will compel reflexivity in the neocolonial center. But this illumination would not be possible, or at least not nearly as powerful, without attending carefully to the American context of Rocco's life and career and without giving due attention to the particulars of his life, family, and humanity. The book therefore moves across disciplinary oceans, just as Rocco moved across a liquid one.

Chapter 1 details Rocco's early life, from his birth in 1915 through the apex of his stardom in the late 1940s. This chapter makes a freestanding argument for Rocco as an important figure in the history of jazz and the early development of rock and roll, steeped in Black queer performance modes. This chapter establishes the performance and identity context of Rocco's life in the United States, giving close attention to musical and biographical details.

Chapter 2 then turns sharply from the world of American nightclubs toward Thailand in the 1950s. As the Cold War accelerated, Thailand moved into the political orbit of the United States. Thailand began developing local infrastructures, from roads and bars to laws, that would suit American visitors and ideologies in the years to come. This chapter focuses on the construction of two spaces that would eventually house cosmopolitan encounters in the 1960s: the Bamboo Bar in the Oriental Hotel and Bangkok's New Phetchaburi Road, where a busy American military bar strip would soon be built. Both spaces, though quite different from each other materially, were emblematic of how Thailand began building infrastructure to serve *farang* visitors, especially Americans, beginning in the early years of the Cold War.

Chapter 3 returns to the story of Rocco, examining his professional decline in the 1950s, and detailing his turn toward leaving the United States permanently. This chapter covers the same approximate period as chapter 2, ending in 1964, when Rocco moved to Bangkok. Rocco's ebb in popularity in the United

States in the 1950s was owed to factors ranging from the precarity of working in the culture industries, especially for Black artists, to the lingering effects of World War II on American nightlife. Rocco compensated for his faltering opportunities in the United States by seeking more work abroad. World War II opened this frontier, which increasingly afforded him both security and compensation. In effect, playing abroad became a second act. Rocco began trying it out in partial fashion in the 1950s before becoming an expatriate in 1959.

Chapter 4 begins to synthesize the two distinct stories that have so far run mostly in parallel. This chapter historicizes Thailand's cosmopolitan nightlife in the 1960s in Bangkok and other Thai cities, examining its development over time. How did foreign nationals during the war begin to patronize forms of music and nightlife tourism that have since become indispensable to the Thai economy? Who were the laborers working in this nightlife? What choices did they make, what incentives did they respond to, and how were their lives—musical and otherwise—altered by the American era?

Chapter 5 is similarly syncretic, tracing the excluded or invisible zones of Thailand's cosmopolitan nightlife culture, namely Black bars and the early emergence of a visible gay culture. In contrast with the largely heterosexual, white *farang* spaces discussed in chapter 4, these scenes mostly stayed out of public view. Rocco found a comfortable, private life there. But his cover slipped away as the war wound down. In the 1970s, as combat in Vietnam declined, the United States began withdrawing troops from Thailand. The chapter ends in spring 1976, as the United States prepared for its final troop withdrawal. In the ensuing power vacuum, Thailand was rocked by violence, both politically driven and opportunistic. Amid this chaos, Rocco was murdered.

The conclusion describes a trip to southern Ohio in spring 2022, when an Ohio Historical Marker devoted to Rocco was unveiled in Oxford's public cemetery, where his ashes now lie. In Oxford, Rocco's memory matters enormously to the local community. This final chapter summons hope for a historical revision in which Rocco might be reimagined as a meaningful (if complicated) part of the history of jazz and rock and roll, of Cold War music in global circulation, and of the mobility of Black artists in the twentieth century. Acknowledging Rocco in each of these ways can also aid in acknowledging the forms and extent of American neocolonial influence in Thailand, including its lingering effects.

After more than five years of archival and ethnographic research, I view nearly everyone who was impacted by the upheavals of the war to have been victimized by their experiences, even though some also enjoyed privilege. People's sacrifices are irreducible and cannot be easily compared. But the ways that different subjects were differently impacted by cosmopolitan encounter interest me greatly, for the histories offered in this book are ultimately composed not of two broad, national groups (Thais and Americans) but of a head-spinning array of subjects whose identity positions affected how they profited, suffered, or simply lived. By the time of the full American withdrawal from Thailand in 1976, many identity categories had changed or been created anew. To be Black, Isaan, *kathoey*, gay, *lûuk khrûng, mia chao, farang,* and so on was to occupy novel or altered positions in Thailand by the time the war ended. Each of these positions retains a specific character that cannot be disentangled from neocolonial histories.

The history of the American war in Vietnam has been written in English, through the eyes and ears of Americans, from countless angles. By comparison, there are very few treatments of Thai experiences of the war (even though some five thousand Thai soldiers fought alongside Americans in Vietnam, as Richard Ruth describes).[41] For that reason, this book is anchored by interviews and engagements with Thai people, as well as research in Thai archives both formal and informal. In particular, chapter 2 draws from Thai state ministry and archival documents. Chapter 4 utilizes funeral books, interviews, fiction, journalism, song lyrics, and message board threads. Thais who lived intimately with foreign visitors during the war are the book's most important sources. I do not speak for these people. I acknowledge them.

The book has also been written in active correspondence with Thai scholars, musicians, artists, and activists who at the time of this writing are pursuing projects related to Thai Cold War history. I have been lucky to get to know people like Oui (Panachai Chaijirarat) and Som (Punyisa Silparassamee), the two head curators of the Noir Row gallery in Ubon Ratchathani in Isaan (Northeast Thailand), who organized an art exhibition at a long-abandoned American radar base known as Camp Ramasun in 2019. New works were installed in situ in the crumbling ruins of subterranean conduits and overgrown grass around a massive circular antenna array called the Elephant Cage. Oui and Som took me and a fellow researcher, a Thai music specialist and friend named Peter Doolan who was integral to this project, on a half-day tour of the sprawling grounds. At their request and in thanks, I shared every primary-source document I had about the American presence in Ubon with them. Although our personal stakes in researching this history are different, our interest in the war era overlaps. That period shaped the economy and culture of Isaan in the present, and the 2010s were a late opportunity to understand that shaping through interviews with living subjects. Researcher Arthit Mulsarn meanwhile developed a traveling exhibition called the Molam Mobile Bus Project, which in 2017 presented histories of Cold War *mor lam* music to contemporary audiences throughout Isaan. An amateur historian named Suphawat Muangma runs a Facebook page called วันนี้ที่ตาคลี (Today in Takhli), which maintains documents, images, and memories of the American era. In brief, people in Isaan are highly invested in these genealogies. The ways that *Bangkok after Dark* might resonate with the continuing concerns of Thai stakeholders are a paramount reason for writing the book. I acknowledge the histories, personal experiences, rigorous research, and incisive curation of Oui and Som, Arthit, Suphawat, and many others.

The research for this book involved a roughly equal mix of archival and ethnographic research. Fieldwork and archival research in Thailand was conducted during the summer of 2019 and was concentrated in four cities (Bangkok, Rayong, Ubon Ratchathani, and Udon Thai), with routine follow-up conversations by phone, email, and video chat in subsequent years. Further ethnographic fieldwork in the United States was conducted in Queens, New York, and Oxford, Ohio. I meanwhile worked in approximately fifteen different archives, some in person and some remote (especially during the height of COVID-19 pandemic travel limitations). The line between ethnography and history was often blurred, however, especially when communicating with subjects whose lives continue to be shaped by the American era. I frequently asked these people questions about the past, which turned out to be also inquiries into their present. Although the research was undertaken ostensibly as a history, work with living subjects frequently became ethnographic. My inquiries were rarely quick shots; rather, they unfolded over lengthy periods, through different media, in some cases over years.

The research process was also notably social. In Oxford, Maurice Rocco's hometown, Valerie Elliott of the Smith Library of Regional History had been studying Rocco's background as a topic of local history for years before I reached out to her in 2019. Val and I began a near-daily correspondence, eventually adding another correspondent to the thread, a highly knowledgeable Rocco fan named Bob Orlowsky. Our conversations were one of the best things I've ever been part of as a researcher, not in terms of information gained (though there was lots of that) but in terms of shared excitement.

Meanwhile, though the average reader of this book may not be concerned with local genealogy, it was imperative to me that all materials about Rocco be made fully available to the public and especially to people in Oxford, including Rocco's living relatives. I came to care as much about this book as a document of genealogical value to Oxfordians as I did about it as a scholarly intervention. These same principles have been applied to relevant research findings from

Thailand. I often had occasion to share materials with Thai people who were connected by family or musical lineage to the subjects of the book. Although academic books, including this one, are principally argumentative, the research had the dual purpose of locating information of interest to historical subjects and their communities. Being in regular contact with so many people, in both Thailand and the United States, transformed research and writing from an often lonely task into one of great fulfillment and friendship. If I might offer one lesson about my experience to other researchers, it is that building true mutual bonds with those whose interests dovetail with your project, holding yourself accountable to them, and sharing the fruits of your inquiries are healthy scholarly habits. For much of the drafting of this book, I refreshed an otherwise desiccated professional identity in the depths of the pandemic by corresponding with people who shared my bottomless appetite for historical questions about Maurice Rocco and Thailand during the Cold War.[e]

A Final Word on Acknowledgments

In this book, acknowledgment is both a grand structural frame and a feature of the writing. Rather than aggregating all thank-yous into a single, isolated section before the introduction, individual acknowledgments are distributed throughout the text. In other words, acknowledgments are part of the story.

Walter Mignolo thinks with Anibal Quijano's notion of a "colonial matrix of power," meaning that the West and its others are tethered together in a common network of exploitation and domination.[42] The history of the non-West is therefore always also the history of the West and vice versa. In both the colonial past and the neocolonial present, the two realms cannot be decoupled. In fact they remain intimately linked. In the case of Thailand, an anti-colonial history must be one that resists the secrets, the redactions, and the exoticist marketing that insist Thailand is a world apart from the United States and Europe. Acknowledgments can help refuse this fetishistic distancing. An anti-colonial history must show how the intimacies between Thailand and the West (especially the United States) have constituted these geopolitical entities mutually, if often less than equitably.

Acknowledgment can of course refer to *the revelation of knowledge*. But acknowledgment can also mean a public recognition of who and what made

---

e ACKNOWLEDGMENT: My children, Julius and Mae, sustained this project through their patience and presence. They are funny and good.

something possible, the support systems which are pillars of any project—that is, *an expression of gratitude*. This latter sense describes what an author typically does in a book's acknowledgments section. But it is useful to reflect on how much these two different senses of the word have in common. Showing gratitude reveals the truth that work is never done in isolation. Perhaps revealing historical truths shows gratitude in turn.

Often even more than citations, acknowledgments sections offer views into the deep structures of research projects. And yet acknowledgments, rarely cited or understood as part of a book proper, are usually brief and relegated to front matter. This book is an acknowledgment from beginning to end.

1

ROCCO BLUES

In 1943, nearing the peak of a fame soon to fade, boogie-woogie pianist Maurice Rocco starred in "Rocco Blues," an example of a type of short musical film called a Soundie. His performance is virtuosic, and the clip, though just three minutes long, offers plenty to analyze. For a dime per showing, viewers in taverns and transit hubs around the United States could watch "Rocco Blues" and other Soundies on "jukebox movie" machines that looked like tall wooden television consoles.[1] Rocco was a minor Soundies star, appearing in four separate productions. Although the format would not last long (the company that made them folded in 1947), Soundies remain noteworthy today both because they prefigured music videos by several decades and because they documented the performances of many World War II–era musicians, particularly Black Americans, who were otherwise rarely or never recorded. Rocco's legacy, and evidence of his talent as a performer, is preserved mostly on film, in part thanks to Soundies. Despite once significant renown as a nightclub star and screen actor, however, Rocco is now at best a footnote in jazz history. This book reconsiders his import, not only to jazz and rock and roll but also within the channels of American global influence that the conflicts and alliances of the Cold War carved. "Rocco Blues" is a fitting entry point for this discussion.

In the Soundie, Rocco plays a thrilling if unusual variation on a 1940 Decca Records recording of one of his original compositions, also called "Rocco Blues." This performance might be read as a foreshadowing of the human displacements caused by new and intimate relationships between nations after World War II, including between Thailand and the United States. Rocco would soon be enveloped by that global relationship. But even in the 1940s he was already caught in the volatile transnational currents of World War II, within which geopolitics and musical commerce were often inseparable. (The Soundies corporation was, to this point, cofounded by a son of Franklin D. Roosevelt.) Rocco's biography reveals twentieth-century global intimacies at a microhistorical scale. In the end, Rocco was much more than a footnote in the history of twentieth-century popular music, not least because his career illustrates some of the furthest limits of that music's circulation. "Rocco Blues" anticipates the migration, the displacement, the floating signification, and the excess that would characterize so much of his life.

Rocco was also an exceptional musician. He left his imprint on American jazz from roughly 1937 through 1952. During that time, he was in demand at top venues in big cities as well as in the film and TV industry. He was a singular performer, both on-screen and in nightclubs. He also prefigured (and, the evidence suggests, was likely a model for) the dynamic styles of Little Richard, Jerry Lee Lewis, and other notable pianists from the early years of rock and roll. The later phase of Rocco's career, spanning the late 1950s through his death in 1976, most of which he spent far from rock music's First World epicenter, was invisible to American audiences. This later invisibility almost completely obscured his earlier success. But the years after 1959 were nevertheless a windfall, albeit in a way that saw Rocco disconnect from popular music in America and refashion himself as a decontextualized icon of Black American music in Asia. This second half of his story, examined in later chapters, opens toward crucial questions about American colonial influence, new global identities during the Cold War, and emerging categories of subjectivity in Asia. The 1943 Soundie once again seems to presage his mobility.

As the brief film begins, an unseen big band orchestra plays an introductory phrase, as the title card fades to reveal the star posed standing at a piano, faced by a trio of women in evening clothes. The tune then hands off from the orchestra to Rocco, who lights into a rapid-fire blues. The viewer witnesses his allure, his confidence, and soon enough his skill. He crouches at the key-board rather than sitting, rolling his eyes ecstatically from the start. The first two measures of the song feature an upbeat walking bass line, punctuated by stylish and heavily syncopated melodic runs with the right hand. The influence of both stride piano and boogie-woogie are immediately clear. He's playing *fast* and in the groove from the opening phrase.

Let's pause the clip momentarily to flesh out the context. Rocco's performance is framed in several ways. The first frame is economic. He is playing at the behest of the myriad companies that produced and distributed Soundies, as well as a distributor called Official Films that later bought the Soundies catalog. As with any recording, the artist is subject to commercial intermediaries, who by 1943 were mostly concerned with selling physical recordings, including both visual and audio media. By the mid-1940s, live stage shows had ceded market primacy to film and records. Rocco "photographed well," and he had an electric stage presence. These were major assets for a company like Soundies, whose busi-ness was to rent the experience of watching music. Rocco thus found himself a cog in a musical economy that, in those years, depended on the movement of recorded media—acetate discs, Hollywood films, and Soundies among them. His face and his performances helped set these media into circulation.

The second is a normative sexual frame. Rocco, as a man, performs by cin-ematic convention in front of an audience of adoring chorus girls (including dancers Ferebee Purnell and Elaine Munroe Ellis), who watch him starry-eyed, stepping along with every phrase, leaning across the piano toward their Casa-nova. Bertram Ashe describes this convention in Soundies, and in reference to "Rocco Blues" specifically, as a "females-draped-around-male-star arrangement."[2] This representation diverged sharply from the real-life scenes where Rocco, as a boogie-woogie pianist, had made his name in the 1930s and 1940s. In those scenes, queer identity could often be openly expressed.[3] But Soundies were constrained both by marketing expectations and censorship boards, which reviewed each film prior to release. The heteronormative representations that survived these filters belied the rich queerness of jazz worlds.[4] Ultimately the "Rocco Blues" Soundie, meant for mass circulation (and the audience pre-sumed to be watching), tells a stylized and fictitious story about the social worlds of jazz. This framing was not only a matter of the Soundies company hiring Rocco for his looks and musical skill but also of Rocco conforming in turn to the values of a new audiovisual format and its industry.

The third is a medial frame, a set of cinematic conventions that Soundies tended to follow. These conventions demanded a way of playing that differed from the scenes in Rocco's earliest live venues, including at the Cotton Club, the Roxy Theatre, and the Kit Kat Club in New York, as well as clubs in Chicago, Cleveland, Pittsburgh, and Toronto. Soundies compressed an unpredictable, improvisatory style into a neat two or three minutes. They exemplified the "massive decontextualization of music making from the environment in which it was often performed."[5] Meanwhile, the films were full of tight close-ups, which centered the musician as an individual star while turning away from the all-important audience and dancing crowd. By their very form, Soundies thus reduced the expansive, dynamic world of jazz performance. This is not to say that one or the other was more authentic, simply that live performance and recorded artifacts presented very different social realities.

Soundies were played on devices called Panorams, usually found in bars and similar establishments. The Panoram was marketed as a visual riff on the standard audio jukebox. It gave whoever spent their own dime a chance to call the tune, with the added novelty of seeing it performed. In this way Soundies were a distant precursor not just to music videos but to the Walkman, MP3 players, streaming devices, and other technologies that allow individuals to select content more or less on demand. The Panoram, as well as the cinematic style of Soundies, framed Rocco's performance through particular medial affordances and conventions.

Panorams were widely adopted, with more than four thousand units installed throughout the United States, before the format declined after the war. Notably, and much like later individual mobile media devices, Panorams targeted an audience that not only gathered in public space but *passed through* that space. The machines could thus be found in train stations, bus depots, hotel lobbies, and bars and restaurants near ports. The location of Panorams suggests that Soundies were aimed at viewers on the move. In an effort to connect emotionally with these viewers, directors of Soundies often staged scenes of transience. During World War II, amid a wave of labor migration in the United States, themes of mobility resonated with soldiers and migrant workers, among others. Many Soundies unfolded as miniature travel stories, showing sailors or workers heading home to their families after long journeys.

"Rocco Blues" told just such a story, as I will explain momentarily. But suffice it to say that through these three frames—the economic, the sexual, and the medial—Rocco was immersed in a world of musical commerce and circulation that he had not chosen when he filmed "Rocco Blues." This world embraced him unevenly, and it would later convey him on trips both enriching and tragic. Both now and later, he was swept up in transnational movements more turbulent than any one person could hope to steer through. Throughout his life, he would be channeled in such ways.

Still, in the film Rocco sometimes manages to escape the frame. Let's resume the clip. Rocco begins by playing an eight-to-the-bar boogie-woogie bass line with the left hand while pounding out a series of riffs with the right. He flashes top-tier technique, keeping pace with Gene Rodgers, Louis Jordan, Pete Johnson, Albert Ammons, and others who would soon orient jazz and blues toward the advent of rock and roll in the early 1950s. Rocco would also play a role in this effort. Blues-based genres like boogie-woogie, gospel, and Delta blues were in the 1940s transmuted into the new guitar techniques and styles of performers like Sister Rosetta Tharpe, their song forms mostly intact but their presentation modified and modernized.[6] Still rock and roll was never only about form. It was also from its very beginning a performance of excess, an overflow of emotion that seemed always on the brink of transcendence. Gayle Wald describes Sister Rosetta as playing "the guitar as an instrument of ineffable speech, of rapture beyond words."[7] Early rock and roll distinguished itself in part by dramatizing such a quasi-religious surfeit of feeling, rooted in Black expression and spirituality. Rock and roll stars routinely performed at the edge of song, stage, or screen. In the ensuing decades, rock's most powerful moments of excess—shouting, convulsing, smashing instruments—have become conventions as vital to its identity as any aspect of rhythm or harmony.[8] Rocco, like Tharpe, was an innovator of that kind of excess, the performance of escaping the frame, more than a decade before rock and roll was codified as a genre. He accomplished this in several distinct ways, the details of which suggest that he might be reassessed as a catalyst of rock's early development.

The first way Rocco signaled excess was by standing at the piano. Rocco refined this technique at least twenty years before Jerry Lee Lewis and Little Richard became famous for the same move. For his entire career, it would remain Rocco's trademark. He played without a piano bench during his childhood in the 1920s and became regionally known for the practice in Ohio in the 1930s. By the 1940s Rocco was almost never mentioned in print without reference to his standing. Whether or not he began to play this way by circumstance, because he preferred it, or simply as a gimmick is unknown. But for audiences, standing up signified Rocco's inveterate energy.

An example of the second way Rocco signaled excess can be seen about one minute into the "Rocco Blues" clip, when he moves down a register with his left hand to the very bottom of the keyboard. Here he begins playing intermittent measures with sixteenth-note subdivisions, speeding up as he goes. The bluesy bass figure grows abstract, and the song becomes muddy, tense, even melancholy. Rocco is no longer playing a blues exactly but rather opening into something like an automatic reverie, or a performance that implies such a reverie. It is exhilarating. The three dancers smile and twist as if the tune were still danceable—even as, for several measures, it decidedly is not. (This also results partly from sound-syncing issues, but the result is the same.) Rocco begins playing even faster, riffing separately with each hand, stretching right and left to polar registers of the keyboard. With this excess, Rocco puts pressure on the coherence of form, threatening to leave it behind in favor of unbridled ecstasy. His excess seems to open toward the promise of a certain freedom. Eileen Southern details how ragtime piano players used their left hands to play bass parts that substituted for the rhythmic role that "stomping and patting" had played in slave song performance, while the syncopated melodies of the right hand emulated "fiddle and banjo tunes."[9] Rocco's boogie-woogie was a close cousin of ragtime, popular just a few decades earlier, and he divided the roles of his two hands in similar ways. This sound of the promise of freedom would often be decontextualized from Black expressive forms, even as it arguably generated much of the value of early rock and roll.

The third instance of excess comes from Rocco's performing body. More than anything else, he escapes the frame of the film with his eyes. Soundies were usually recorded in a single take, using multiple cameras, some focusing on the face and some encompassing the full stage, shot from several different angles.[10] The performers played along with a recorded version audible to them from off-stage. Image and sound were later synced in postproduction. This process caused visible hiccups in the alignment between performers and sound. But the single-take approach helped Soundies capture some of the energy of a live performance. About one minute into "Rocco Blues," the camera switches to a close-up of Rocco's face. His eyes roll up and around emphatically, as they do again several times later in the clip and as he routinely did on film. The eye-rolling gesture, much like standing at the piano, is a move that Little Richard later adopted, quite possibly emulating Rocco. Throughout the Soundie, Rocco avoids looking at the three dancers, instead gazing coyly at the camera, perhaps at an audience that he believed was watching, whether or not the director, William Forest Crouch, was in on the signal. There is a subtle performance of intimacy here, a direct solicitation of some unseen viewer beyond the frame, perhaps a coded gesture. Each of these details points toward excess, a striving to evade the limits of the medium.

Then, about ninety seconds into the three-minute clip, Rocco bends his knees, almost squatting, eyes darting around. Abruptly after a modulation, the song moves to its final section, which is not included on the 1940 Decca recording of "Rocco Blues" or in any other version. This is the point where the film becomes something more unusual. Rocco plays softly, in a lower register, and then begins—unexpectedly, given what he's done so far—singing. His voice is tender against the intense flurry of his piano riffs. Throughout his life he was a competent but not extraordinary singer, yet his voice here conveys a vulnerability that complements his playing quite beautifully. The vocal section marks the end of the excess, of escaping the frame. Here, instead, Rocco becomes wistful. It is late in the brief three minutes of the Soundie, and the piece has been otherwise entirely instrumental so far. To this point Rocco had given the impression of improvising. But now he begins singing lyrics adapted from a standard. Not a jazz or gospel standard, or anything remotely contemporary, but a centuries-old Irish ballad called "Sweet Molly Malone." The transition is quick but complete, like jetting across the world to start a new life. In the most common version of its lyrics, the song is the tragic story of a fishmonger named Molly Malone who falls ill and dies, her wandering ghost thereafter selling fish from a wheelbarrow in the streets of Dublin. But in Rocco's phantasmagoric alternative, there is no wandering and there is no death. His modified lyrics transform the piece from a tragedy into a mythic triumph over the disruptions of transience, a narrative arc true to the Soundies brand. This time Molly Malone does not meet an untimely end. Instead, her male suitor proposes marriage and offers to bring her out of Ireland. Molly is intrigued, but as Rocco sings it, she will accept the proposal only if her suitor remains with her in Dublin, their shared home: "He asked her to marry, she said 'twould be grand' / but to leave her dear Dublin, she'd not give her hand."[11]

For Molly, the relationship can only continue if she and her partner can stay together without being uprooted from the city where they already live. The song ends happily, hopefully, perhaps naively: "So they both wheel a barrow through streets wide and narrow / crying 'cockles and mussels, alive-alive-o!'"

What led Rocco to insert lyrics from an old Irish standard into a boogie-woogie film clip made to entertain wartime itinerants in American bars and bus stations? It is likely that "Molly Malone" was chosen in part because the song was in the public domain. But Crouch and Rocco were also doing what Soundies so often did, producing fantasies of stability for transient audiences by adding lyrics about overcoming migration and displacement. They made the song a story of home.

Still, it is noteworthy that Rocco did not title his version "Sweet Molly Malone," as it was generally called when played as a standard. Instead the song *bore his own name*, and gestured toward his own burden: "Rocco Blues." The autobiographical title suggests that the song, a strange hybrid of proto-rock-and-roll excess and the death-scrubbed text of an old Irish folk song, encapsulated something fundamental about Rocco's experience and perhaps about his art.

Indeed, Rocco by this time had already been thrown into a life of near-perpetual travel. Most of his gigs were in New York and Chicago, a displacement from his home and family in southern Ohio, and as he became a successful film actor in the late 1930s, he increasingly played on the West Coast as well. His transience would increase during the Cold War. In 1948, he played an extended tour of England and possibly the European continent. In 1946, he was scheduled to tour Panama, until at the last minute a racist policy led to him being denied entry. He would later tour Scotland, the Netherlands, Cuba, Japan, Hong Kong, Australia, and possibly Vietnam and the Middle East before finally settling in Thailand. By 1943, Rocco had already embarked on a nomadic career, which would not end until his death (and even for a while after that). The "Rocco Blues" Soundie anticipates all of this. Perhaps Rocco's adaptation of "Sweet Molly Malone" voiced his desire to hold displacement at bay. The stark structural shift within the song even mirrors the eventual transition in Rocco's life around 1959. Following a surge of notoriety, and then a steady professional decline, he moved abroad forever. Perhaps like the version of Molly Malone that he authored, part of him longed to simply stay home. But figuring out where home was would prove a lifelong struggle.

Early Life Mythscapes

Maurice John Rockhold (he would take the stage name Rocco in the 1930s) was born June 26, 1915, in Oxford, Ohio. His father, John Westly Rockhold, worked as a butcher's assistant, and his mother, Ruby May Rockhold (née Young), was a cleaning woman, performing pianist, and piano teacher.[12] Ruby was an excellent musician and Maurice's first instructor. She played regularly in her local African Methodist Episcopal church and also served as an accompanist for silent films at the Oxford Theater. Both Ruby and John were born in Indiana, he in a tiny town called Liberty in 1885 and she in Richmond in 1891, according to census records. They met in Ohio and then married in 1908. The couple settled on Sycamore Street in Oxford, less than a mile from Miami University, where one of their sons would later work and where at least one of their daughters would attend college. The Miami library now holds a small archival collection devoted to Rocco, the only one in the world.

Maurice had at least five siblings, named Ohmer (sometimes spelled Omar), Thomas, Malcolm, Geneva, and Charlotte, as well as a cousin, Samuel, who at one point lived in their house. Both sides of the family had been free from enslavement since well before the Emancipation Proclamation and, although they had little formal education, could read and write. According to older census records, Maurice's great-grandmother on his father's side named America Rockhold (née Arnold) was born in 1826 in Kentucky. She relocated with her family to Cincinnati as a young girl. There, she worked for several years as a servant to the abolitionist author Harriet Beecher Stowe in Ohio, until Stowe left for Bowdoin College in Maine around 1850. America and her husband, John, later moved to Oxford, where they had a son, Charles, who would become Maurice's paternal grandfather. Both sides of the family moved several times during the nineteenth century—through Kentucky, Tennessee, Indiana, and Virginia—before settling in Ohio, a free state with an active abolitionist movement as well as good employment opportunities around the time of the Civil War.[13] John Rockhold, America's husband, registered to be drafted into the Union army while living in Oxford. Another of Rocco's ancestors, Thomas (possibly Maurice's great-great-uncle), served as first sergeant in the Civil War from 1863 until 1865, when according to military documents he was discharged after being "wounded in Right Foot and . . . completely disabled."[14] Maurice's family history involved great labor and sacrifice, as well as valor.

Many members of his family on both sides were also musical. Ohmer Rockhold contributed an article about his family's musicality to the *Oxford Press* in 1938.[15] He wrote, "Since our mother is musical, I guess it's no more than right that the rest of the family should have something musical about us, and we do. Everyone in our family does." Ohmer went on to describe his mother's regular impromptu playing at home, listing his family's talents at length. Ruby "played in two theatres, a number of churches, and minstrel shows of all kinds. My father used to be a comedian in several small towns. He also was a dancer. When mother plays, he pulls his cane across his finger to make the sound of a bass fiddle. . . . My brother Malcolm plays a bass fiddle. . . . My sister Geneva plays the piano. . . . My other sister, Charlotte, plays the piano and dances. . . . My other brother, Thomas, is learning to be a tap dancer."[a]

Maurice began playing the piano around age four. He practiced for hours at a time while tagging along with his mother as she cleaned houses. She preferentially sought jobs in homes with pianos so that her son could practice while she worked.[16] Ruby played a mostly classical repertoire, but she tolerated

a ACKNOWLEDGMENT: This history of Maurice's family and young life owes a special debt to researcher Paul Watson, who uncovered layers of genealogical information and located military and civilian information from the National Archives and Records Administration. Watson also read draft chapters of this manuscript for clarity and accuracy and helped shape vital parts of the argument. His insights and research acumen have made the book deeper and more complete.

Maurice's emerging preference for jazz. Maurice later told a friend that a local white piano teacher, a Mrs. Williams, recognized his talent and offered him lessons when he was very young. But during practices he would rebelliously add syncopation, which Williams heard as incorrect. His lessons ended after just a few months. By age six, Maurice regularly played the piano to accompany march-in and march-out time at Stewart Public School in Oxford. By age nine, he was playing paid gigs at Miami University fraternity parties. Maurice would not resume formal instruction until at least 1931, when he was sixteen. In his late teens he took a job performing solo at Cincinnati radio station WLW, which at the time had one of the highest-wattage transmitters in the country, so powerful that it used the slogan "The Nation's Station" because its signal could be picked up as far northeast as New York City and as far southeast as Florida, even into Cuba. The WLW gig may be what brought Maurice to the attention of Noble Sissle, a leading Black composer and Harlem bandleader, who subsequently invited the young pianist to play in New York City at the original location of the Cotton Club on 142nd Street.

The evidence about Maurice's early life presents certain complications. Namely, key details from his youth are drawn from an unpublished memoir written by Louis Rodabaugh, a white resident of Oxford just a few years older than Maurice, who often described Maurice as his best friend. Rodabaugh was a jazz musician too, and so in his writings he could explain musical details at a level that surpassed most other sources about Rocco. Rodabaugh also clearly loved his friend, writing of Maurice with awe, devotion, and intimacy. There is much to glean from his recollections. But Rodabaugh's descriptions at times reflect the haze of decades (he was in his seventies when he wrote his memoirs), as well as the issues that tend to arise when white people speak on behalf of Black people, especially in contexts of legal segregation and routine racial violence. Simply put, Maurice Rocco was never empowered to represent himself in the same ways that his childhood friend could. There are also a number of demonstrable, significant errors in Rodabaugh's writing. Rodabaugh is not a reliable narrator. I thus treat his memory as a source of partial evidence but note where and how his historical accounts might be skewed or incomplete.

According to Rodabaugh, Maurice first toured at length outside Ohio at Noble Sissle's invitation, possibly in 1934.[17] As Rodabaugh recalls:

> He spent the summer when he was 17 and I was 21 in Cincinnati. When I saw him I asked what he had been doing. He replied, "Oh, I was toppin' for Noble all summer at the Cotton Club." Noble Sissle, one of the better bandlead-

ers, used <u>two</u> pianos. One pianist played chords in the lower and middle registers, and the other played chime-like figures in the upper register—this was called "topping." When we reached his parents' home after this conversation his mother, Ruby, was frantically waving a telegram. It was from his agent, and it read, "COME NEW YORK NOW STOP HAVE JOB RKO THEATER CIRCUIT WITH DUKE ELLINGTON." At Sissle's suggestion, Maurice had adopted the stage name of "Rocco." Maurice Rocco left at once for New York. . . . He arranged with Principal Milholland to complete his High School work by correspondence.[18]

The 1940 census indicates that Maurice finished all four years of high school, perhaps partly by correspondence. But establishing even these basic details requires sorting through rumors and dubious claims. Many aspects of Rocco's life were either narrated loosely by others or told with the inflated language of the show biz press. Contrary to one of Rodabaugh's claims, for example, there is no evidence that Maurice ever attended Miami University. And he was probably never directly hired by Duke Ellington, least of all to play in a Radio-Keith-Orpheum Corporation, or RKO, circuit that by the early 1930s had converted almost entirely to screening films rather than hosting live performances. The memoir excerpt is therefore in doubt.

Ambiguity and myth cloud the archives. I note this in the midst of historicizing Maurice's early life because I understand this cloudiness not as an impediment to writing a true biography but rather as a firmament of racist mythmaking that is simply part of the history at hand. As Michel-Rolph Trouillot famously argues, narrativity and the processes of history are entangled.[19] Human beings tell reductive or fictional stories about themselves not just in history books but also *while history is happening*. Such stories are sure to be full of ideology and self-promotion, but inasmuch as fantastical stories are a primary component of history-in-time, they should not be ignored when history is written later on. Thus I take seriously (if not always factually) press accounts from outlets like *Billboard* and *Variety* as well as regional newspapers in the 1930s and 1940s, which were often imprecise and outlandish, routinely printing rumors as fact. Examples include the claim that Maurice attended Oberlin College or that Rocco was his surname from birth, two falsities that appeared in one 1944 article from the *Milwaukee Journal*. Perhaps this happened because newspapers were compelled to print exaggerations, especially when writing about entertainers. Rocco himself played the same game sometimes, for example reeling off stories of dubious authenticity during radio interviews or falsifying his birth year, as he (like many entertainers) often did.

Exaggeration and fantasy are common in coverage of celebrities, including in their own strategic self-representation.

But the exaggerations were not always innocent. The mainstream press tended to employ racist caricatures when discussing Rocco. Journalists overstated his physical features, including the claim that he had large hands. These features were sometimes said, without evidence, to account for his skill at the piano. Scholars of music have noted that in several hundred years of academic and everyday discourse about global music, the capacities of Black and brown musicians have been reduced again and again to supposedly inherent biological capacity, rather than to erudition, skill, or intellect.[20] An obsession with Rocco's body in the popular music press was an expression as well as a reinforcement of this myth.

The press also tended to exaggerate Rocco's relationship with Duke Ellington. It is true that Rocco was acquainted with Ellington, and Ellington, one of the greatest musicians in American history, even refers to Rocco in his own autobiography as an "old friend."[21] Rocco's friends and relatives have said that Ellington regularly visited Rocco's Chicago apartment in the 1940s. Still, there is no evidence that Ellington ever employed Rocco directly, as Rodabaugh claimed in his memoirs. The two musicians certainly crossed paths in New York in the 1930s and 1940s, including playing on several concert bills together in 1944 and 1945.[22] Ellington may have seen Maurice play in Cincinnati as well, as legend has it, inviting him for an informal audition after his own performance in that city in 1936. But their relationship does not appear to have been any deeper than that, at least professionally.

In sum, mythmaking was always part of Rocco's story. He never publicly disputed the many mischaracterizations or hyperboles that made the rounds about his life. Indeed he gave few interviews at any point in his career, aside from scripted radio segments that provide little insight into his feelings or beliefs. He was a private person who used media representations to savvy career advantage but who kept his private life walled off from those representations. Nevertheless, racial prejudice and violence were ingrained in Oxford during Rocco's upbringing, as they were throughout the United States, and he could not evade their effects. At every point in his life, one finds racist attitudes in his public representations.

The Oxford of Rocco's youth was a place of typically acute racial inequity, less than thirty miles from the Mason-Dixon Line and by many accounts well south of that line in spirit. "We [Black residents of the city] couldn't swim in the municipal pool," recalled Ennis Miller, one Black former resident of Oxford who knew Rocco growing up and who often saw him perform. "We had to swim in the creek. And the cows and the farmer's animals had access to the creek and if they were upstream that stuff floated down the creek. Growing up in Oxford there was the fact that you couldn't go in the restaurant in the front, you had to go in the back in the kitchen. Opposite all of that, when we were in grade school, they had separate restrooms. Black and white. Whites go in one, Blacks go in the other."[23] Segregation and related attitudes were, unsurprisingly, common even in northern states like Ohio.

Some details about Maurice's early years can be known with relative certainty. But many facts have been narrated through powerful filters of racial hierarchy or distorted by celebrity news coverage. This would remain the case throughout his life.

Scenes of Performance

Using his new stage name, Rocco began playing in New York City in 1934, shuttling between Manhattan, Cincinnati, and Pittsburgh for about two years. He was now entering performative scenes organized in some ways by the old rules (including long-standing racialized expectations), even as these rules were being actively fractured by new media, especially film. Now and into the future, Rocco's career depended on navigating both old and new strictures of performance.

A fresh face in the New York jazz scene, Rocco spent a relatively quiet first year in the city. His name appeared in few newspaper advertisements during 1934, although he may have been part of Noble Sissle's Cotton Club shows as soon as he arrived. He first played the Apollo Theater in Harlem in December 1935. An article from the *Oxford Free Press* that same month suggested that Ellington was to some degree his sponsor, although the actual extent of that sponsorship is unknown: "Talented piano playing [Maurice Rockhold] is playing this week in New York City in the Harlem district with two girls who also are members of Duke Ellington's orchestra," the paper reported.[24] "Young Rockhold soon will go on the road on the RKO circuit. He also will make a number of shorts for the Metro-Goldwyn-Mayer moving picture producers." As Rocco had not yet graduated high school, the article further noted that "Duke Ellington has hired a competent tutor who travels constantly with Rockhold's unit and holds classes with him every day." In fact, Rocco never traveled on the RKO circuit, nor did he appear in any MGM films. But it is true that before his twentieth birthday, he had left Ohio to make a career in New York.

By 1935 Rocco had begun generating buzz. The young pianist's name showed up in a trickle of New York City newspaper stories and concert reviews and then soon in a torrent. He also drew attention for collaborating with a Philadelphia-born dancer and singer named Dorothy "Dotty" Saulters, who later partnered with Cab Calloway. Saulters would die in 1962 at the age of thirty-nine, and she and Rocco teamed up only until the mid-1940s. As with many Black entertainers, Saulters's career and life were tragically short. She and Rocco first performed as a duo in 1936 at the Kit Kat Club, an upscale Black nightclub on 55th Street in midtown Manhattan, near the heart of the nightclub district.[25] Their debut engagement was a popular revue called "Harlem Goin' Park Avenoo," along with a group called the Three Roccos, an alter ego of the Rogers Sisters. The show earned positive reviews, and Rocco was widely seen as a standout. The *Brooklyn Daily Eagle* noted in 1936 that the Kit Kat Club's "new show is really something about which to drop a card to the folks back home. There's a chap there—Rocco by name—who goes to town on a piano in a hammer and tongs manner. ([Manager Charles] Lucas says the piano repair bills are terrific.)"[26] Rocco developed his reputation from commentary like this, which cast him as thrilling and uninhibited.

Almost as soon as Rocco and Saulters began performing together onstage, they looked toward Hollywood for further opportunities. Stage shows were by this time most useful as a launching pad for movies, then entering a commercial heyday. Rocco and Saulters's earliest break on-screen came in 1935, when they were hired to play in a fictional group called the Kit Kat Club Orchestra in the film *Temptation*, directed by the legendary Oscar Micheaux. Micheaux was a Black South Dakota homesteader born to former slaves who became a pioneering moviemaker. He was remarkably prolific during the eras of both silent and sound film, an experimentalist and auteur who worked deftly with political topics, especially around race. Micheaux became the first African American director to make a feature-length silent film in 1919, and then in 1931 the first to make a feature-length sound film as well. And he was not only early but trenchant. His *Within the Gates* (1920) was a pointed response to D. W. Griffith's white supremacist *Birth of a Nation*. The segregated structure of the white-owned film industry meant that Micheaux's work was not marketed toward an audience beyond Black Americans in his lifetime, but his talent was significant, and multiple biographies now attest to his importance.[27]

Micheaux often thematized jazz in his films, including *Swing!* (1938) and the short *The Darktown Revue* (1931). His process for casting musicians involved attending nightclub shows, approaching the artists backstage, and then inviting them to perform their revue in its entirety at his studio in Fort Lee, New Jersey. This is precisely what he did with Rocco and Saulters after visiting them at the Kit Kat Club. Micheaux paid what little he could afford, given that he was unable to access the investment sources used by mainstream white directors. Rocco and Saulters were up-and-coming performers but not yet beyond Micheaux's budget. Thus they earned a shot in the movie industry, working with one of the first great African American directors. All existing copies of *Temptation* are now considered lost, so the specifics of Rocco's role are unknown. His early association with Micheaux is still significant. Within two years in New York, Rocco was already building a serious career in the twin worlds of stage and screen. Soon after Rocco's film debut, in March 1937, Rocco and Saulters left New York together for Hollywood, this time under a two-year contract with an established white producer/director, Walter Wanger (who also had seen the pair play live at the Kit Kat Club), to make two more movies.

These turned out to be *Vogues of 1938* (released in 1937) and *52nd Street* (1938). *52nd Street* tells the fictionalized story of the titular thoroughfare in New York City, nicknamed "Nightclub Row" in the 1930s for being one of the most active nightlife strips in the city. The Kit Kat Club on 55th Street, where Rocco and Saulters broke out, was only a few blocks away. In the film, Rocco and Saulters act out a stylized version of their stage show. They play the role of nightclub entertainers who sing, tap dance, and play piano in front of an audience of well-to-do young white people. In the scene, a two-minute cameo, Rocco and Saulters provide the hyperbolic physical expression that allows the white concertgoers in the film to witness but not sink too deeply into after-dark debauchery. This racialized trope of the nightclub scene, pro forma in that cinematic era, would be reprised in nearly all of Rocco's movie roles.

The nightclub scene in *Vogues of 1938* has a slightly more complex staging than the equivalent scene in *52nd Street*. Here Rocco again accompanies Saulters, as she joins a trio called the Cotton Club Singers, an uncredited group of female dancers, and a quartet of male performers called the Four Hot Shots. The women dance in fur and pearls. With Rocco on piano, the band plays an arrangement of Bunny Berigan's 1937 hit "Turn On That Red Hot Heat (Burn Your Blues Away)." The six-minute number dramatizes the distinction between elegant music of the intellect, coded as European, and instinctual music of the body, coded as Black. The film sets up this binary by switching from an opening medley that includes snippets of Russian ballet, opera, and music by Frédéric Chopin and Franz Liszt to an interloping jazz arrangement that introduces syncopation and blue notes. As the jazz edges in, Saulters and the other dancers respond with faux shock, singing demurely, "What's that music they're playing so hot?" Soon the band's soulful sound draws them in, however, and the dancers remove their furs to reveal skimpy cabaret outfits. The tune transitions to an up-to-the-minute jazz hit. Rocco is in the background as the scene opens, pantomiming at playing the piano with exaggerated intensity. But no actual piano can be heard in the arrangement until more than halfway into the scene, when Rocco appears in close-up. As in *52nd Street*, he pounds the keys far harder than he ever would on a real stage, thrusting his head up and down, hyperbolizing himself.

The scene is highly choreographed, from the performances to the audience, and would not be readily mistaken for the goings-on at a real nightclub. Moreover, the action of the musicians only thinly corresponds to the music on the soundtrack. Among other things, instruments that do not appear onstage are heard as part of the diegetic arrangement, while some of the visible instruments go unheard. Meanwhile, most of the audible notes are wildly out of sync with the gestures of the performers. But verisimilitude was not the point. In fact, Rocco's principal role in the film was not to play his own music, or to reveal his considerable talent at entertaining, but instead to exaggerate his own raced body, as Black performers were routinely made to do in cinematic nightclub scenes staged by a white-owned film industry. Ultimately, Rocco performs a phantasmagoric, anything-goes nightlife culture far more than the brilliant stagecraft that had made him a budding star in New York during the previous few years. He is tasked in the film not with showing off his artistry but with performing tropes to show his own social position. At the end of the scene, the camera cuts away to reveal the implicit audience, a young, straight white couple out on a date. The couple is venturing outside the constraints of their upper middle-class life, with Rocco, Saulters, and the other dancers and musicians "presented as a commodity for white consumption," lending literal and figurative color to the couple's adventures.[28]

Racist as this depiction may have been, jazz's role as a carnivalesque excursion for middle- and upper-class white audiences in 1930s New York was not limited to film. Jazz clubs in the city were in fact a common site of "slumming" for white professionals in the early twentieth century.[29] These professionals, especially but not exclusively men, could tour the working-class worlds of Black, Irish, or Italian fairy life in order to see or even partake in nonnormative sexuality without being stigmatized by it in the morning. Black neighborhoods were especially popular areas for slumming in the 1930s, in part because they were less stringently policed than white areas like Greenwich Village and Times Square.[30] In this way, slumming granted middle-class white men access to prohibited sexual experiences without subjecting them to violent medicalization and policing. Slumming also reinscribed class difference. Jazz and its spaces offered temporary excursions for middle-class nightclub patrons, but the same spaces were *home* for working-class people. The touristic character of middle- and upper-class visits to these clubs affirmed who belonged where. Slumming happened in other urban centers as well. The Cabin Inn in Chicago's Bronzeville neighborhood was famous for queer performance, and some venues openly alluded to such performances in their advertisements.[31] Amber Clifford-Napoleone writes of clubs in Kansas City's queer-of-color jazz scenes during the same period, which overlapped significantly with similar scenes in New York.[32] Clifford-Napoleone historicizes jazz's musical development as part of a social assemblage that included nonnormative and often illegal sexual practices, gender expressivity, and sexual experimentation, ranging from slumming to gender impersonation, from buffet flats (apartments where one could sample a wide sexual variety) to sex work. Throughout the United States, spaces of jazz performance doubled as spaces of sexual alterity in the 1930s, where whites were periodic visitors.

Rocco got his start as a live performer in these spaces. In New York, he played most often in Times Square and Harlem, two of the most active neighborhoods in the city for both jazz and queer life in the 1930s. Harlem was home to a variety of sex and gender expressions. Noted queer performers like Gladys Bentley and the drag queen known as Sepia Gloria Swanson were onstage most nights. "Bentley trashed the gender norms and family ideals central to the project of racial uplift—self-regulation, monogamy, fidelity, wedlock, and reproduction," notes Saidiya Hartman.[33] George Chauncey characterizes the late 1920s and early 1930s, the time of Rocco's arrival in New York, as "the heyday of lesbian and gay clubs and performers in Harlem."[34] Eric Garber locates the end of the height of this period around 1935, by which time Rocco was already in town.[35] Chad Heap notes that "Black lesbians and fairies [were] so common in Harlem and Bronzeville that slummers began to encounter them even in the districts' more high-toned cabarets."[36] In sum, a queer milieu of live jazz was fully active when Rocco arrived in New York City.

The reasons white audiences ventured to these clubs were often quite different from what Rocco's films could portray during a homophobic era. Mainstream Hollywood movies could not, either normatively or legally, come anywhere close to representing jazz as part of the scenes of queerness and slumming that in fact fostered the music. Rather, the version of jazz nightlife depicted by these films minimized the degree to which jazz and queer culture were linked or even co-constitutive. In sum, Rocco was a markedly different performer on the live stage than he was shown to be in his films. For all that Rocco's turn to Hollywood did to boost his career, it also radically altered the indices and contexts of his music. *Vogues of 1938* and *52nd Street* tell stylized, limited, and heteronormative versions of his story as a live performer.

After returning to New York from his first extended trip to Hollywood in August 1937, Rocco was in greater demand than ever. His "Harlem Goin' Park Avenoo" show at the Kit Kat Club was held over for several months due to its box office success. He played ensemble concerts, including a charity benefit in Los Angeles in 1937 alongside Art Tatum. In the same year, he also formed his first band, a ten-piece ensemble called the Rocking Rhythm Orchestra, or Rocco's Rockin' Rhythm Orchestra. As he toured with that band, both *52nd Street* and *Vogues of 1938* were widely acclaimed in the press, and he and Saulters were often named as highlights.

In late 1937 and into 1938, Rocco continued to perform at the Kit Kat Club in Midtown, starring in a revue called "Christmas Night in Harlem" in December, followed by another revue in February. Rocco was mostly inactive in 1939, perhaps resting on the financial success of his two recent films or taking a break from the exhausting performing schedule he had kept the previous two years. He may also have been preparing for the studio recordings he would make for Decca in 1940 and 1941.

The years 1938 and 1939 saw a sharp increase in demand for boogie-woogie, Rocco's specialty. This owed to a pair of now-legendary Carnegie Hall concerts held in December 1938 and December 1939 called "From Spirituals to Swing." These concerts, which featured top jazz and blues musicians, generated a durable narrative of African American musical lineage whose full span was implied by the show's title—from slave spirituals to the ultramodern swing styles of jazz. Boogie-woogie was central to the later part of this narrative. The concerts featured pianists Meade Lux Lewis and Albert Ammons, two major names. "From Spirituals to Swing" led to a nationwide boogie-woogie craze in the ensuing years, and Rocco profited handsomely from the vogue.

Rocco's initial studio recordings were made for Decca between 1940 and 1941, when he was based in Chicago. He was by then a leading draw among boogie-woogie performers (if not quite as famous as Lewis and Ammons), so it was fitting that he would record for the same label as Ella Fitzgerald and Benny Goodman. He released at least twelve recorded sides in these two years, including several original compositions.[37] He also periodically published sheet music or piano solos. However, neither his records nor his sheets sold very well, and these formats are rarely mentioned by fans or commentators. Speculatively, this may result from the failure of either sound recording or sheet music to capture what Rocco excelled at most—live performance. The Decca recordings are restrained and somewhat antiseptic, conveying little of the energy of his film appearances or club shows. The tempo is slower than in his live playing and the notes more clearly articulated. The records possess what might be called refinement, but they lack the sense of excess that arguably made Rocco a star. A 1945 *Metronome* reviewer wrote of one of his recordings that "Rocco is a great showman, but on records you can't see him standing up."[38] Remembrances of his studio recordings are, perhaps as a result, quite rare compared to commentary about his live and filmed performances.

This is one possible factor in Rocco's near-total erasure from the canons of jazz history by scholars, critics, and contemporary listeners. Performing, especially compared to composing and songwriting, has been underappreciated in the historiography of popular music, including both jazz and rock. It is common to analyze a musical composition as a text, to describe its systems, patterns, and polysemy. But it is much less common to offer the same analytical treatment to an accomplished live performer, despite the complexity and labor of stagecraft. Guthrie Ramsey identifies a clear hierarchy in the assignation of "genius" to certain artists by jazz fans and critics: literary production (i.e., composition) at the top, musical skill in the middle, and performative prowess at the bottom.[39]

This hierarchy is both raced and gendered. Critics and scholars assign intellectual value mostly to inscribed works of a certain tangibility or textuality, such as compositions, arrangements, or studio productions. Jazz historian Frank Driggs tellingly refers to jazz arrangers as the genre's "intellectuals."[40] In late capitalist aesthetics, inscription is regarded as primarily the domain of Euro-Americans or men, ideally both. By contrast, women's musical expressions are often regarded as a natural result of their gender.[41] Nonwhite performance is often similarly characterized as primal. These biases help explain, in the case of gender, the decades-long history of Svengali-like male studio producers who lend an imprimatur of arcane technical wizardry to the allegedly mindless female pop stars with whom they collaborate, such as Max Martin for Taylor Swift or Nile Rodgers for Madonna.[42] Similar biases map onto race, underlying the routine description of Black jazz performers like Rocco as titillating rather than artisanal. In this hierarchy of musical brilliance, composition and production are (mostly white and male) achievements of the mind, while performance is the (mostly nonwhite and nonmale) result of bodies acting without agency, especially as the music edges toward something called "entertainment." Leonard Feather's 1984 *Encyclopedia of Jazz* puts it bluntly: "Rocco is an entertainer rather than jazz musician, despite the intensity of his fast boogie-woogie performances."[43] In Feather's view, jazz as *music* and jazz as *entertainment* are mutually exclusive. Paige McGinley identifies commentary like this as evidence of a "widespread antitheatricalism in blues criticism, which dismisses the theatrical trappings of blues performance as secondary, feminized, derivative, or affectively excessive."[44]

As a result of his specialization as a performer rather than a composer or arranger, Rocco has been mostly absent from jazz historiography.

Academic studies of music have often reproduced these biases, mainly by omission.[45] Thus there are plentiful scholarly analyses of jazz composers in which scores are read as rich texts. But there are comparatively few analyses—and comparatively few analytical tools—for interpreting live performance as an intentional, symbolic, and thoughtful craft.[46] Lisa Barg offers an important corrective to the heteronormative historiography of jazz by examining Billy Strayhorn as a queer artist, for example, but it is telling that she focuses on a composer in doing so.[47] Rocco is not discussed in Barg's piece, yet Strayhorn's and Rocco's lives overlapped significantly. They were born within months of each other in 1915, less than fifty miles apart in southern Ohio. Strayhorn was a close associate of Duke Ellington, while Rocco traveled in an outer ring of Ellington's circle. Both were gay and Black, and they worked and socialized in similar artistic worlds in New York in the 1940s. And yet the brilliant composer Strayhorn, whose work was written down, makes a far more legible musicological subject than the brilliant performer Rocco, about whom almost nothing has been written in musicology or jazz studies. Perhaps it is possible to approach Rocco's performances as layered texts as well, including layers of queer expression, just as has been done for Strayhorn's compositions. In Rocco's case, this leads toward sites of analysis, especially stagecraft, that a study of his studio recordings cannot reveal but that a consideration of his live and filmed performances might.

Black Queer Stagecraft and the Prehistory of Rock and Roll

One dimension of Rocco's performance that bears deeper analysis is his signature move: standing at the piano. Understanding the queer stagecraft of standing allows us to see how rock and roll was shaped by performative innovations that began in jazz and blues, including little-analyzed genres like boogie-woogie. It also helps to show what kind of musical figure Rocco was. The symbolic baggage of standing would stay with him for his entire career, from Oxford in the 1920s through Bangkok in the 1960s and '70s.

Standing signaled an energetic performance, even wildness, and it accounted for much of Rocco's box office draw. Wildness is a racialized and frequently racist notion in American music. Rocco was pigeonholed by it from a young age. "Rocco at the piano doing a solo," wrote one *Pittsburgh Courier* critic in 1937, when Rocco was twenty-one, "smacks more of a jungle witch doctor's dance than of a man playing the piano."[48] However, even this overtly racist framing should not diminish the move's remarkable craft and innovation. Not only did Rocco popularize the technique, but he thoughtfully honed it over years and decades. It is only due to their greater commercial success that Jerry Lee Lewis and Little Richard are now more closely associated with standing at the piano than Rocco.[b]

The origin of Rocco's standing technique likely dates to the first half of the 1930s, if not a bit earlier. He told different stories about it throughout his career. According to one version, offered to the *New York Post* in 1943, he began standing spontaneously one night at the Capitol Lounge in Chicago, three years earlier:

> The Lounge was a long, but narrow room—always packed. One night I went up to play and looked around for my chair. Somebody had taken it. Well, I was jammin' with the Three Bits Of Rhythm and they started their number off before I could find the chair, so I had to stand. Finally somebody shoved my chair up on the stage, but I was getting such a laugh, I kicked it aside. I found that standing up was a good selling point. People got to asking me to stand up. It was tiring. I developed muscles in my legs and also learned that I could rest one foot by dancing around on the other.[49]

But Rocco would contradict this story many times. He offered a more minimal explanation to an Armed Forces Radio Service host in 1943, the same year he was quoted in the *Post*: "I'm not tired, so I stand up."[50] In fact earlier newspaper stories suggest that his practice of standing must have begun at least a few years before 1940 and probably much earlier than that. One 1937 article suggests that "[Rocco's] technique of pounding a keyboard in the current red-hot swing style involves only occasional, very fleeting contact with the piano stool."[51] A 1935 *Oxford News* article mentions that "Rockhold, while still small and attending Stewart school, would stand at the piano and pound out dance music for the pupils during intermissions."[52] An even earlier article from the *Hamilton Evening Journal* in 1932 offered that "he showed his talent from the time he was too small to reach the keys, except by standing on tiptoe."[53] And each of his surviving late-1930s films shows him without a bench. The story about the Capitol Lounge in 1940 is therefore clearly a yarn. Rocco stretched the truth for the press by framing the standing technique as one born of the spontaneity

---

b ACKNOWLEDGMENT: I thank Jean-François Pitet, author of the *Hi De Ho Blog* (www .thehidehoblog.com), for ongoing conversation about this section. Pitet and I shared many primary-source materials, especially related to Rocco's early career.

FIGURE I.I. An advertisement for Maurice Rocco in *Variety* magazine shows him standing as he plays piano. *Variety*, January 5, 1944.

of nightlife rather than training and the deliberate labor of stagecraft. This was savvy marketing, and he was not alone in doing it. But it also disguised his own performative craft.

The kinetic practice of standing at the piano is too difficult to have been invented on the fly. Standing upright, a player's arms drop straight onto the keys, which alters the sound as well as the mechanics of playing, in addition to being rapidly tiring for the legs. Although sometimes used as a training exercise, a player's usual touch and tone would be affected by standing during a performance. Thus Rocco (like Little Richard and Jerry Lee Lewis, following in Rocco's footsteps) had to compensate by learning how to play with bent knees. Rocco crouches in almost every one of his film clips. Crouching granted him a posture and arm angle that resemble what he would have had with a piano bench. But playing in that awkward position must have required significant practice, as well as focused muscular training. Staying in a crouch, especially for an entire concert, requires powerful quadriceps, hamstring, gluteus, and core muscles. The necessity of muscular development is coupled with an altered center of gravity and a different angle of approach to the keys, both of which would have required ample trial-and-error adjustment. The benefit of standing was not just entertainment value but also a unique sound. According to jazz historian John Tennison, Rocco's standing partly accounts for his grace, speed, and articulation. It offers an ergonomic advantage "if you want to attack the notes in a certain way."[54] Tennison adds that standing allowed Rocco to dance and otherwise move around as he played, which made his act "elegant and suave." These benefits accrued from countless hours of experimentation and training. Although critics like Leonard Feather dismissed Rocco as a shallow entertainer rather than a serious jazz musician, the standing technique was clearly not invented by chance, or spontaneously, but rather from years of labor. Rocco combined boogie-woogie piano with choreography in rare and remarkable ways.

Standing was exactly the kind of trick that boogie-woogie pianists (and ragtime pianists before them) had long used to entertain audiences, but no other pianist had ever earned a reputation expressly for it. Yet from the 1930s onward, news articles made note of Rocco's standing as a matter of course. Often these stories highlighted the uniqueness of the move. Radio host Barry Gray called Rocco "the only man in the music business who plays the piano standing up."[55] Rocco was the opening guest on Bob Hope's first televised special in April 1950, no small emblem of his prestige. Hope introduced him in that episode as "the world's only stand-up boogie-woogie pianist."[56] He continued to stand throughout his later years in Thailand. One longtime friend of Rocco's from that period told me that it remained his signature move at the Oriental Hotel in Bangkok in the 1970s.[57]

This is one point of evidence for Rocco's likely influence on Jerry Lee Lewis and Little Richard, two originators of rock and roll. Simply, there was no other pianist whom Lewis and Richard could have looked to as a model for this technique.[58] By the time Lewis and Richard were young and breaking into show business, Rocco was already nationally known. Lewis first played locally around Louisiana in 1949, making his first commercial recordings for Sun Records in 1956. Richard's timeline was similar, although his background was not. Richard debuted as an opening act for Sister Rosetta Tharpe in 1947, playing in drag under the stage name Princess Lavonne on the minstrel circuit before cutting his first single, "Tutti Frutti," in 1955.[59] Both Lewis and Richard were teenagers with fledgling careers in the 1940s, while Rocco was performing at major venues, appearing in Hollywood films, and recording for national labels like Decca and Musicraft. It would have been almost impossible for Richard and Lewis not to know who Rocco was, even in the American South, no less to stand at the piano without drawing comparisons to him. Indeed, other musicians who stood were broadly understood to be performing in Rocco's shadow.

A 1945 *Billboard* review of the Loumell Morgan Trio noted that "Morgan does a Maurice Rocco on piano" by standing up.[60] Forrest Sykes, another boogie-woogie pianist who played standing in the late 1940s and early 1950s, was regularly billed as "the Junior Maurice Rocco." A 1949 article in the *Detroit Free Press* described Sykes as "styling his playing in [a] Maurice Rocco manner."[61] A 1946 *Variety* summary of a Chicago revue featuring pianist Sammy Ross suggested that the "act really gets hot when [Ross] does his harmonica bit and a stand-up boogie, a la Maurice Rocco, at the piano."[62] And so on. Even after his star dimmed in the early 1950s, the association remained for those with long memories. John S. Wilson, writing about Keith Jarrett's improvisations in the *New York Times* in 1975, called Jarrett's crouched posture "a cross between Maurice Rocco and Chopin."[63] Quoted in the *New Yorker* in 1973, Tony Bennett described seeing Rocco play at the Greenwich Village Inn and in a one-sentence recollection duly mentioned his standing.[64] Especially between the late 1930s and the mid-1950s, Rocco and his standing technique were all but synonymous.

Neither Lewis nor Richard ever acknowledged styling their playing after Rocco. Then again, neither of them ever spoke much about their mentors or models. One of Richard's only comments about his standing came in a 2011 interview, with little context: "I had started standing at the keyboard so I could do my stage routine without having to get up."[65] Aside from Tharpe, Richard's most frequently cited influence was his friend Billy Wright, the jump blues singer. Traces of both Tharpe's and Wright's styles are apparent in Richard's gospel-inflected approach to rock and roll. To this list, scholar Vincent Lamar Stephens adds the gospel-turned-secular pianist Esquerita (born Eskew Reeder Jr.), whose stagecraft and flashy appearance were a template for the self-presentation that Richard began experimenting with in the 1950s. Esquerita played frenetically, with his hair in a high pompadour and his face caked in makeup. His look and approach drew on Black queer aesthetics, especially those of the Chitlin' Circuit, and he had moderate success as both solo artist and session musician. There is no surviving film of Esquerita, but in photographs the resemblances to Richard's stage persona are clear.

Still, there are two aspects of Richard's playing that none of Richard's three major influences (Esquerita, Wright, and Tharpe) could have taught him. The first is standing at the piano. Wright and Tharpe were not pianists, and Esquerita is not known to have stood when playing. And yet, in the earliest available films of Richard from the 1950s, he stands throughout every song, sometimes lifting his leg onto the body of the piano, dancing in place, or swinging his arms. Like Rocco, Richard bends his knees, bouncing or standing in a crouched posture. He and his band play either shuffle rhythms or (later) eight-to-the-bar blues, just as Rocco did, while crowds of mostly white heterosexual-presenting couples thrill to Richard's energy and excess, precisely like the audiences in nearly all of Rocco's film cameos and shorts. Esquerita may have been a more direct influence on Richard's fashion, but the overall similarities in performance between Rocco and Richard are unmistakable.

Second, like Rocco, Richard performed queerness overtly with his eyes. This gesture does not appear to have been borrowed from Esquerita, Wright, or Tharpe. Richard famously performed in heavy makeup. But he also communicated with his eyes onstage. The action shots on the covers of *Mono Box: Complete Specialty/Vee-Jay Albums* and *Directly from My Heart (Best of the Specialty and Vee-Jay Years)* both show him with a familiar expression—mid-shout, eyes wide. In some of his early film clips, including a cameo in the 1956 film *Don't Knock the Rock*, Richard sports long, thick lashes, eyes darting up and around as he pounds the keys. By comparison with the standing technique, it is less certain that Richard copied these ocular gestures directly from Rocco. However, the two artists certainly drew on a common lineage of suggestive eye use in their performance.

Queer studies scholars have identified the gaze, including the exaggerated use of eyes, as an important part of queer gestural communication, particularly in the twentieth century.[66] Chauncey writes that tweezed eyebrows were a "telltale" signal of gay identity in early twentieth-century New York, quoting one sailor who calls "the expression with the eyes" a helpful way to discreetly discern whether someone else is gay.[67] Chauncey quotes another man similarly: "The eyes, the eyes, they're a dead giveaway."[68] The cartoon character Betty Boop, whose appearance was based on actress and singer Helen Kane, was drawn with giant eyes and long lashes as symbols of her femininity. Her character debuted in 1930 and remained popular throughout the decade. That cartoon likely strengthened the perceived link between hyperbolized eyes and feminine expression.

Eye gestures were a vital part of Rocco's queer stagecraft, as they would later be for Little Richard. In his Soundies, Rocco not only opens his eyes wide but rolls them repeatedly while staring at the camera, sometimes fluttering his lashes. As one music blogger notes, "Although, to the best of my knowledge, Little Richard never cited Rocco as an influence (he never credited anyone as an influence claiming loudly to be utterly unique) you only need look at Rocco in performance—standing up playing, eyes rolling and sometimes fluttering, and that direct gaze to camera/audience—to see something of Little Richard who turned all that up to 11, with make-up."[69]

Richard and Rocco also styled their hair in similar ways, while sporting contoured eyebrows. In Stephens's analysis of Richard's persona, the value of queer gesturing was not simply in its showcasing of excess (although that did help sell records) but in a finely tuned use of "queering tools," or strategies of self-presentation that aided the navigation of both racial and sexual constraints. Richard, writes Stephens, was a "consummate manipulator of queer tools."[70] Richard often told interviewers that his stage persona was calibrated intentionally to defuse the risk of white, straight audiences rejecting him for being dangerously appealing to white women. "I wore makeup and wild outfits to keep white people from focusing on me as some kind of a sexual threat," he told the *Wall Street Journal* in 2010.[71] Richard telegraphed just enough sexual alterity that audiences would read him as thrilling rather than threatening, while leaving room for conservative audiences (especially in the South) to miss the markers of his nonnormative sexuality altogether. Richard "self-enfreaked and self-neutered situationally in service of navigating intra- and intercultural expectations."[72] Given that Rocco was a gay Black man performing under precisely the same homophobic conditions as Richard, often in the same performative circuits, he may have made a similar calculation about how to adjust appearances of sexuality in his stage persona.

Even though eye-rolling could in some cases be a gesture reminiscent of minstrelsy, as for example in Louis Armstrong's "Shine" Soundie, Rocco and Little Richard engaged in a different kind of signaling that instead drew from Black queer performance traditions.[73] Unlike many of his contemporaries, the white director of "Rocco Blues," William Forest Crouch, was avowedly opposed to the use of blackface and minstrelsy in his productions. A viewer would not confuse the widened eyes of the performers in "Shine" with the playful darting and fluttering, feminized lashes of "Rocco Blues." These two different modes of ocular gesturing should thus be disambiguated. In sum, Rocco and Richard shared a common genealogy of response to oppressive heteronormativity in popular music during the early years of film and television, using their eyes to implicitly signal their sexuality.

If the exaggerated use of eyes was a key sign not only of queerness (to certain viewers) but also wildness (to others) in early rock, it is worth following the thread that links this gesture from the queer socialities of jazz and rhythm and blues to the less overtly queer early moments of rock and roll. This is because queer, Black performativity was a vital, if often sublimated, ingredient in the heteronormative version of rock and roll that appeared and became extremely popular in the late 1950s. This performativity was widely dismissed by rock's earliest critics as shallow entertainment, or as the autonomic effects of primitive bodies. But its gestures drew from deep and meaningful histories. Put another way, rock and roll was blessed from birth with elements of queer performativity that it rarely acknowledged.

Jerry Lee Lewis is instructive in this regard. Rocco also influenced Lewis, another figure of early rock and roll closely associated with standing at the piano. There is even a secondhand suggestion that Rocco directly taught Lewis how to play standing up. Robin Rodabaugh, one of Louis Rodabaugh's sons, told me a story dating to the 1960s, when he visited home from college. By circumstance, Robin was sitting at his parents' kitchen table when Maurice Rocco called Robin's father on the telephone, as Rocco periodically did from Bangkok. As Robin recalls, Rocco told Louis a remarkable story during the call: "What Maurice Rocco told him was, in 1942 or '43, I believe, after a concert when he [played standing up], a kid came up afterwards, twelve- or thirteen-year-old kid, and said he thought that was really neat and interesting, and would like to incorporate that into his own act, and asked if Maurice would show him the fine points. And he did. And the kid was Jerry Lee Lewis."[74] The story may be an exaggeration—either by Robin, Louis, or Rocco. One red flag is the date. In 1942–43, Jerry Lee Lewis was only seven or eight years old, not twelve or thirteen. Robin might have been mistaken about the year. Regardless, his anecdote does not prove a direct connection between Rocco and Lewis. But if Lewis was to learn the standing technique from anyone in the 1940s, it would have been Rocco, and the possibility that he did so in person is intriguing. Whether or not Robin's story is accurate, Lewis was essentially in the same position as Little Richard. In the performance circuits of the 1940s and 1950s, he could not have played standing up without being compared to Rocco. As with Richard, none of Lewis's other influences, such as country boogie-woogie pianist Moon Mullican, used such a technique. Maurice Rocco was the only available model.

Lewis's concerts in the 1950s, when he began standing at the piano, do not reflect the same calculus of racial or sexual self-presentation as those of Little Richard, because Lewis was white and straight. Nor had Lewis emerged from the religiously inflected, queer-of-color scenes that nurtured boogie-woogie. But he nevertheless performed excess in a manner reminiscent of Rocco. Lewis made his television debut on July 28, 1957, playing his then new hit single "Whole Lot of Shakin' Going On" on *The Steve Allen Show*. The song is a stripped-down version of a boogie-woogie piano number, played with a country feel. During an instrumental break halfway through the performance, Lewis begins pounding the keys so hard that his unkempt hair tosses about. He then plays softly for a few measures, entering into a calm talk break that sets up a wild finale: "Now let's get real low. All you gotta do, honey, kind of stand in one spot, jump around just a little bit, that's when you have flat got something, you know? Now let's go!" Then Lewis screams the word "Shake!" again and again, demonstratively kicking away his piano bench while playing the last few measures of the song with exaggerated energy. He stands in precisely the crouched position that Rocco had made famous more than a decade earlier. This performance among others earned Lewis the nickname "rock and roll's first great wild man."

Like many other white rock and roll stars, Lewis broke through commercially by adopting the stagecraft of Black performers, especially boogie-woogie and gospel artists, as his own. But those Black performers had worked in a rigidly segregated music industry that limited their audience by default.[75] Lewis developed a reputation for wildness in part by emulating Rocco's maneuvers and carrying them out in places and ways that Rocco was not given license to do. Though Lewis was less skilled than Rocco as a pianist, he evoked a similar spirit.[76] And he did so in the latter half of the 1950s, when the kind of excess that Rocco performed was no longer regarded as a sideshow. By that point excess was the animating substance of rock and roll, a genre that increasingly conveyed artistic depth and a generational consciousness. Yet Rocco, rather than being acknowledged as an innovator, was by then so bereft of opportunities in the music business that he would soon leave the country altogether.

The evolution of Lewis's style shows how the high stakes of performance for Black people in the early twentieth century ("Choreography was an art, a practice of moving even when there was nowhere else to go," writes Hartman) were transformed into "white metaphor," a source of pleasure for privileged youth in scenes of early 1960s rock and roll.[77] Lewis's career temporarily nose-dived in 1958, after it was revealed that he had secretly married his own thirteen-year-old cousin. This scandal led to a significant fan backlash and prolonged absence from the *Billboard* charts. Before reinventing himself as a country star in the late 1960s, Lewis attempted a comeback as a rock musician. In a 1964 live performance of "Whole Lot of Shakin' Going On," the same song he played in his television debut in 1957, Lewis showed clearly how standing at the piano bridged rock's earliest years with its later maturation in the 1960s. In the 1964 performance, the crowd huddles around Lewis, dancing with increased frenzy as he plays. Lewis extends the song beyond its original two minutes to a sprawling and improvisational seven minutes. The scene of white teenagers rapturously discovering themselves in musical wildness is kindred to Beatlemania, at its peak exactly then. This time Lewis kicks his bench away much earlier in the song, and plays standing for several minutes after doing so. He improvises lyrics as well as dissonant runs on the piano. The rowdiest

FIGURE 1.2. Maurice Rocco backstage at the Playdium Club in Cleveland, Ohio, 1947. Rocco is in a white collared shirt and suspenders. Images courtesy of Smith Library of Regional History, Oxford, Ohio.

segment, played for just a few measures in the 1957 performance, lasts a full three minutes in the 1964 version. Lewis enters a deep crouch as he strikes the piano with his hands and later his feet. At one point he stands with his full weight on the keyboard, before nearly diving into the crowd heaped around the piano. The similarities to Rocco's performative style are clear, even though Lewis's act was less choreographed and decidedly more unhinged. In the early 1960s, Lewis amplified a sense of secularized, euphoric freedom that had been comparatively new in rock in the mid-1950s, but which would greatly increase in popular music as the 1960s wore on, charting a path toward the psychedelic freak-outs of 1967 and beyond. In tracing the links between Rocco and standing pianists like Little Richard and Jerry Lee Lewis, it is apparent that the Black queer gestures of boogie-woogie as well as the ecstasy of gospel did more than seep into early rock and roll. They persisted and remained part of rock's DNA in later phases as well. Rocco was, however quietly, a contributor to the styles and gestures of rock and roll.

American Rise and Fall

The years between 1942 and 1947 were the apex of Rocco's career in the United States. After a long and successful stint at the Capitol Lounge in Chicago, he signed a seven-year contract extension with booking agent Phil Shelley, who also represented pianists Dorothy Donegan and Martha Davis. Shelley's agency, Stanford Zucker, coordinated shows for George Burns and Gracie Allen, among others, and for Rocco this deal promised exposure. His nightclub performances were by now increasingly split between New York and the Midwest, especially Chicago and Cleveland. During the American Federation of Musicians' recording strike of 1942–44, intensive touring was an important source of income for musicians, and Rocco had no trouble finding work at theaters, nightclubs, and cocktail lounges.

He continued dividing his energies between stage and screen. In 1943 he filmed four Soundies, "Rocco Blues," "Rhumboogie," "Beat Me Daddy Eight to the Bar," and "Rock It for Me," each showcasing a different dimension of his talent, from ballads to protorock to blistering boogie-woogie. He stands in all four films, gesturing with his eyes, dancing, and approaching the edge of excess, especially with his powerful left hand. The accolades piled up. Rocco was featured in the debut lineup at the new and fashionable Café Zanzibar on Broadway and 49th Street, perhaps the most prominent Black nightclub of its time in New York. The Zanzibar was a successor to the recently closed Cotton Club, though unlike the Cotton Club the Zanzibar admitted Black customers. There Rocco played with Ella Fitzgerald and Don Redman. A full-page ad listed his most recent achievements: five weeks as headliner at the Roxy Theatre, another residency held over, and fourteen weeks at Le Ruban Bleu on 56th Street, plus an announcement that he would soon go into production on several new films with Paramount Pictures. In October he played on a radio variety show with Lena Horne, and in December on *Jubilee!*, an Armed Forces Radio Service show aimed at building the morale of Black servicemen. The Armed Forces Radio Service showcased some of the most elite Black musical talent in the United States, a group that now certainly included Rocco. His headline appearance came between one episode starring Count Basie and another featuring Louis Armstrong. He was thriving.

By 1944 and 1945, journalists began calling him rich. Columnist Walter Winchell reported that Rocco paid a quarter of a million dollars in taxes on his film and record earnings in 1944. A Chicago musicians union called him "the highest-paid colored single act since 1902."[78] He owned "a six-flat apartment in Chicago, a summer home and farm near Oxford, [and] several pieces of property in Oxford proper," and he bought an additional house for his parents.[79]

He was now a national star. A 1944 *Billboard* review gushed: "Maurice Rocco . . . not only entertains but almost astounds with his deft keyboard manipulation. . . . While Rocco surpasses everything seen here under the guise of a boogie-woogie pianist, there is something vastly different about his treatment of this type of music. . . . Rocco not only stopped the show cold—he put it on ice."[80] He debuted at Carnegie Hall on May 2, 1944, with Duke Ellington as bandleader, in a tribute to socialist labor organizer A. Philip Randolph. Rocco would play Carnegie Hall four more times that decade. He shared a bill with Louis Armstrong around the same time, at Café Zanzibar, for a revue called "Zanzibaranian Nights." In at least one ad, his name was listed above those of Louis Jordan and Meade Lux Lewis.

Meanwhile his Hollywood profile kept rising. In late 1943 and early 1944, he filmed cameos in two major films set for release in 1945. The first was a variety picture starring Bing Crosby called *Duffy's Tavern* and the second a Betty Hutton vehicle from Paramount called *Incendiary Blonde*. Both were among the fifteen highest-grossing films of that year. Rocco's cameo was likely edited out of the final cut of *Duffy's Tavern*, but his appearance in a nightclub scene in *Incendiary Blonde* was central to the film. That movie was far more widely seen than his earlier screen work. With the recording ban now over, Rocco also went back into the studio, cutting tracks this time for the Guild and Musicraft labels. He was nearing the height of his fame and success, where this chapter began.

On June 7, 1944, the day after Allied troops landed at Normandy, Rocco appeared on Eddie Cantor's radio show *It's Time to Smile*. The host reverently called him "the king of boogie-woogie piano players."[81] During a bit of scripted chatter, Cantor added, "Maurice, I've seen you play in nightclubs many times, and I notice you never use a piano stool." Rocco replied with a jocular origin story, this time not stretching the truth but deflecting the question good-naturedly. He then launched into a boogie-woogie number, going low and hard as ever with the left hand, breaking intermittently from the blues as he so often did. But the war was now over, and Rocco's situation was about to change. By the end of the decade his opportunities would begin drying up, as boogie-woogie waned in popularity and he himself largely aged out of popular music. Rocco would soon shift his marketing approach as well as his geographical focus, with periodic successes. But in the end, he would fail to keep his career in the United States afloat.

The turbulence began in late 1944. Rocco's mother, Ruby, passed away in October, at fifty-three years old; Rocco was then just twenty-nine. His father came to live with him in Chicago thereafter, but he, too, would pass away within a few years. Less than a year after his mother's death, in July 1945, Rocco married a woman named Santha Moore in New York City. The two separated the following June, with Santha filing charges against Rocco for multiple alleged acts of domestic violence, including stomping on her in front of houseguests, pulling her hair out, scarring her with a bathroom scale, rendering her unconscious, and at one point causing a miscarriage.[82] Santha wrote in her complaint:

> I became pregnant shortly after my marriage to the defendant, and while we were in Baltimore, Md., my husband, being engaged there at the time, continued his beatings of me and beat me so badly that that he caused a miscarriage. The doctor who treated me in Maryland for this miscarriage spoke to my husband and advised him of my condition. My husband, nevertheless, never came home that night but instead went to Washington, D.C. for the following day, only returning that night to dress for his appearance and he did not even appear sorry for what he had done.[83]

These detailed allegations of violent spousal abuse were not reported by the same mainstream newspapers that routinely praised Rocco's musical prowess. Black newspapers were the only outlets that covered the story of Santha's abuse, including the Baltimore *Afro-American* and the Harlem-based socialist weekly the *People's Voice*. Rocco failed to appear in court when subpoenaed. Santha pursued alimony payments through at least 1950. This was not the last time that Rocco would stand accused of committing acts of violence, including against women; another instance occurred at a nightclub in 1957, when his career was near rock bottom. A patron called him washed up, and he hit her with a champagne glass. With regards to his abuse of Santha, Rocco was undoubtedly affected by the homophobic pressures that presumably led him to marry a woman to keep up appearances. There is no evidence at any other point in his life that Rocco was bisexual, and mixed-orientation marriages were common in the twentieth-century United States, especially for people with prominent public careers. Still, the homophobic pressure to marry a woman that Rocco might have experienced was not Santha's fault, and it cannot excuse the violence he committed against her. Rocco's abuses during that yearlong relationship are a terrible but important part of his story. Santha's torment, which comprises its own evidentiary gap, bears acknowledgment.

In what appeared to be a step forward in Rocco's career, *Incendiary Blonde* began playing in New York before screening nationally, just weeks after his marriage to Santha in July 1945. Rocco's cameo would be the most prominent Hollywood role of his life. The film is a biography of a real historical person named Texas Guinan, a daughter of Irish immigrants born in Waco, Texas, who became a nightclub impresario in New York during Prohibition. Betty Hutton plays Guinan, the titular incendiary blonde, a fearless small-town woman who endures sexual harassment and romantic trouble on her way to becoming Broadway's "queen of the nightclubs" before dying at the peak of her career. Motivated equally by money and fun, Guinan scorns temperance laws, throwing fabulous parties at which her white customers learn to overcome their own prudish reservations. Unsurprisingly given the racialized cinematic tropes discussed earlier in this chapter, a Black musician was solicited for the film's climactic party scene, in which the white patrons lose their inhibitions at last. It is thus both a nod to his talent as well as a racist irony that Rocco was featured as the film's lone musical cameo, with a major role in its marketing effort to match.

Rocco begins the scene playing a waiter in Guinan's nightclub. Amid the revelry, she crosses his path, reminding him that everyone in the venue must pull their weight by entertaining the customers in one way or another. He replies sheepishly that he can "sorta knock around the piano a little bit," to which Guinan replies, "Well, let's knock brother, let's knock!" Hesitating dramatically for a beat while the patrons hush, Rocco launches into "Darktown Strutter's Ball," a jazz standard written by Black Canadian composer Shelton Brooks in 1916. Rocco kicks the piano stool away, spinning on his heels, tap dancing, and playing the piano housing percussively with one hand while keeping the bass going with the other in a smartly choreographed arrangement. His eyes are active throughout. This is classic Rocco, including a division of the song into a soulful portion with lyrics followed by a faster segment that nearly breaks from its own form. When he finishes playing, the audience erupts, stoked by Guinan's upthrust arms. Guinan approaches Rocco: "You're terrific! What's your name?" Standing stiff and dutiful before her, he replies, "Rocco, Maurice Rocco." And she judges him worthy: "You're through being a waiter. Come in in the morning and I'll give you a contract!" "Thank you ma'am!" he answers, before running offscreen and out of the film to wild applause.

This role was an important opportunity. A widely seen film brought press coverage that raised Rocco's star. But it also demonstrated the limits of what he not only would but could achieve in American popular media. *Incendiary Blonde* implicitly celebrates the mobility that was available to white ethnic minorities like the Irish American Guinan. But such mobility was almost completely unavailable to Black people. The film's title plays jovially on the term *incendiary bomb*, implying that Guinan is a figure apt to cause chaos. She is depicted as sometimes scheming but ultimately moral—or at least a lot of fun. In other words, the film gives her latitude to bend the rules in pursuit of social and professional advancement. Her transformation from small-town Texan to Broadway magnate parallels her journey from an Irish immigrant identity to an assimilated and generally unmarked whiteness later on. There are Black characters in the film but only in subservient roles, and none of them experience anything like Guinan's dynamism or opportunity. But impressive as Rocco's performance is—and is recognized as being by the other characters—by this point it is Guinan, the white protagonist, who has the authority to validate his talent and then to decide to hire him (or not). She has become the boss; he works for her. They have settled into familiar positions of racial hierarchy, talent be damned. Black musicians regularly faced this imbalance, and would not cease to face it, on-screen as in real life. The cinematic encounter between Guinan and Rocco reveals a sticky structure in which mobility and assimilation were available to certain light-skinned ethnic groups but not to Black people.[84] The film shows race as the ultimate limiting factor in Rocco's professional success in the US entertainment industry.

There are other reasons to interpret this film as the beginning of the end of Rocco's peak. Though released in 1945, *Incendiary Blonde* was set during Prohibition, in the late 1920s. By the mid-1940s boogie-woogie was no longer the cutting-edge trend that it had been a few years earlier (although it would retain moderate cachet for a little longer). Selecting Rocco for a musical cameo in the film was thus a subtle signal that his style had grown anachronistic, that perhaps that style suited a scene set fifteen years earlier. As strong a draw as

Rocco was, he was no longer at the cutting edge of jazz and popular music. Instead, he was now a classic who embodied jazz's erstwhile golden age.

Compounding this, Rocco's most lucrative live performance scene, nightclubs, was in severe decline in the waning months of World War II. "[Cocktail lounge] managers report that business has dropped off sharply," noted *Billboard* in early 1945.[85] "Customers prefer to spend their evenings near their radios, awaiting news of American successes, rather than in a bar." This lull continued through most of the decade. "Further indications that neighborhood vaude houses are not the bonanza they formerly were for standard acts is seen by the fact that the Loew one-night vaude stands are getting a consistent run of performers in the $1,500 and $2,000 class who during the war years wouldn't consider hitting this time unless they were breaking in a new act," noted *Variety* in 1946.[86] The same article reported that Rocco was accepting less prestigious gigs during the downturn. The end of World War II, among other factors, shifted the music industry's center of gravity from the East Coast and Midwest to California, Florida, and various international locations. Phil Shelley moved his office from Chicago to Los Angeles in April 1945, selling the right to represent many of his artists to the William Morris Agency in the process (although in an affirmation of his value, Shelley decided to continue representing Rocco). New York, where Rocco had established himself, was no longer the only epicenter of the US music business.[87] Thus 1945, although in many respects the most successful year of Rocco's career, was also the moment when he began his slow personal and professional decline.

For the remainder of the 1940s, he continued to play New York gigs, although their frequency declined, as did their profitability. The trade magazine *Film Bulletin* reported in October 1946 that "Maurice Rocco on the Roxy Stage . . . will only stay three weeks after slipping badly following a $100,000 opening stanza."[88] Another show at the Roxy in March 1949 received a disappointing box office take. He continued to make high-profile appearances, including a May 1946 bill with Ella Fitzgerald and as the recipient of an award from the International Negro Press and Harlem Citizens Committee that October. But the prominence of his gigs, the strength of his draw, and the enthusiasm of critics all began to wane in the second half of the decade.

All of this was compounded by the ebbing appeal of boogie-woogie, especially as bebop came to dominate jazz, along with the rise of a new blues-based ferment that would soon be called rock and roll. Bebop introduced a degree of rhythmic complexity that earned it a reputation as both elite and elitist. With bebop, jazz was received for the first time (fairly or not) as high art, at least in the United States.[89] But with this came a reduced listenership, concentrated among aficionados who could appreciate smaller combos, freer rhythms, an emphasis on soloists, and a strong push toward experimentation—what Guthrie Ramsey calls a "demanding avant-garde."[90] These changes eviscerated the market for Rocco's style of playing, which was rooted in swing and boogie-woogie and not easily adapted to bebop. It also affected the position of the piano as the instrumental centerpiece of jazz ensembles. John Szwed claims that "in 1949 and 1950 . . . many groups dropped the piano from their instrumentation."[91] It is unclear whether there were actually fewer positions for pianists in the bebop era by the numbers. The success of figures like Thelonious Monk, Bud Powell, and Dave Brubeck in the 1940s suggest that there was still plenty of room for piano in jazz. But the role of the instrument had certainly changed. "By the mid-1940's . . . the orchestral approach to the keyboard of a Tatum or Ellington was too thick, too textured to work in the context of a bebop rhythm section. Instead, the new generation of modern jazz pianists looked for a sparser, more streamlined approach."[92] Rocco's skills were ill-suited to the new vogues.[c]

Rocco responded not by adapting but by seeking new audiences in new places for the same product he had always offered. In addition to giving concerts in smaller cities—such as Portland, Oregon; Holyoke, Massachusetts; and Atlantic City, New Jersey—Rocco began traveling abroad. His first scheduled trip was to Panama in February 1946. However, that country, under pressure from the United States, passed a series of Jim Crow laws that remained in place until the end of World War II, after which time local white business owners, including nightclub owners, still attempted to bar Black Panamanians as well as West Indians from their venues. This prompted a series of union-backed lawsuits filed by Black people against the nightclub owners, which in turn led the government to temporarily ban all Black entertainers (including African Americans) from entering the country at all.[93] The two most prominent musicians affected by the brief ban were Rocco and Art Tatum. Rocco's trip was canceled.

Still, even the possibility of the Panama trip suggested that international gigs were an increasingly appealing option for him. According to *Variety*, Havana's Campoamor Theater began booking American acts in 1947, hoping to lure tourists from Miami. Rocco played Havana in March. A few months later, the William Morris Agency, which had begun actively shopping its talent abroad, announced that Rocco would play an extended tour of England and

c ACKNOWLEDGMENT: I acknowledge the assistance of music theory professor (and SUNY Stony Brook PhD candidate, at the time of research) R. J. Wuagneux in thinking through the ideas in this part of the book.

parts of Europe in early 1948. He would not return to the United States until September.

Naturally, as Rocco spent more time overseas, his American engagements began to decline. His name gradually disappeared from newspapers. His *Variety* mentions became small-print reports of travel back and forth between New York and Europe, with fewer reviews of his actual music. The details of his journeys are most clearly outlined in the manifests of the steamships he boarded. These documents reveal that he was often at sea for as long as a week, his age and birthday almost never printed the same way twice. He listed addresses on commercially zoned blocks (perhaps the offices of attorneys or agents), with his occupation noted each time simply as "artist." The late 1940s marked the beginning of a career phase when Rocco moved out of the American limelight. He continued to work but cultivated a life of increased privacy as well as distance from the American music industry. The list of destinations where he performed would grow longer and farther from home in the 1950s. Chapter 3 will describe what happened during the 1950s for Rocco, an outcome that resembles that of other Black artists who found sanctuary and opportunity abroad during the Cold War. The postwar period launched an era of global travel and commerce that transformed life and work for many musicians. This era just happened to arrive at a moment when Rocco badly needed something to revitalize his career.

Rocco's situation in the United States continued to worsen. His loyal agent Phil Shelley died on a business trip to New York in 1949, at forty-eight years old. Many of Rocco's friends and associates were gone. And he was no longer a novelty, or young. His style of playing was out of fashion, the nightclub scene had dried up, and the American entertainment market, including Hollywood, no longer embraced him as it once had. Bleak as things were, they would get much worse in the 1950s. By the middle of that decade, there was little awareness and in some circles not even a memory of the electric star that Rocco had been from 1935 through the late 1940s, where the narrative leaves him for now. No wonder that his commitment to foreign performance circuits increased, until at last he became an expatriate, never to return to the United States in his lifetime. One can imagine him identifying with Molly Malone, the protagonist of his 1943 "Rocco Blues" Soundie, as his life took this discomfiting turn. Perhaps he wished that, like Molly in her fictive courtship, he had the leverage to insist on simply staying home. But there was no longer any place that Rocco could rightly call home. So he traveled. It would take more than ten years for him to find somewhere to stay.

2

HEART OF NIGHTLIFE,

ARTERY OF WAR

The cost of building a kilometer of road must be millions of baht. But that's nothing if you think of it as an artery of war. —RONG WONGSAWAN, สัตหีบ: ยังไม่มีลาก่อน (Sattahip: There's no goodbye yet) (2009)

As Maurice Rocco stumbled into the 1950s, Thailand was also stumbling—without much strategy or intention—under the patronage of the United States. American imperialism was rapidly opening new markets in Thailand, including markets for nightlife. As a result, patrons of the kinds of American urban nightlife scenes described in chapter 1 could increasingly experience similar scenes in other parts of the world. Conduits were developed between heretofore discrete places like Manhattan and Bangkok, with outposts catering to denizens of the former sprouting rapidly in the latter. A fresh wave of globalized racial capitalism resulted, and within its spaces, displaced Americans like Rocco would soon find profitable opportunities for their musical labor. This chapter is a history of the early development of some of these profitable new spaces in Cold War Thailand. This is where Rocco, still struggling in the United States for the time being, would soon enough revive his career. But first an infrastructure for that revival needed to be built.

The years immediately following World War II were the beginning of a deeply entwined Thai-American intimacy, a bond that has often been described as a "special relationship." Years before the American military buildup in Southeast Asia became war in Vietnam, this relationship bloomed at the twin levels of the state and the market. Thailand became at once an anticommunist ally of the United States and an attractive frontier for capitalist development. These roles complemented each other. In the postwar period the United States courted Thailand as an anti-communist outpost. That courtship opened markets. Daniel Fineman describes the results: "In 1941, only one American firm other than oil company agents did business in Thailand; in the three years after the war, the number increased to thirty. The number of American businessmen in the country, in the meantime, mushroomed from several dozen to more than three hundred."[1] By 1956, Thailand had an active American chamber of commerce to serve a growing international business community. This trend advanced through the 1950s, until Thailand not only was aligned with the United States but had become its de facto client. The knot of military, economic, and strategic dependencies between the two countries grew ever tighter and more complex. Their mutual interests became so entangled that, as historian Thak Chaloemtiarana notes, by 1960 it was impossible to tell which aspects of Thailand's latest national development plan had been written by the Thai prime minister and which by the US government.[2] In this moment of intimate geopolitical engagement, Thailand was becoming a prime place where a down-on-his-luck American entertainer might seek a second chance.

But what kind of sense would the aesthetics and identities described in chapter 1, in the context of American nightlife, make here in Bangkok? How would they be reinterpreted, misinterpreted, or otherwise altered? These are mainly questions for chapters 4 and 5, but their answers are set up by this chapter, which will describe two small-scale, everyday spaces of nascent Thai-American intimacy: a bar in Bangkok's old city and an entertainment district nearby. Both of these spaces developed between the end of World War II and 1960, before the war in Vietnam began. These spaces were not at all unique. In the postwar period, Thailand was full of neocolonial entanglements with the United States, ranging from the transnational silk trade to the Thai king's obsession with American jazz.[3] But this chapter's particular spaces have been chosen because they are narrowly related to the book's narrative—the story of Maurice Rocco specifically, and Thai wartime music and nightlife more generally. By the 1960s, neocolonial spaces would allow international visitors to live, work, and do business in Thailand. The spaces historicized in this chapter offer an intimate view into performance venues, urban nightlife areas, and musical labor, the very contexts where Rocco would soon rekindle his career.

Reflecting on spaces grants insight into the nascent "special relationship" between Thailand and the United States at the level of interpersonal intimacy. The relationship shared by the two countries during the 1950s was not only forged through trade agreements, arms shipments, or memoranda of understanding, as historians have often examined.[4] It was also part of daily life. Everyday intimate spaces available to both Thais and non-Thais in the 1950s incubated the even deeper engagements that would arrive in the 1960s, including the continuation of the story of Maurice Rocco. Everyday intimacies—musical, sexual, linguistic, aesthetic—led to modes of political and economic engagement between Thailand and the rest of the world that have remained decisive. These intimacies often took shape in spaces of nightlife such as bars and clubs, where music was a lucrative product, a source of livelihood, and a tremendous vector of symbolism for identity-building and self-expression. The role of music in Thailand's economic and social growth was considerable. Music both filled spaces and was itself a space crucial to the intimacies that propelled Thailand's postwar growth.

Borrowing from human geography, I understand space as the product of iterative social relations rather than fixed physical architecture.[5] Space must be produced and reproduced in order to be coherent. This mirrors how the word *space* is used in everyday speech. Safe spaces, hard drive space, and parking spaces, for example, are all understood as spatial phenomena, despite their very different materiality. What is similar about these seemingly far-flung spatial types is not their shape, size, durability, or even tangibility but rather their qualities of affordance: each space *affords* certain actions while foreclosing others. A parking space, for example, must have suitable dimensions to fit a vehicle. But its affordances are not ensured by its shape alone. Its surface must be regularly maintained, and there must be regulations and enforcement mechanisms to ensure that it is not used for other kinds of storage. Should this labor stop, the parking space would lose its affordances. Similarly, a functional safe space requires the active, ongoing labor of building trust and discouraging hurtful communication. Safe spaces do not have linear boundaries or hard surfaces like parking spaces. And yet they, too, must be maintained. All spaces, no matter their materiality, have histories that make them amenable to certain actions. In the framework of human geography, spaces are defined—made meaningful and productive—less by their linear borders than by the ongoing processes that keep them coherent.

This chapter tells the story of two spaces in Thailand that afforded intimate nightlife encounters between Thais and non-Thais during the Cold War. These spaces were part of a general infrastructure that allowed Thailand's entertainment and hospitality industry to flower in the subsequent decade of the 1960s, eventually enabling new forms of musical cosmopolitanism. But before such cosmopolitanism was possible—before, for example, Maurice Rocco could become an expatriate in Bangkok—these new spaces had to be built and implemented.

To briefly summarize, the first space to be described is a jazz club inside the Mandarin Oriental Hotel in Bangkok. Since the 1950s, the Oriental has been one of Thailand's most elite secular venues, a place of sun-dappled colonial verandas and luxury handbag stores. In recent years the hotel has charged about $800 for a single night in one of its standard rooms. It boasts a long list of global celebrities among past guests, including John le Carré, Eleanor Roosevelt, Louis Armstrong, and Princess Diana. The Oriental was built in the late nineteenth century, but it was not until its total renovation in the 1950s that it became a leading high-culture destination. Among the hotel's modernizing postwar amenities was the Bamboo Bar, the club that would eventually hire Maurice Rocco as its house pianist, where he would be recorded by Doris Duke in 1965. The renovation of the Oriental just after World War II, including its symbolic use of jazz, pointed to a new kind of cosmopolitanism that depended on music to signify taste and status.

The second space is New Phetchaburi Road, an extension of an older east–west artery called Phetchaburi Road in central Bangkok. Along New Phetchaburi, designed in the late 1950s and opened in the early 1960s, the busiest nightlife strip catering to US soldiers on rest and recuperation (R&R) anywhere on the planet would open around 1966. The construction of New Phetchaburi had many dramatic effects. It displaced poor Sino-Thais, connected major roadways throughout Thailand's central plains with an eye toward the coming war in Vietnam, and contributed to the obsolescence of Bangkok's once-thriving canal network. New Phetchaburi was built with the money and managerial expertise of American government agencies and contractors, and it was backed by a Thai prime minister, Sarit Thanarat, who was eager to please his American patrons. The road's construction signaled a strengthening Thai-US geopolitical intimacy. But the bar strip that was afforded by its construction eventually became its own strange, seedy world, housing nightlife intimacies that were integral to Bangkok's economic and social life in the 1960s, the very lifeworld that Rocco would enter beginning in 1964.

This chapter is a bridge between chapter 1 and the remainder of the book. The developmental work of the 1950s made Thailand a ready launching pad for the war in Vietnam. Indeed, Thailand's neocolonial development was logistically essential to that war. The same development that facilitated war also facilitated nightlife, making it easy and profitable for a musician like Maurice Rocco to emigrate to Thailand and to remain there in comfort and prosperity. The entrepreneurial labor of opening a jazz club permitted military officers and jet-setting tourists to realize their cosmopolitan aspirations in an unfamiliar place, to the tune of music transplanted from American nightlife scenes. The strategic military project of extending Phetchaburi Road gave young American soldiers a place to hear note-perfect covers of the Lovin' Spoonful before passing out wasted under the hot lamplight of their own mortal terror. New Phetchaburi, artery of a changing world, flashed an auditory hallucination of cross-cultural unity across a vast neocolonial gulf. Development afforded fertile if surreal spaces, where the scenes described in chapter 1 were restaged awkwardly, imperially on another continent.

Thailand's Cold War development followed the contours of American militarism, from the movement of troops to the launching of air sorties, from the operation of radar bases to the promise of arms deals. This same development also created a spatial infrastructure for the music and nightlife intimacies where Maurice Rocco would soon reinvent himself.

The Oriental Hotel

The Oriental was built early in the history of western-facing Siamese global commerce.[6] In fact, it was the country's first hotel. Its original building was constructed in 1865, mere months after Siam was opened to British trade by the signing of the Bowring Treaty. Over the course of seven decades of liberalized global commerce, a succession of Americans, Danes, Italians, and Japanese owned the Oriental, marking it as distinctly international. But after World War II, the building fell into severe disrepair, becoming nearly worthless. Its silverware and furniture were plundered. Around 1945, US Air Force personnel barracked inside unused rooms. At its nadir in 1946, the entire facility was purchased for less than $2,000 by a consortium of Thais and westerners, including Office of Strategic Services (oss) officer and silk magnate Jim Thompson, Thai politician (later ambassador to the United States and acting prime minister) Pote Sarasin, and a

European photojournalist named Germaine Krull.[7] This elite consortium typi-fied a wave of postwar international entrepreneurialism. Its members planned to restore the Oriental just as the dynamics of the Cold War were taking shape.[8] The new owners took various steps to revive the building, but of chief interest to this book is the opening of the Bamboo Bar, a jazz club conceived by Krull as a sophisticated, cosmopolitan salon. The Bamboo Bar would become a center-piece of the Oriental's ambitious vision for cultivating wealthy clientele from among the growing wave of international businesspeople and civil servants ar-riving in Thailand in the mid-1940s. The bar was intended as a new kind of space serving a new kind of foreign customer in Thailand.

Krull's worldview typified the attitude of western entrepreneurs in South-east Asia in the years between World War II and the war in Vietnam. For Krull and her business partner Jim Thompson, Thailand was not just a place of op-portunity but a blank slate. Krull wrote that Thompson "visualized beautiful Thai-style rest houses with American comforts which he would design and erect in various beauty spots. From these dreams and ideas he worked out a programme of large-scale tourist promotion. . . . A hotel in Bangkok was an integral part of our tourist plans."[9] Krull and Thompson favored Thailand as a tourist destination because they found it friendly. ("It was and is a happy country. . . . What a difference from the hostile faces in Indonesia.") But they were also developers, and developers need room to build. The country appeared to them to be open territory because they saw it as lacking worldliness, history, or significant institutions. The consortium thus appointed themselves the task of dictating parts of the country's modernization. Krull found Thailand Edenic ("Where will you ever find such a heavenly spot again?") but under threat from the wrong kind of modernity.[10] She felt that her own approach would be more tasteful and even more moral than that of other, less attentive capitalists. In mul-tiple books and memoirs, she wrote about scoundrels, diplomats, and intrepid businesspeople who fled the law or sought fortune in Thailand, sometimes both. She wrote of a womanizing French colonialist who meandered into the country after the war seeking business opportunities; national traitors on the lam, some known to her from her days as a war correspondent; and a British former medi-cal adviser to the Siamese royal court who, although an open white suprema-cist, wooed and married a Thai woman. Krull detested them all.

Instead, her models were those rare figures whose extractions were tempered by intimate, allegedly authentic knowledge of the country.[11] Krull's *Tales from Siam*, published in 1967 (after her co-ownership of the Oriental had ended), opens with the sonic trope of leaving Bangkok's urban noise for the "solitude of the mountain triumphs" in the northern countryside.[12] There, Krull sought what she judged to be the real Thailand. Even the title of her book, which used the decades-outdated name Siam, rather than Thailand, brimmed with nostalgia.

Although Krull presumably meant to be sensitive, she trafficked in troubling colonial notions of Asian primitivity. For example, her framing of virginal rural landscapes as authentic—and in need of preservation by people like her—positioned Thailand as a kind of "feminized Asian other," a helpless place in need of stewardship by westerners.[13] In the same vein, colonially minded Europeans had long imagined Siam/Thailand as a prelapsarian paradise, as indeed they had imagined many nonwestern places.[14] French researcher René Guyon, for instance, devised a grand theory of sexual liberation from his home in Thailand in the 1940s.[15] Guyon, so enamored of the country that he became a naturalized Thai, "saw in primitive societies a sexual freedom that 'no longer' existed in modern Europe."[16] Guyon regarded Thailand as an untainted laboratory for understanding human nature, where people remained open to pleasures that the West had come to prudishly deny. Krull harbored similar presumptions.

The attitudes held by Guyon and Krull prefigure the "intimate economies" that Ara Wilson argues have been crucial to the marketing of Thai tourism since the 1960s. Intimacy remains the primary selling point for touristic experiences in Thailand today, and in tandem the country continues to promise sexual hedonism to foreign visitors. In this regard, Guyon's writing in the 1940s and Krull's memoirs in the 1960s both foreshadow intimacy's enduring touristic value in the twenty-first century. Appropriating Karl Marx, one might say that Thailand has appeared twice in the colonial imagination: first as sexological field site, then as bachelor party destination.

The book *Tales from Siam* most overtly expresses Krull's desire to protect a vanishing Thai authenticity. In it, she chides foreigners who exploit the country. Yet she herself subjects Thailand to pet theories of development, representing it as exotic and pristine even as she tacitly asserts her right to turn parts of it into vacation destinations for Europeans. These contradictions and condescensions were already normal in her time, and they have long outlasted that era. Janit Feangfu refers to a category of visitors, already well known to Thais by the 1970s, who seek to "differentiate themselves from other tourists by going independently or at least traveling in the same way that they assume Thai people do."[17] Often this self-differentiation has served, intentionally or not, to justify exploitation.

It was on these self-differentiating terms that Krull renovated the Bamboo Bar as a space for the postwar global rich. Her bar would be a site for western expatriates to experience Thailand in fashionable comfort and for certain Thais, in turn, to "seek access to the European-centered world, to learn about imperial social practices and develop networks with colonial representatives."[18] Historian Joshua Bollen describes nightclubs as paradigmatic spaces during the twentieth century's waves of travel: in nightlife venues, dislocated people (including Rocco and his audiences) could make sense of a world in motion.[19] This sense-making was profitable, and Krull was prescient in identifying it. The US government would not make a comparable investment in Thailand until several years later, and the foreign business community was thus far only a fraction of what it would become in the 1950s and 1960s. Krull, paternalistic though she may have been, was a savvy entrepreneur, years ahead of a coming wave of investment driven by both affordable air travel and war.

One of Krull's first moves in enticing a new and distinguished clientele to the Oriental was to build a space where people could eat, drink, and listen to live jazz. Her Bamboo Bar began as an informal gathering space on the ground floor of the hotel, but as demand among local expatriates grew, her goals came to include a French American kitchen, the training of a competent service staff according to "European standards," a dress code, beautiful furniture and wallpaper, and the hiring of a world-class jazz combo. In her memoir she describes the effort of cobbling together the decor and training the staff. As she tells the story, this work depended on the ingenuity of western experts in a forbiddingly alien place.

The Bamboo Bar's first house band was led in the late 1940s by Trevor Mac, an Irish Portuguese drummer who previously lived and worked in the United Kingdom and India, where he specialized in orchestral jazz, before coming to Southeast Asia (he would stay there at least into the 1960s). At the bar, Mac led an English women's orchestra beset by infighting. Efforts to replace the musicians piecemeal initially met with rancor and resignations. One pianist was accused of throwing ashtrays at guests. Despite the tumult and turnover within the house band, the bar proved popular, and by the early 1950s it was a fashionable nightspot. Krull had already identified jazz, a totem of global culture throughout Southeast Asia and beyond, as the appropriate genre to match the atmosphere she wanted to create. The stage was quite literally set for Maurice Rocco, who within a decade would be hired for a daily residency at the Bamboo Bar (see chapter 4). This is the history of the nightspot that would become his first employer in the city, and his entrée into a stable life in Bangkok.

The Bamboo Bar soon had company among venues seeking wealthy customers. The first of what would become a city full of cosmopolitan restaurants, clubs, and nightlife venues opened around the same time and with similarly global management. Among these was the Silver Palm Club in the Patpong neighborhood, well known as a CIA clubhouse. Other venues had even higher commercial aspirations. "The latest development," reported Krull, "was the first elegant, air-conditioned night-club, 'Chez Eve,' financed by a group of wealthy Chinese and some police colonels, and operating under Hungarian management in the form of the beauteous Vera and the suave Nick."[20] Much as Krull played up the French and American connections of the Bamboo Bar, Chez Eve advertised the international character of its Hungarian management and menu. This marketing effort matched the growing cosmopolitanism of Bangkok itself. Major Thomas Sheppard, an American soldier on R&R from Vietnam a few years later, recorded an audio letter to his wife in which he narrated the experience of dining at Nick's Number One Hungarian, the successor to Chez Eve. He addressed his wife with excitement: "Boy, we had some real fine chow. I had Hungarian 'gulyas.' And by the way I found out it's not 'goulash,' it's 'gulyas.' G-U-L-Y-A-S. We had gulyas, and we started with a margarita. And oh, was that good! It was a little one. It was the first one I've had since I had one with you, and boy was it tasty. And once again I thought 'oh, gee, if only she was here to try this out.'"[21] This meal hailed Major Sheppard as a worldly tourist, the kind of customer presaged by the rise of venues like Chez Eve in the 1950s. *Gulyas* and margaritas were global delicacies (even if not often paired together), and Sheppard consumed them not only as food but as part of a worldly education. This was the model of consumer identity to which the Bamboo Bar, Chez Eve, and other new venues in Bangkok had begun to appeal.

Across town, the Atlanta Hotel opened in 1952, not long after the Bamboo Bar.[22] Its owner, a half-Jewish German chemist named Max Henn, had left Germany as a refugee in the late 1930s, bouncing from visa to visa in different countries for almost a decade while trying to find sanctuary in South America. He never got there. Henn was waylaid and broke for so long in Thailand in the late 1940s that he decided to get married and start a business in Bangkok. Drawing on his background as a chemical engineer, he launched a pharmaceutical company and later opened the Atlanta Hotel. Ten years before the war in Vietnam began, the Atlanta was not yet oriented toward military visitors but rather toward the global diplomats and developers who were increasingly populating Bangkok. Once the war began, Henn's hotel—with its ornate art deco details and strict prohibition against sex workers—appealed to career officers more than young soldiers. Generals William Westmoreland and Creighton Abrams each stayed there in the 1960s. Like the Bamboo Bar and Chez Eve, the Atlanta was part of an emergent generation of Cold War spaces in Thailand that served cosmopolitan western elites.

Global money and power were beginning to flow through Bangkok, and the Bamboo Bar competed with other nightlife venues for the patronage of rich, politically connected people. "The guest list [at the Bamboo Bar] was as incongruous as the menus," wrote Krull. "Generally there were at least two high-ranking princesses, one or two diplomats and a few business people. . . . The ambassador and his wife were hosts at [dinner]. . . . Bangkok was booming and more and more business people arrived to avail themselves of the money-making opportunities."[23]

Because of the ways that nightlife lubricates such opportunities by helping people make sense of a world in motion, bars, restaurants, and hotels became increasingly important institutions for the city. And although the Bamboo Bar was still struggling to stabilize the lineup of its house band in the late 1940s and early 1950s, jazz was already vital to its affective environment. Maurice Rocco would begin his residency at the bar in 1964, when even more money and status were at stake. By the 1960s, the bar afforded part of an intimate nightlife scene that transformed Thailand economically and culturally. Anticipating such a future fifteen years before it arrived, Krull had built a gilded space.

New Phetchaburi Road

One morning during the rainy season of 2019, I walked the full length of New Phetchaburi Road's original two and a half kilometers. The road is now marked by dilapidated, mid-twentieth-century buildings, a bit more modern and a few stories taller than traditional shophouses. Many of these date to the time of the road's development before and during the war in Vietnam. New Phetchaburi, once nicknamed "the American Strip" or the "golden mile," was Bangkok's primary bar and nightlife area for GIs during the American era. It was as vibrant as it was squalid. In the 1960s, it was also an epicenter of live music. "Out past Soi Asoke was full of GI bars, short time hotels, the Morakot inter alia, and massage parlors, catering almost entirely to R&R visitors from Vietnam," recalled one American serviceman. "Many of those GIs never saw any other part of Bangkok during their R&R."[24] One Thai woman sex worker claimed that the bars on New Phetchaburi were among the city's seediest nightlife spaces.[25] *Bangkok World* columnist Bernard Trink called the road's conditions "shockingly poor" in 1968.[26] Yet the American Strip thrived throughout the war. By 2019, however, that world was almost half a century gone.

Today there is little new construction along New Phetchaburi, with the exception of a few government buildings and offices. The value of the land is low compared to that of nearby neighborhoods.[27] The area's condition (and land value) contrasts especially with Sukhumvit Road, a roughly parallel road about one kilometer south that also catered to international visitors during the American era. Most of the 1960s businesses along New Phetchaburi closed many years ago. The R&R party ended when American troops left in the mid-1970s, culminating in a full withdrawal by 1976. "When Phetchaburi opened up, it was all GI bars," one American who lived through that time explained to me, but "Phetchaburi was a dump by the early 1980s."[28] According to a guide to Thailand published by a US supercarrier stationed in-country, by the end of the 1970s most of the road's bars and clubs had closed or moved to other parts of town.[29] The neighborhood was surpassed by the Sukhumvit and Patpong nightlife areas, and it has never recovered. Many of its war-era structures now sit unoccupied or have been repurposed as fresh markets. Much of the artery has the feel of a highway rather than a walking street. And there is no more music. From the GI era, the only surviving street-level commercial presence is massage parlors, and there are relatively few even of those. My walk showed mere glimpses of a bygone vital nightlife scene.

New Phetchaburi is contiguous with the original Phetchaburi Road, which preceded it, and today there is no visible indication that New Phetchaburi was built separately. For its entire length, the road runs alongside Saen Saep canal, the last remaining commuter *khlong* (canal) in Bangkok, at certain points rising just a few meters above its banks. Saen Saep is one of many artificial channels first dug by Chinese and Lao laborers in the early nineteenth century as maritime expressways for Siamese troops moving between the Chao Phraya River and the provinces adjacent to Bangkok. The canal's western leg is still used by Bangkokians to get across the city by boat. The eastern end of New Phetchaburi is an intersection called Pratunam, meaning "water gate." This name refers to Saen Saep's sluice gate, although the gate itself can no longer be seen. Malls, hotels, markets, and of course pavement now cover it like the layers of a palimpsest.[30] In many ways, the road's past, including its once boisterous nightlife scene, is now invisible.

Before the road's construction began in 1959—just five years before Maurice Rocco moved to Thailand—the area slated for construction was swampland dotted with rice fields, orchards, and rain trees, all lying outside the developed core of Bangkok.[31] Like the vast majority of Bangkok's metropolitan area at the time, it was a mix of agricultural fields and undeveloped land. The fertile soil was worked by poor Chinese and Muslim laborers, who lived in slums alongside the canal. Unlike the Sampheng district a few kilometers to the south, also populated by Chinese laborers, this area was not yet of administrative concern to the Thai government or monarchy. In fact, it was barely part of the city at all.

Like large swathes of Bangkok in the mid-twentieth century, the area where New Phetchaburi would eventually be built was aqueous, fed by the waters of the Chao Phraya River. Urban transportation in Bangkok occurred by boat through a labyrinth of canals, which were crucial public spaces not only as transportation arteries but also for everyday living. Waterways were used for trade at floating markets, bathing, fire protection, irrigation, fishing, and religious worship. Although the canals had originally been built to serve military ends, they were later thoroughly integrated into the city's social fabric. It was thus a major disruption when many of these waterways were covered with impervious surface in the 1950s and 1960s.[a] Canals were surfaced to support the construction of new roads, highways, and buildings. The changes were rapid and dramatic. One study based on historical aerial maps of Bangkok found an overall reduction from 170,500 total meters of canal in 1932 to just 44,763 meters by 2017.[32] In sum, paved arteries like New Phetchaburi displaced former features of the floodplain—both waterways and the communities that used them—en masse during the Cold War. By the late 1970s, new paving had slowed, but war-era infrastructure projects had permanently changed Bangkok, among other things transforming it into a car-dependent city.

Today, New Phetchaburi's lack of recent development reveals buried layers of the palimpsest. Parts of the road are elevated above the mud below, where ample shanty housing remains. The train tracks that bisect the artery have been partially reclaimed as footpaths or for small-scale commerce. Upon crossing Pratunam, one of Bangkok's most imposing intersections for pedestrians (fortunately there is an overpass), one sees immediately how New Phetchaburi hosts fragments of community that coalesce around the site of a past rupture. People raise chickens on tiny slivers of land between road and canal. Palm trees peek over guardrails. Stilted homes open directly onto the water, which residents still use for daily purposes. The massive infrastructure projects of the twentieth century altered landscapes and lifeways, but when those projects ended, past lifeways returned like wandering specters.

How and why did these disruptive development projects come about? The United States had a heavy hand in the paving of Bangkok, including New Phetchaburi Road. The paving of the city was one facet of an anti-communist campaign active from the mid-1950s through the early 1970s. US president Dwight Eisenhower prioritized checking the regional spread of communism. Infrastructural development, key to Eisenhower's fight against communism in Asia, began in Thailand soon after he took office in 1953. Northeast Thailand was of special concern, as it lay close to hotbeds of communist activity in Laos

a ACKNOWLEDGMENT: My thanks to University of Pennsylvania geophysics professor and surfing instructor Dr. Douglas Jerolmack for reading and commenting on this material with respect to the landscape and geology of Bangkok.

and it was poor (and thus allegedly vulnerable to communist recruitment). The Eisenhower administration felt that Northeast Thailand needed a massive economic stimulus to prevent its proverbial dominos from falling. Before such development could occur, however, the northeast had to be physically linked to the economic heart of the country: Bangkok. American development work brought the remote northeast into Bangkok's administrative orbit, centralizing and expediting everything from travel to communication. Above all, this required roads, which were built at a pace Thailand had never seen, connecting places where infrastructure had never reached. In unintentional ways, the feverish building of roads would help bring active, profitable nightlife and music scenes to Thailand within a decade.

The entity that managed road-building projects on behalf of the United States was called the US Operations Mission (USOM) in Thailand.[33] USOM's purview was broad, encompassing not only roads but also education, TV and radio broadcasting, sanitation, and quite a bit more. In fact, almost all American development work in Thailand aside from intelligence, propaganda, or military operations was at that time under USOM's authority. USOM spent several years in the early 1950s both mobilizing resources *and* articulating justifications for its projects. By the end of the 1950s, well before the war in Vietnam, the mission had brought in hundreds of Thai and American personnel, procuring foreign construction contracts and managing an array of projects with cumulative lifetime costs greater than $100 million.[34] This work was accompanied by a rhetorical effort to cast development as magnanimous rather than what it actually was: part of a cutthroat global fight against communism.

Transportation was USOM's primary focus as it modernized and connected Thailand internally. According to Sean Randolph, "Between 1955 and 1960 . . . USOM involved itself in virtually every major highway project in Thailand. Between 1951 and 1965, $350,000,000 was spent on highway construction."[35] For perspective on how important transportation was to the American development effort, in one period in the 1950s USOM self-reported spending $51.7 million building roads and highways, compared to $13.2 million on health and sanitation, $12 million on agriculture, and $9.8 million on education.[36] None of USOM's other endeavors came close to matching its expenditures on paved roads.

The first major transportation project overseen by USOM was a "Friendship Highway" that connected the remote northeastern province of Korat to the central province of Saraburi, near Bangkok. Begun in 1954 and completed in 1958, the Friendship Highway reduced travel between Bangkok and Korat from "8 or 9 hours of dangerous, car-busting travel" along four hundred kilometers of "tortuous and rough" road down to a manageable three and a half hours over just 150 kilometers.[37] Funds authorized for the project totaled more than $20 million, much of which was paid to American civil engineering and construction firms. A similarly modern asphalt highway was built between the north and northeastern regions between 1955 and 1961, employing the same American contractors who built the Friendship Highway. Although USOM often boasted of the training it provided to Thai engineers, machine operators, and technicians, the bulk of its payments flowed to American firms like Sverdrup and Parcel in Missouri and Raymond Construction in Texas. A telegram from the US embassy in Bangkok to secretary of state Dean Rusk summarized the Thai perception of this as graft: "Under the loan agreement, bidding can only be done by American companies. . . . The lowest bid was almost twice the Thai Highway Dept. estimate of the construction costs. . . . It looks as if the American companies have taken advantage of the condition in the loan agreement to cooperate in keeping bids high and ensuring a big profit."[38]

Nationalist nepotism aside, USOM's primary goal in building roads was to control and surveil Thailand's outer provinces. "Highway 223 will help counter communist insurgency by improving communications and the road to Sattahip will be important for its economic value to the Northeast," noted the *Bangkok Post*.[39] Before 1965, "counterinsurgency officially became USOM's highest priority; that is, all aid projects were selected or rejected on the basis of assisting the Thai government in defeating the Communists."[40] From political rationales to financial beneficiaries, road-building in Thailand during the Cold War served American anti-communist ends.

Once the Friendship Highway was finished, USOM began building or improving a series of roads inside Bangkok itself. Though much shorter than the highways that linked rural provinces, inner-city road-building followed a similar logic of enhanced integration. Highways and city roads were different components of the same ambitious transportation network. Most of USOM's work in the capital fell under the aegis of the "Bangkok-Bangkapi Roads" project, which included widening and resurfacing Sukhumvit and Rama IV Roads, constructing or repairing bridges, and finally extending Phetchaburi Road to create what would eventually be called New Phetchaburi Road, or Phetchaburi Tat Mai in Thai. In its quarterly reports, USOM described these projects as efforts toward national connection. For example, the renovation of Sukhumvit Road was important not only for transportation inside the city but because it served as a link from Bangkok to "the only highway to south-east Thailand."[41] USOM's report emphasized the economic benefits of national road-building. But the authors were also surely aware that the southeastern city of Sattahip was being eyed as the future site of a large American military base. Sattahip's U-Tapao airfield was already in use at that time by the Royal Thai Navy. By 1965 it would become a frontline base for the US Air Force, vital for launching B-52 bombing missions in Vietnam. Economic development was critical to USOM's anti-communist mission. But the increasing overlap between local economic growth and military capacity-building in the early 1960s is also in evidence. Intimate economies, including musical spaces, would soon follow. "[In 1965] we asked ourselves what we should do to welcome the American soldiers?" one Sattahip resident remembered asking. "Around the end of the year, the first bars opened. The sweet smell of the dollar tempted us."[42] No sooner was pavement laid than nightlife grew along its edges, which turned out to be a fertile loam for capital.

Roads in urban Bangkok posed unique logistical challenges. In densely populated areas, engineers had to relocate water, electric, telephone, and sewer lines, among other existing infrastructure, and they had to build sidewalks. Developers also needed to fill in and pave many of the canals that crisscrossed the city, as these hampered the growth of a comprehensive infrastructure for vehicle traffic. But before any of this could occur, the Thai government had to relocate citizens whose homes were in the way of planned thoroughfares. Among the elements of the Bangkok-Bangkapi project, the New Phetchaburi extension involved the most new development, and thus it required the most extensive human displacement.

It so happened that many of the people who lived in the path of the planned road were poor Chinese immigrant laborers, a class and identity position that was multiply vulnerable in Thailand in the 1950s.[43] Chinese people had long faced discrimination in the kingdom but most acutely since a large wave of Chinese immigration to Siam in the early twentieth century. In 1914, Siamese king Vajiravudh published a pamphlet in which (drawing on anti-Semitic comparisons already at least a decade old) he used the protofascistic term *Jews of the East* to refer to the Chinese in Siam, blaming them for a range of national ills in spite, or perhaps because, of their economic success. The fact that Vajiravudh was himself part-Chinese suggests the deep complexity and ambiguity of Siamese Chinese identity. Nevertheless, the networks of close kinship that characterized Siamese Chinese businesses aroused political suspicion. The Siamese government began to classify the Chinese in effectively racial terms. "The Chinese first of all were said to be unassimilable: because of their racial loyalty and sense of superiority, they remain always Chinese," notes William Skinner.[44] Lawrence Chua has demonstrated that the Chinese were treated as a distinct racial category by the Siamese census as early as 1910 and that the Siamese government used this categorization to manage, compete with, and profit from Chinese enterprises.[45]

By the time New Phetchaburi was built, a number of Chinese families had grown rich and powerful and were in some cases insulated from the effects of racism, even granted pathways to assimilation. Bangkok was well on its way to becoming a Sino-Thai city. But during the Cold War, ethnic Chineseness remained persistently suspect and poor Chinese laborers subject to violence and deportation. Anti-Chinese slurs were common in everyday speech. In the 1940s, Field Marshal Phibun Songkhram feared uprisings in Thai Chinese communities amid strained relations between Thailand and the newly communist government in Beijing. As prime minister, Phibun actively harassed Chinese people. In September 1945, the police and eventually also the military engaged in a nightlong shootout with ethnic Chinese who had failed to display the flag of Thailand during a parade earlier in the day.[46] Such repression worsened in the 1950s, especially after Sarit Thanarat came to power as prime minister in a 1957 coup. Courting American support even more aggressively than his predecessors, Sarit scapegoated poor Chinese people (the Chinese merchant class fared better) in order to demonstrate his opposition to communism. In one infamous incident, Sarit ordered the summary execution of five Chinese men accused of arson.[47] The United States, appreciative of Sarit's opposition to communism, openly tolerated his racist authoritarianism. This led to a toxic symbiosis: the US government was circumstantially Sinophobic because it feared the spread of communism among Thai Chinese, while the Thai government was circumstantially anti-communist because it distrusted the Chinese.[48] Caught in this double bind, poor ethnic Chinese laborers who lived in housing labeled as "blighted" near Saen Saep canal were powerless to halt their displacement at the hands of the Thai government and USOM in the late 1950s and early 1960s.

It is not clear when or even whether displaced residents of the area slated for New Phetchaburi were ever compensated for their land. A 1958 USOM report makes passing reference to the legal process for displacing current residents: "The municipality requested authority to advertise construction of the Phetchaburi extension prior to securing right-of-way. A letter was written in reply stating that we believed advertising should be withheld until right-of-way was secured and arrangements made."[49] In fact, right-of-way may never have been formally secured. One man from a wealthy Thai Chinese family who lived on the north side of Saen Saep canal when New Phetchaburi was built told me that the construction was a complete surprise to him as a young boy:

PETIPONG PUNGBUN NA AYUDHYA: My family lived on the left side of Saen Saep canal. My grandparents lived there for a very long time. I had to take a boat and then take a tram [to school]. . . . So my parents bought a car. And every day we had to cross the canal by a boat, and then take a car to go to work. I think it was 1958 or '59. Then I think in 1961 or '62, while I was playing with my friends, this captain came along in the backyard of my house, which was formerly a vegetable garden run by a Chinese man and the rest of the piece of land was rented out to the Chinese. And then one day this captain came without me knowing, and he just started building his road.

BENJAMIN: They started building the road without telling you? And did they take any of your property?

PETIPONG: Yes.

BENJAMIN: They seized your property without giving you any warning?

PETIPONG: I don't think we raised any objections, because we were very happy that the road came along. I felt good because I didn't have to use the *khlong* anymore. I can go by bus or something like that. Everybody was happy except for the Chinese.[50]

For someone from a rich, noble family, Petipong's experience was rare. Not only did his family own a car, making them direct beneficiaries of New Phetchaburi, but they also soon invested in land along the new road, which they would develop into bars and clubs when the American era arrived in the 1960s. Nevertheless, Petipong acknowledges that most Chinese residents near Saen Saep were less fortunate than he, and those residents had a far worse experience of displacement.

In 1946, the Chinese government accused Thailand of preparing to steal land from ethnic Chinese residents in order to give that stolen land to Americans.[51] At the time, those accusations must have come across as propaganda. But in fact that is exactly what happened when Chinese people were forced from their homes to allow for the paving of New Phetchaburi Road. Within three years of its completion, this artery would become Bangkok's most popular GI nightlife area, a place where American-style capitalism could proceed unchecked, with live music at its center. New Phetchaburi was built to promote capital (and thus to fight communism) by advancing national development and aiding the American war effort. The anti-Chinese dimensions of its construction were merely an animating force.

Even as the chief reasons for building New Phetchaburi were plain to see—internal connectivity, economic development, and militarism as barricades against communism, with Sinophobia also in the mix—USOM and its Thai allies tried to offer nobler justifications in public. They deemphasized American interests while playing up the benefits of development for sanitation and traffic flow. One March 1960 letter from Thai major general Sathien Pojananond to Thomas Naughton, director of USOM, described American aid as selfless. "The aim of the U.S. economic aid is to 'help us help ourselves,'" wrote Sathien, making no mention of American interests or policy. His letter cast development as generous and rational, while making the need for neocolonial projects seem self-evident.[52] This kind of language "legitimated U.S. expansion while denying its coercive or imperial nature."[53] USOM sought to minimize America's neocolonial designs under cover of rationality and reciprocity.

A master's thesis written by a Thammasat University student named Radom Setteeton in 1960 echoed such language. Radom later became an economics professor in Bangkok, after earning an American PhD. His training, as well as his regular travel to the United States, helps explain his comfort with American development. In his thesis, Radom suggested that the impetus for road-building in Thailand emanated from the wisdom of aristocratic Thais, including the king, who traveled to "the great cities of the world," where they saw what great roads should ideally look like.[54] Radom breathlessly described the new roads built or improved in Thailand at the suggestion of aristocrats as "so modern, so wide, and so beautiful." Radom saw Europe at the apex of a hierarchy that Thailand should try to ascend.

Making direct reference to the Bangkok-Bangkapi Roads project, Radom explains road construction as a project led by great men. He tells a reverent story about Prime Minister Sarit touring a subdistrict outside Bangkok one day, looking for solutions to traffic and sanitation problems. Afterward, Sarit calls a meeting with his top ministers to propose solutions, which are then dutifully enacted. In this fanciful story, the paternal Sarit sees the flaws in urban design and makes policy suggestions that are immediately translated into action. Power flows frictionlessly from the great leader, a political model less democratic than divine. "With the exception of persons of high rank," suggests Radom, "the impact of individuals to the decision-making in street administration is little."[55] The prime minister derives his authority from a magical sense of rational urban development (which just happens to genuflect to the West). This mirrors the absolute authority of the king himself. Mythomania keeps the neocolonial reality of urban development out of sight.

Invoking the designs of London, Copenhagen, Chicago, and New York, Radom argued that new roads would reduce congestion and traffic accidents. By contrast, he considered *khlong*s a risk and a threat. Some existing canals that could not be salvaged due to sanitation problems or logistical inconvenience, he argued, might need to be dredged and filled. A few could be preserved for the sake of traditional lifeways or to attract tourism but only if kept sanitary. "They tend to be one of the major sources of filth and a major source of disease dispersion if they are used for consumption," wrote Radom. The filling of canals was explained and justified not as part of a politicized American vision of development, anti-communism, and militarization but as sound public health. This supported the fiction that, as Christina Klein puts it, "America did not pursue its naked self-interest through the coercion and subjugation of others, but engaged in exchanges that benefited all parties."[56]

Radom refers approvingly to the Greater Bangkok Plan of 1960, a sweeping document produced by an American firm called Litchfield, Whiting, Bowne, and Associates.[57b] The Litchfield firm shared consultants as well as a developmental vision with USOM, and the Greater Bangkok Plan was a "joint undertaking" between USOM and the Thai government. The plan mapped out the next thirty years of Bangkok's development through the eyes of Americans with significant global development and military connections. But, echoing Radom, the authors described their plan as merely providing a "rational, consistent framework" focused on "water supply, storm and sanitary sewerage, transportation, schools, etc." Safety, efficiency, stability, and public health became warrants for remaking the Thai capital. Like Radom's thesis, the Greater Bangkok Plan avoided any mention of US development or military priorities. The authors took care to list all of the Thai engineers and technicians involved in its preparation and thanked the Thai government profusely. This made it appear that the plan was a shared vision, if not a primarily Thai vision, for the future of Bangkok. In reality, US strategic interest drove the plan at every level.

New Phetchaburi Road was completed in 1962 and opened to traffic in 1963. As USOM and the American government hoped, the capital quickly became more amenable to motor vehicles and also more connected to the rest of the country. Cars and trucks, including those that might carry munitions or

---

b ACKNOWLEDGMENT: I thank SUNY Stony Brook PhD student Christine Pash for helping to locate historical information about the Litchfield firm.

manufacturing material, could now move quickly from western Bangkok to air force bases and other facilities beyond the city—at times, in fact, too quickly; the earliest newspaper headlines about the road complained of a scourge of speeding. The new artery was part of Thailand's emergent car culture; the number of cars in Bangkok increased 650 percent from 1947 to 1957, and the number of vehicle registrations nationwide more than doubled between 1959 and 1964.[58]

As a means of internally linking the country, promoting car travel, and making remote places more accessible, New Phetchaburi was a success. But an optimistic vision for traffic mitigation and sanitation—if such a vision was ever sincere—failed. Traffic jams and pollution have greatly worsened in Bangkok since the 1960s. The paving of canals has shifted the city from having a tendency to experience frequent small floods to experiencing rarer but more catastrophic events. Urban development left the city more vulnerable to the effects of climate change in the twenty-first century while also contributing to the intensity of those effects. But as of 1962, when Cold War concerns precluded almost any other kind of political thinking, USOM had accomplished a major strategic goal: building a connective network to steel Thailand against communism.

Still, within three years of its completion, New Phetchaburi would take on a different and unintended purpose. Around 1966, New Phetchaburi was informally designated as the primary R&R enclave for visiting American soldiers. Bars, massage parlors, and music venues catering to soldiers began appearing along its pavement. As chapter 4 will describe, by the mid-1960s, money flowed easily along New Phetchaburi, and intimate relationships prospered there. The road had not been built prognostically as a center for R&R nightlife. Documents related to its construction never mention the road as a space in its own right, merely as a route between other locations—in effect a nonplace. The Litchfield plan refers to New Phetchaburi only as part of an industrial bypass route. Nevertheless, by 1966 nightlife intimacies would fill the spatial container of New Phetchaburi to its brim. The contexts of music and nightlife that would prove so central to GI experiences of Thailand during the war, and transformative to the country's culture and economy, were built directly on the surfaces described in this chapter. Transnational nightlife was an outgrowth of militarism. Its music was incubated by neocolonial domination.

Such ad hoc effects are typical in Bangkok, where urban planning routinely fails.[59] The Greater Bangkok Plan is a fitting example. Despite its sweeping vision, the plan was never implemented. Government agencies could not coordinate with one another, and USOM eventually abandoned its blueprint. "These grand plans," writes Claudio Sopranzetti, "if coherent and definitive in the pages of the Litchfield Plan, crashed against the messiness, contingency, and contradictions of daily practices in the city and the fragile and fragmentary state apparatus that was supposed to control and implement them. The abstract idea of re-writing the city looked, in practice, more like a confused entanglement of scribbles than a tidy overlay."[60] Lacking central planning, Bangkok increasingly became "a city of congested infrastructure networks and broken social services."[61] It also became a place of increasingly unregulated foreign tourism, including intimate nightlife.

During my 2019 walk along New Phetchaburi, I wondered whether the CIA or a large conglomerate like the Ital-Thai company might have had a guiding hand in the road's development. But there is no clear indication that this was the case. Rather, it seems that New Phetchaburi was built as part of an American-led, nationwide push for connectivity. Contrary to Radom's story about Sarit's divine intuition, power—let alone planning—did not flow from a single source. The transformation of New Phetchaburi into an American nightlife strip typifies a shambolic regime of urban development. The beginning of the war in Vietnam in 1965 gave the road a new and urgent purpose. But there was no great man leading it there. Instead, fresh pavement, piles of money, racist impulses, and frightened, horny soldiers congealed within a neocolonial war machine to yield a fashionable new nightlife area. Sometimes spaces, even those that serve a profound purpose, are produced and reproduced without intention.

New Phetchaburi would soon be a space that not only served the American war effort but also housed intimate encounters. Like the Bamboo Bar, the American Strip would become an important node in Bangkok's musical culture in the next decade. But unlike the Bamboo Bar, the road had not been built deliberately with such ends in mind. For the first two years of its existence, before the bars were built, it was mostly an artery of war. As chapter 4 will describe, when war arrived the most logical use for the road *as a space* turned out to be in service of Bangkok's cosmopolitan nightlife.

Conclusion

In 1950 Thailand was of fledgling interest to the United States. By 1955 it had become more significant, and by 1960 it was an indispensable ally. The fates of the two countries intertwined as the war in Vietnam approached. The amount of money and infrastructure that the United States invested in Thailand during the 1950s was so massive that Thailand arguably ceased to act as an independent nation. In turn, the United States relied heavily on Thailand as a regional partner. What would soon be called a quagmire in Vietnam was foreshadowed by an American approach to foreign policy in Thailand so blinkered in the 1950s that it proved impossible to pull back later without inviting catastrophic effects. The two spaces this chapter historicizes developed during these years of heedless intimacy. At every scale of life and business in Thailand, the conditions of possibility for the American era and its messy involvements were being established. The conditions that enabled Maurice Rocco's arrival were now set in place.

The list of globalizing moves made by Thailand in the 1950s is long indeed. Prime Minister Sarit accelerated economic development, counterinsurgency, privatization, and foreign investment. In the late 1950s, he built on a decade of increased alignment with the United States, introducing reforms and initiatives that furthered the two nations' intimate relationship. The infrastructural investment in New Phetchaburi Road was just one consequence. Around the same time, Bangkok became headquarters for the Southeast Asian Treaty Organization (SEATO), an anti-communist group modeled after NATO. Meanwhile, as an anti-communist measure, Sarit took steps to revive royal symbolism. King Bhumibol Adulyadej's profile as a jazz composer and saxophonist figured prominently in this revival; the king invited Benny Goodman to Bangkok in 1956 as part of a State Department tour, then later jammed in 1960 at Goodman's Manhattan apartment. The king's facility with a culturally western musical idiom suggested Thailand's cultural proximity to the United States and thus to anti-communism as well. Simultaneously, the government directed Thai universities to begin teaching students English.[62] Sarit established the National Economic Development Board in 1958 and the Board of Investment in 1961 and lifted limits on foreign landholding. His 1958 national development plan called for expanded American aid, beefing up security at the expense of social welfare. Sarit oversaw a massive rise in managerial approaches to both culture and economy; the National Economic Development Board created new criteria for "first-class" hotels, whose construction by international conglomerates was incentivized.[63] The Tourist Organization of Thailand (later Tourism Authority of Thailand) was conceived in 1959 and officially launched in 1960. Retail stores that met specific criteria for modernization received a special sticker from the Tourist Organization to place in their windows to show that they were, according to the *Bangkok Post*, "approved shops as a guide for tourists."[64] And on and on. Thailand's war-era music and nightlife were built upon this globalizing, American-facing foundation.

Suddenly much of Thailand was international, tourist-focused, and perhaps above all friendly to Americans. All of this dovetailed with the increasing presence of western soldiers, diplomats, and businesspeople. This period saw the first major wave of tourists to visit and spend money in Thailand during the Cold

War, and Sarit's expansive vision for a tourist-focused, cosmopolitan national development was created with them in mind. The proto-American-era spaces described in this chapter were shaped in significant ways by Sarit. The groundwork for the American era, both as a geopolitical movement and a context of intimate everyday spaces, was established in the 1950s, even before the war in Vietnam began.[65]

The next chapter returns to Maurice Rocco, detailing his life in the United States during the 1950s, the same decade that chapter 2 has described in Thailand. Chapter 3 will examine the turbulence that led Rocco to leave the United States. He would soon avail himself of the spaces and opportunities that Thailand was now ready to provide. In doing so, his experience would exemplify the nightlife intimacies that became possible amid Thailand and America's burgeoning "special friendship."

3

"WHAT EVER HAPPENED TO

MAURICE ROCCO?"

My father was the Maurice Rocco fan, and he would have me learn his songs and play them for him. Then one day he just stopped requesting them. —RAMSEY LEWIS (2019, interview with the author)

Like most musical genres, rock and roll has no birthday.[1] Its name was foreshadowed, over decades if not centuries, by the innumerable blues, boogie-woogie, and rhythm and blues songs and by spirituals that all used words like *rockin'* with meanings both sacred and carnal. Critics used *rock and roll* on occasion to categorize the music of Sister Rosetta Tharpe in the early 1940s, but it was not until a decade later that the term described anything like a fixed generic form. In hindsight, driving blues anchored by distorted guitar, including Ike Turner's "Rocket 88" (1951), sound like rock and roll's first complete realizations. Yet even before the genre was codified, many of the songs that foreshadowed it were major hits, lifting young artists to stardom. The key symbols of the new music, touched on in chapter 1, were excess, exultant young bodies, and a sense of joyful recklessness escaping the frame. Anchored by these symbols, a new cultural and commercial juggernaut was born.

Maurice Rocco played no part in any of this. By 1950 he was thirty-five years old, antique as popular musicians go. As chapter 1 argued, Rocco's live performances in the 1930s and 1940s were part of the blueprint of rock and roll, especially his standing pianistics. He was connected to Black, queer night-life worlds, whose fashions would eventually be transformed from novelty into art through the racial-capital alchemy of rock and its cognoscenti. But Rocco was ten to fifteen years older than Little Richard, Ike Turner, Elvis Presley, Ruth Brown, and others of a generation who launched their careers in a newer mass media moment. Rocco helped create their milieu. But as an artifact of war-era nightclubs, a master of last decade's style, he helped build a house for rock and roll that he would never himself occupy.

This chapter follows Rocco from the early 1950s, the ebbing years of his commercial peak, through 1959, when he left the United States forever, on his way to a second act in Bangkok. As the last chapter discussed, this was the same decade that Thailand was actively building spaces that would accommodate Americans and their fantasies of international nightlife. In 1964, Rocco renewed his career in Thailand in precisely these spaces. But the decade-plus journey to his renewal was anguished. His cachet fading in the early 1950s, Rocco fell out of fashion and into legal trouble. By the middle of the decade, he spent lengthy stints away from music, mired in court cases and at times in jail. Rather than riding the wave of rock and roll, which he had helped set in motion, Rocco's career in the United States washed ashore. But this same moment was also one of new opportunities for American performers abroad, albeit for a troubling reason: American militarism. In the wake of war, Rocco would remake himself as an international symbol of jazz in Europe and eventually Asia.

Humiliations of Home

Rocco hustled as a live act in 1950, playing held-over nightclub gigs, though now rarely in New York or Los Angeles. His year was dominated by twice-nightly shows at a hotel bar in Saint Louis (the Zodiac ballroom of the Chase Hotel), a gambling and dinner venue in northern Kentucky (the Lookout House), and a casino in Reno (the Mapes). Many of these were also regular touring stops for "Rat Pack" entertainers like Dean Martin and Frank Sinatra.

The gigs were decent, but they paid less than the clubs in bigger cities where Rocco had played in the 1940s, and the venues had rough reputations.

His schedule was dotted with only a few high-profile appearances, including one on Bob Hope's first television special, *Star-Spangled Revue*, in April 1950. After a decade on radio and playing for troops, Hope's TV debut was widely anticipated, so much so that NBC paid him the gaudy sum of $40,000 for the program, which became, in effect, the pilot episode of *The Bob Hope Show*. Given Hope's platform on the new show, it was a vote of confidence for the host to feature Rocco as his first act. But the accolade was marred by a racist incident, albeit one that the press did not seem to notice. After opening with a short comic monologue, Hope welcomed Rocco to the stage, referring to him as "boy." Rocco then tap-danced his way through two numbers, including W. C. Handy's "St. Louis Blues" (infused with a few measures of Dizzy Gillespie's "Salt Peanuts," perhaps to show that he could handle bebop), moving the piano around the stage and engaging in a complex choreographed dance routine as he played. The power of his left hand had perhaps never been so evident. The performance was among Rocco's best on-screen, but Hope's casually racist introduction was a reminder of Rocco's debased position in show business. A choice opportunity became, with that word, a fresh reminder of the racial hierarchies that Rocco could never escape in the United States. Rocco's performance was meanwhile dismissed in the newspapers. Ed Sullivan wrote that "the Maurice Rocco opening was a TV cliché."[2] His most prominent appearance of 1950 looks impressive in retrospect, but at the time it did little to quell the sense that he was a fading star, and it affirmed some tenacious indignities.

The year 1951 was much the same. Rocco played at casinos, a café in Montreal, and Grossinger's, a Jewish resort in the Catskills. The language of his advertisements began to allude to rock and roll—one 1954 ad implored audiences to "rock and roll with Rocco"—but this belied the fact that he was tangential to rock and roll's emergent moment. Live, he continued to play much the same repertoire as he had in the 1940s, primarily boogie-woogie, even as that music fell further out of style. By 1951 the press was beginning to forget him. Jazz publications like *DownBeat* and *Metronome* had covered his shows and recordings extensively in the 1940s; by 1951 they had moved on.

The declining prestige of Rocco's gigs also meant, of course, declining income. After regularly earning double salary in the mid-1940s, his typical payments fell to less than $1,000 a week. Rocco's ownership of numerous properties gradually became untenable. He sold all four of his lots in Oxford, originally purchased for his mother on Sycamore and Poplar Streets, in 1949. Despite still being a regular on Jackie Gleason's vaudevillian TV show *Cavalcade of Stars*, Rocco had no media appearances that paid nearly as well as the previous year's show with Bob Hope. He began to spiral. His clothing was stolen from a Saint Louis hotel room in February 1951. In 1952, segregationist Georgia governor Herman Talmadge publicly denounced Rocco's appearance alongside a white woman on television. Hurting on many fronts, Rocco was charged with passing bad checks for the first time in July 1950, at a Cincinnati clothing store.[3] He was cleared in court after paying the balance. But his career remained at a nadir throughout the decade. He would face bad check or loan default charges again in 1953, 1956, 1957, and 1958.

The early 1950s were a grind. Rocco kept touring, playing small-time television shows, appearing in Miami, playing a GOP convention in Rochester, New York, and traveling between cities from coast to coast at a backbreaking pace. Rarely taking more than a few days off, he cycled through about twenty different North American cities for more than three years. As his fortieth birthday approached, he was primarily a casino act, featured in small towns like Windsor, Ontario, and Reno, Nevada. Compounding the indignity, he was now regularly billed in the press as a novelty performer rather than an artist. The papers called him "Madcap Maurice Rocco" or a "frenzied comedian at the piano."[4] Review after review in the 1950s tagged him as a novelty pianist, a designation he never would have accepted in the 1940s. The *Cincinnati Enquirer* announced one of his homecoming shows in 1951 by noting acidly that "he doesn't waste much time with the more serious music."[5] Although the press had always hyperbolized Rocco's wildness, this condescension was new. There was no longer any sense of trajectory to his career, only a stream of work-for-hire gigs. In 1953, a club called the Brass Rail in Ontario brought a union claim against him for his alleged failure to pay back a $150 loan, an amount that would have been insignificant to him a decade earlier. Rocco was broke and flailing.

Meanwhile, many of the key pieces of rock and roll were falling into place all around him but never to his benefit. Rock had its commercial breakout in 1955 after several years of priming. Big Mama Thornton recorded "Hound Dog" in 1952; Elvis Presley made his first Sun Studios demos in 1953; Guitar Slim's "The Things That I Used to Do" became a surprise hit the same year. These were all pieces of a fledgling rock music industry distinct from the nightclub network that had launched Rocco's career. Rocco showed no desire to adapt to rock, and it had little use for him in turn. Louis Rodabaugh reflected in his memoir that "America had embraced the cult of the ugly in all things: music, theater, television, radio, dress, hairdos, morals.... The list is long. The beautiful big bands had practically disappeared, and bookings for such former stars as Maurice Rocco had become few and far between."[6] Rodabaugh's fusspot view of rock and roll hardly negates his correct observation that Rocco's moment had passed. In the first half of 1955, Rocco's main gig was at a Polynesian-themed hotel in Las Vegas, part of a revue that also included acts called the Zany Madcaps and the Hilarious Halfback Trio. The music press was no longer writing about him at all.

Sydney, a Sanctuary

Then seemingly out of nowhere, 1955 offered Rocco a career lifeline. On June 11, just weeks before "Rock around the Clock" became rock and roll's first number one *Billboard* single, Rocco boarded a Pan Am flight from San Francisco to Sydney, Australia. He would remain overseas for the next nine months with a touring group called the Harlem Blackbirds. Rocco had traveled abroad before, including short trips to Cuba and for many gigs in Canada. He played his first extended international tour in England in 1948. That trip was remarkable. Eleanor Roosevelt sat in the audience as he performed on a ship crossing the Atlantic.[7] The London papers wrote breathless reviews once he arrived. But Rocco was still a leading draw in 1948. The fanfare that greeted him abroad in the 1940s was simply an extension of what he experienced at home. By 1955, however, his career was in shambles, and he desperately needed a high-profile, high-earning opportunity.

The Harlem Blackbirds were created and produced by Larry Steele, a Chicago-born Black impresario and songwriter who had worked with leading jazz artists in the United States for many years. The Blackbirds show was adapted from a similar Steele-produced revue in New York City in the early 1950s called "Smart Affairs." The show toured Australia and New Zealand for almost a year in 1955 and 1956, becoming the first all-Black ensemble to tour either of those countries. Their performances were a stylized representation of Black music in America, not unlike what "From Spirituals to Swing" had undertaken in New York in the late 1930s. The program book heavily hyped the fame of its "32 sepia stars." Thus the duo Leonard and Leonard were "one of the most brilliant dancing duos in the show business," on a bill with "the famous Conga Girls—who have thrilled America" and with "Freddie and Flo [who] played all leading R.K.O. theatres in the U.S.A." Steele had a showman's instincts, and his management helped make the Blackbirds a hit. "Bookings since the cast arrived have been phenomenal, with queues each day at the Palladium," noted the *Sydney Morning Herald*.[8]

During Rocco's time with the Blackbirds from June 1955 through February 1956, he was the headliner, billed in the program as "our star." Betty Frazier, who joined the Blackbirds as a chorus girl when she was a teenager, told me in an interview that Rocco had been "the star of the show."[9] In ads, he was listed first and in the largest print of any member of the ensemble. Headlining a sold-out revue, Rocco was suddenly receiving the kind of attention that had eluded him in the United States for the past five years. Steele's marketing was flattering, and audiences received Rocco as a bona fide star, knowing nothing about his career troubles in the United States. Handsome compensation followed. One article called him a "pianist in the money" and reported that he was earning enough to buy property in Australia.[10] "I can't take out more than 10,000 American dollars," said Rocco in one quote from the article. "I'll have to do something with the rest. Either I'll buy a ranch with it or invest it in a block of flats."

The contrast with North America was glaring. There his career was so moribund that *Cue: The Weekly Magazine of New York Life* asked in 1955: "What ever happened to Maurice Rocco?"[11] For readers who had not seen him perform or read about him in the papers in several years, he was effectively forgotten. Even beyond his crumbling career, America held few comforts. The country was in a period of acute racial backlash and homophobia, even by its own grim standards. In the late 1940s and early 1950s, senator Joseph McCarthy relentlessly targeted people suspected of nonnormative sexuality, claiming they were de facto communists. For years the Wisconsin senator found ample support within the government and beyond. An executive order signed by Dwight Eisenhower in 1953 concretized McCarthy's homophobia by formally designating homosexuals a national security risk. More than five thousand federal employees were fired on mere suspicion of being gay. The "lavender scare" was a profound threat emanating from the apex of American political power. Meanwhile, while Rocco was in Australia, Black teenager Emmett Till was tortured and murdered by two white men in defense of a white woman (who later confessed she had never been threatened at all) in Mississippi. The two men were acquitted in court. Rocco himself faced racial discrimination and diminishment throughout his years in show business. The effects of racism and homophobia, both ubiquitous in the United States at many scales, could only have intensified for Rocco as he lost the thin protections of stardom.

By contrast in Australia, while the marketing for the Harlem Blackbirds certainly invoked racial essentialism, and while Australia still had remnants of a white supremacist legal system, these could not nearly compare with the acute, everyday risks that loomed in the United States. Audiences in Australia and

New Zealand viewed Rocco with reverence because of the lore surrounding jazz. Betty Frazier described the reception of the Blackbirds, and of Rocco in particular: "He was very popular, everybody enjoyed him. . . . He was very well received. . . . Because we were from the United States, we got star treatment. We didn't have any racial issues. Maybe a few might have been, you know, some little personal issues here and there, we went to parties and one lady bumped into me and gave me a dirty look for no reason, know what I mean? Something like that. But other than that they treated us very well. They treated us like celebrities."[12] Larry Steele's marketing elevated Rocco in a transnational jazz imaginary. This was exactly what he needed. An international star turn offered a reprieve from the burdens of the United States, including his sputtering career. The fact that he was not only thousands of miles away from mortal danger but also earning enough to buy property again must have been welcome indeed. Finally, according to Frazier, in Australia Rocco could be reasonably open about his sexuality, if not always sporting: "He did invite me to one of his parties once. . . . I was dating somebody he was interested in . . . a good-looking man. So he invited me to the party because I was dating this good-looking man. He didn't want anything to do with me, or any of the chorus girls for that matter." The picture that emerges from Frazier's recollections of Rocco in Australia is one of renewed status and confidence.

Rocco was among the many Black artists and intellectuals who found succor abroad in the twentieth century. James Baldwin left the United States for Europe in 1948. In his short story "This Morning, This Evening, So Soon," Baldwin speaks through a narrator, a Black American musician living in Paris: "I think of all the things I have seen destroyed in America, all the things that I have lost there, all the threats it holds for me and mine," adding, by contrast, that "I love Paris, I will always love it, it is the city which saved my life."[13] Baldwin said much the same thing in his own voice forty years later: "The fact that I went to Europe so early is probably what saved me." Nina Simone became a quasi expatriate in southern France in 1970. Duke Ellington never lived abroad, but he was a regular in Europe from 1933 onward, playing in twenty-six different cities in France alone. Visual artist Loïs Mailou Jones began splitting her time between Washington, DC, and Paris in 1937, citing the French capital's comparative racial tolerance. Miles Davis once said, "I loved being in Paris and loved the way I was treated."[14] The French capital offered Josephine Baker opportunities that Broadway did not, and she not only became an expatriate there but in fact aided the anti-Axis Free French movement during World War II. France was surely no paradise of racial tolerance.[15] But by contrast with their experiences in the United States, many Black Americans in the twentieth century identified Paris as particularly livable. It was also unquestionably a rich commercial frontier. Jazz had been critically validated in Europe by the 1920s, much earlier than in the United States. By the 1930s, jazz musicians could usually earn much more in Europe than at home. Many musicians toured or even moved there, taking advantage of both social and commercial opportunities. As Ellington once said, in Europe "you can go anywhere and talk to anybody and do anything you like. . . . When you've eaten hot dogs all your life and you're suddenly offered caviar, it's hard to believe it's true."[16] This was not limited to stars like Ellington. Even nonmarquee names were in demand on the continent. Well past her prime, Sister Rosetta Tharpe toured Europe with great success and a warm reception in 1957 and 1958.

A smaller number of Black Americans went to Asia during the Cold War for similar reasons. Singer LaVern Baker, like Rocco, made her first extended tour abroad in Australia, performing there in 1957. Like Rocco, she traveled to Asia in the 1960s, ultimately staying in the Philippines for more than twenty years, during which time she also played in Bangkok. Eartha Kitt toured Asia throughout the 1960s. Trumpeter Buck Clayton spent the years 1935–37 in Shanghai, where he enjoyed respect and compensation of a kind he had never known in the United States.[17] Tellingly, as Andrew F. Jones notes, the major instances of racism that Clayton experienced in China were at the hands of American soldiers or white Americans in the United States who sent intimidating letters to the venues where he played in Shanghai. Dizzy Gillespie and Ellington played extensive, State Department–sponsored tours of Asia in the 1960s and 1970s. Civil rights activist Robert Franklin Williams lived for four years in China in the late 1960s, avoiding the FBI.[a] Asia could be challenging, and for Black Americans in the twentieth century it was never quite as welcoming as Paris. But for some, it was a haven.

Asia meanwhile was a vital site of third-world global affiliation in the postcolonial moment. A major international Afro-Asian summit, the Bandung Conference, was held in Indonesia in 1955. The conference was an effort to build new forms of political and cultural solidarity between Black and Asian people. It took place in April, just two months before Rocco began his tour with the Harlem Blackbirds. Attended by representatives of thirty countries, whose aggregate populations totaled more than half the people in the world, Bandung was a profound statement of nonaligned solidarity. Its speakers, including a number of

a ACKNOWLEDGMENT: I thank Dr. Ronald Stephens (Purdue University) for bringing my attention to Williams, about whom Stephens is currently writing a book, and for correspondence about many topics in this chapter.

heads of state, explained problems of the modern world order as the result of European colonialism. They proposed that Africans and Asians should form an international political bloc to resist colonialism collectively. Novelist Richard Wright, himself an African American expatriate in France, attended the conference, describing it in his 1956 book *The Color Curtain*. Wright recognized the conference as a space for common cause. "The despised, the insulted, the hurt, the dispossessed—in short, the underdogs of the human race were meeting. Here were class and racial and religious consciousness on a global scale. Who had thought of organizing such a meeting? And what had these nations in common? Nothing, it seemed to me, but what their past relationship to the Western world had made them feel. This meeting of the rejected was in itself a kind of judgment upon that Western world!"[18] Colonialism had made Third World bodies into a kind of living archive of oppression, which the conference sought to reveal: "The agenda and subject matter had been written for centuries in the blood and bones of the participants."[19] The conference solicited Wright, as a Black American, to affiliate with those who had experienced oppression akin to his own. Wright was already an expatriate in Europe, but this event suggested Asia as perhaps an even more logical postcolonial home for nonwhite people. Bandung demonstrated that Black-Asian connections were not only possible but arguably already latent around the world. In any case, modern Blackness would not be sutured to the West. Although Rocco did not attend the Bandung Conference, it is striking that his longest tour abroad to that point occurred in the Asia Pacific region at nearly the exact same time as Bandung, which framed Asia as a place of brotherhood for nonwhite people. Rocco would soon live squarely within that frame.

One could only guess why Rocco returned to America at all after the Harlem Blackbirds tour. There was little left for him socially or professionally there. Izzy Rowe's *Pittsburgh Courier* column captioned a photo of Rocco on a balcony in a well-appointed Sydney hotel in October 1955: "Famed pianist Maurice Rocco [is] 'at home' in the exclusive Glen Ascham Hotel.... Rocco, perhaps at that moment, was dreaming of home."[20] Perhaps he was indeed homesick, couldn't secure an international visa, or had no opportunities lined up abroad. For one or several of these reasons, Rocco tried the United States one last time, flying back to San Francisco via Tokyo in March 1956. But his engagements in America remained sparse, and the work was no better than before. A few shows in Saint Louis were followed one month later by a single week in Montreal, then three weeks at a Miami hotel, the Lucerne, that was on the verge of bankruptcy. For substantial parts of the year, he appears not to have worked at all. Given his declining earnings, such a sparse schedule was unsustainable.

Rocco then entered a new round of legal trouble in December 1956. He was charged with passing several bad checks at shops near the Chase Hotel in Saint Louis, using them to buy a record player and a watch. After those checks bounced, he wrote an $800 check to the manager of the hotel in January 1957, which also bounced. In March, Rowe reported on another violent incident in her column: "Standup pianist Maurice Rocco got fighting mad when telephone company worker Sandra McDonald called him a washed-up 'former star'! Incensed, he struck out with his champagne glass, and a slight but bloody impression was left on the back of her head."[21] For the second time, Rocco stood publicly accused of violence against a woman. He was never legally charged for the champagne glass incident. For the remainder of the year, Rocco played in an update of "Smart Affairs" in Las Vegas. If not for Larry Steele, he might have had few gigs at all. The newspapers mostly did not cover his shows. After writing another bad check in Cleveland in November 1957, Rocco went to jail, where he remained through Christmas, unable to cover the $1,000 bail.[22]

The year 1958 repeated the same cycle: few shows of note and another bad check charge. He was arrested, tried, and convicted in Saint Louis over the summer and fall. The *St. Louis Dispatch* soon after called him a "stunt pianist."[23] In July a reader wrote to a *Dayton Daily News* columnist named Miss Fairfax: "Where can I write to Maurice Rockhold, the piano player, last heard of in England." Miss Fairfax replied: "I wonder if you mean Maurice Rocco? I do not know that he is under contract with any record company, which would be the only way I can think of that you could communicate with him."[24] His career and life in the United States were effectively over. On probation following his November conviction, he set out for Miami, the only American city left where he could still find regular work.

This final span of three years in the United States, 1956–58, was probably the lowest point in Rocco's career. He had limited contact with his living family members, and retained only scraps of a professional life that had once made him a wealthy national star. But his success in Australia and New Zealand left tantalizing hints to the possibility of a second act. Perhaps beyond the United States, there might be *something else*, even perhaps a rekindling of his international successes of 1948 and 1955. So Rocco boarded a ship on May 1, 1959, from New York City to England, never to return to the United States in his lifetime. His departure offered more than renewed career opportunities, however. It also held the promise of privacy. By boarding that ship, Rocco deliberately entered a gap.

Forms of Absence

Archives are material assemblages, and so are their gaps. Gaps can be places of privacy. Gaps contain layers.

Consider white ants. These creatures, which thrive in Thailand's humid tropical climate, are known in Thai as *plùak* and in English as termites. The most common destructive species of termite in mainland Southeast Asia are *Coptotermes gestroi* and *C. havilandi*, which build sprawling subterranean hills. Millions of foragers can live in a single colony. *Coptotermes* destroy not only wood but paper in their hungry quest for cellulose. Printed matter of all kinds becomes vulnerable, and Southeast Asian libraries and archives struggle to keep their materials safe through various practices, such as treating shelf wood with essential oils or placing small pools of water under wooden supports. Termite damage has been a challenge for many centuries in Southeast Asian paper archives. In the 1980s the Thai government outlined rules and responsibilities for fixing bureaucratic documents with termite damage and for filing reports about documents devoured beyond repair.[25] The problem is widespread. By eating, termites create archival gaps.

On several occasions during fieldwork for this project, *plùak* were invoked as the reason certain documents were not available or certain historical questions could not be answered. For example, I spent months seeking traces of Maurice Rocco's erstwhile nightly residency at the Oriental Hotel in Bangkok. I continued this pursuit through long email threads with staff from the corporate offices of the Mandarin Oriental Hotel Group, the Oriental Hotel in Bangkok, and the historian of the hotel, as well as two trips to the Oriental in Bangkok in person. There are traces of Rocco's former presence, including photographs of him on the wall of the Bamboo Bar (although by 2019, no one there had heard of him, let alone known him personally). But the hotel has only three items related to Rocco in its archives: two photographs and one press release, all digitized. There are no employment records, no pay stubs, no lists of performances, no correspondence, and no tax documents. Nothing on paper remains. Our email threads continued, in many fruitless directions, until I asked the hotel historian directly whether the hotel had kept anything at all. "They have no records of all this—no chance!" he wrote. "Sorry—lack of space and too many white ants."

The absence of documents that might have been kept under different circumstances has a material basis in Central Thailand's freshwater swamp forest environs, where white ants flourish. But the ethology of termites is not the only way to understand how these creatures produce absence. White ants can also be used *rhetorically* by people who want to withhold information. At several points during fieldwork, I was stonewalled, especially by corporate or state entities. Large conglomerates, including those that helped build New Phetchaburi Road, do not maintain public archives. They share nothing unless compelled. The Joint US Military Advisory Group Thailand (JUSMAGTHAI), a CIA-affiliated agency that was a nerve center for the war in Vietnam, now runs a saloon connected to the US embassy in Bangkok. But its archives are locked away. Whatever role the agency might have played in building New Phetchaburi Road cannot be known, at least not by me. Of course that organization never promised anyone transparency. My efforts to locate evidence from the collections of private companies, military entities, and intelligence groups were predictably in vain. The only path through these blockades would have been political power or elite connections. Lacking either of these, in corporate offices I was often instead given a justification: we keep no records because of the white ants. In Thailand's archival culture, termites exist in multiple modalities, from pest to pretense.

The upshot is that absences have forms, just as presences do. Absences are "an ambiguous interrelation between what is there and what is not."[26] Diana Taylor suggests that the field of performance studies was presaged by "absence studies," a broad term for the centuries-old scholarly reckoning with things that were not written down.[27] In Thailand (as in any other place) both absence and presence are given form by the local political terrain. Reflecting on archival collections of Thai state violence, for example, Tyrell Haberkorn found ample evidence of brutal acts committed by the Thai government *fully present* in the country's own national archives.[28] Damning details are visible to anyone with a researcher card. Why does the Thai government allow such evidence to remain in plain sight? Haberkorn explains this striking phenomenon as an example of impunity. Certain state agents have the power to simply ignore the law, even in front of witnesses. This self-endowed privilege, often justified by reference to Buddhist authority, is not flexed capriciously, but because doing illegal things in plain sight reinforces one's right to do such things *at will*. As Haberkorn notes, the public nature of illegal acts becomes pedagogy for all who watch, serving as a reminder of who can get away with what. Thus evidence of state violence is left in the archive deliberately. This is one contour of archival presence in Thailand, one way in which this territory has unique forms of presence.

Although impunity of this kind is flaunted in many places, in Thailand it is part of a system of inscription (and non-inscription) specific to local jurisdictions. What one finds or does not find in a given archive is an expression as well as an instrument of local power structures, pace Michel Foucault. The Thai state is buttressed by a particular archival assemblage, in which some things are documented and some are not, some things are hidden and some are revealed. There is a shape and a style to this assemblage. It assumes a form within which Buddhist notions of hierarchy, military paranoia, powerful currents of libertarianism, and termites all cohabitate. These elements are as incongruous as they are inseparable in Thailand's archival culture, which is governed not only by law and ecology but by practices of disclosure and secrecy that run through the everyday work of archivists and corporate employees, who are more than happy to ally with white ants to turn nosy researchers away. As a historian I felt frustrated. However, and importantly, this is precisely where Maurice Rocco found sanctuary.

In a recent turn presaged by both Foucault and Jacques Derrida, historians have responded to archival absence by turning away from state-sanctioned archives and toward archives otherwise. What is not admitted by a state library can sometimes be found in an attic, in a memory, or along the fibers of a scar. This recognition calls for broader definitions of the archive itself. For example, Davorn Sisavath reads the material remnants of US bombs dropped during the secret war in Laos as an in situ archive. There, war matériel has been recycled as "fixtures in homes and villages, parts for rice milling machines and herb planters, and makeshift museums in guesthouses and restaurants."[29] The artifacts of a secret war are not merely decorative but "reminders of death and violence" that "intentionally catalog US militarized excess in Laos." To read these everyday displays of historical objects archivally pushes past the ideological limits of state-managed collections. Relatedly, Ann Laura Stoler describes the role of "colonial common sense" in shaping archives, such as those kept by the Dutch in Indonesia. Colonial common sense tends to ignore Indigenous people and their structures of knowledge, finding them unworthy of inscription. Yet bureaucratic anxiety about those people is evident in the colonial archive anyway. When read carefully, "words could slip from their safe moorings," revealing the sublimated fears of colonial bureaucrats hiding between the lines.[30] Stoler analyzes archives not for the facts they catalog but for their affective "grain." Other scholars conjure or speculate even when little or nothing is left. This may seem a risky practice, but it can be necessary as well as profound. Saidiya Hartman uses fiction, at the blurred boundary between storytelling and history, to relate the lives of enslaved Africans (in one book) and Black tenement dwellers in New York (in another), whose humanity was not admitted during their lives let alone written down.[31] In this way fiction can be a tool for acknowledging unarchived lives. These three strategies—locating unconventional archives, reading conventional archives between the lines, and historicizing with fiction (termed "critical fabulation" by Hartman)—each contend with ideological forms of historical inscription and non-inscription.

Here, however, I want to consider archival absence in a somewhat different register. Returning to key themes from this book's introduction, and to Maurice Rocco, I note that archival gaps can sometimes be fortuitous for those averting surveillance. Rocco vanished many times in his life, hoping to dodge the law or the spotlight. Lying low is common enough, but when Rocco disappeared he tended to do so completely. I do not know, for instance, where he was in 1939 (there are only bits and pieces of evidence); or in March 1956 (he might have been traveling through Asia); or in spring 1958; or for much of 1963 (possibly he was in Australia or Hong Kong). And I contend that the entirety of his time in Thailand, though I know enough about it to continue telling his story, was a disavowal of the kind of attention that would have left much in the way of archival traces. These gaps in the record are not for a lack of digging; I have combed government, military, personal, and newspaper archives in many languages, often by hand and with the help of French, German, Cantonese, and Dutch speakers where necessary, in addition to conducting interviews and traveling, for more than five years. Sometimes a tidbit will emerge. But no degree of diligence can change the fact that there is *far less archival evidence of Rocco at some moments than others*. Moreover, these absences are clearly intentional. When Rocco wanted to disappear, he mostly could and did. Following Michael Herzfeld, who writes against a "canon of proof that demands presence as its main criterion," I read these absences as meaningful components of Rocco's biography, not necessarily as research dilemmas to be tenaciously solved.[32] Rocco shielded himself from the press, or from certain presses, many times. He dwelled in gaps when he wished. Absence is part of his story. I write beside rather than into these absences, in an effort to forestall what Scott Larson describes as a tendency for queer historical subjects to be "displayed, examined, and categorized."[33]

I am not sure it is my business what Rocco was doing in the time of his deepest archival absences. He may have been resting. He may have been avoiding law enforcement. He may have been pursuing what he wanted or liked. There is pressure in both historical and ethnographic research to document (and to reveal, in a direction oriented always toward imperial knowledge centers) everything. Contra this pressure, Audra Simpson uses the term *ethnographic refusal* to describe a more intentional calculation of "what you need to know and what I refuse to write in."[34] In other words, not all that is said or done in the scene of ethnographic research can or should be reported. The researcher must make this calculation in alignment with stakeholders or else ethnography is merely a synonym for surveillance. Notably, Simpson calls refusal a *form* of ethnography. Although it is a negative construction, an oppositional register, refusal takes a shape. Like the absences in Thai archives detailed above, refusal generates a gap that is not a void but instead a politically determined phenomenon. Historical refusal, especially that which involves deceased subjects with no living relatives, cannot be figured in quite the same way as ethnographic refusal. I cannot ask the long-deceased Maurice Rocco what he wants. Yet it seems to me that Rocco was already clear, by way of his own decisions, about what he did and did not wish to make known. So I enact a historical analog of ethnographic refusal by choosing to stop prying into Rocco's life beyond a certain reasonable point of inquiry, making exceptions where I think ethics demand it. But on the whole, I do not fetishize total knowledge as the measure of a worthwhile biography.

It is a quirk of panoptic times that I can now sit at a computer in Queens, New York, and access enough global databases—newspapers.com, the Swiss National Archives, worldradiohistory.com, Australia's Trove, RIPM Jazz, and many more—to map decades of an artist's performing schedule. When he was out of the spotlight, Rocco exploited the impossibility of this level of surveillance, which did not exist during his life. A Missouri court that issued Rocco a summons for a bad check charge could not easily find him in Miami, even if an ad for one of his shows appeared that same day in a Florida newspaper. The American music press had no way to track Rocco in other countries. His appearances could not be cross-checked. This left an archival gap, a gap that Rocco called home.

Though he no longer faces legal jeopardy or has the privacy concerns of a living subject, I am not convinced that Rocco's death removes all limits on my mandate for investigation. As of this writing I am alive and therefore still implicated in these histories. My methodology thus refuses most lines of inquiry that pass beyond the integument of privacy established by Rocco himself. Instead, I offer simply that the desire to be free of scrutiny and visibility in the United States was the reason that Rocco boarded a ship from New York City to England in 1959, his duration of stay marked "indef." on the manifest. That is perhaps all we need to know.

Through Streets Wide and Narrow

Rocco made no public statement when he left the United States in May 1959. But Louis Rodabaugh recalled speaking with Ohmer Rockhold about his brother's departure:

Ohmer told me that [Rocco] told [his family] "I've had it with this country." Just why he had had it Ohmer doesn't know. Ohmer thought he might have had some tax problems. We don't know what it was. Or he continually felt that he wasn't getting the high-class jobs that he felt he deserved to get with his ability, and felt that the racial thing was holding him back. Well, he had had several bookings in Europe—Paris, London, Hong Kong, and so forth. He already had those and had been treated so much better in any of those places, just like a celebrity. And he just felt I'm going to leave and I'm not going to tell you where I'm going. I just don't want anything to do with the family or this country. . . . At any rate, he left and they never knew where he was.[35]

Ohmer alludes to Rocco's frustration with declining work, legal problems, and racism in the United States. All of this contrasted with the promise of better gigs in Europe and Asia.

But Rodabaugh (like Ohmer) says nothing about homophobia, which must have been a further factor. Throughout their relationship, Rocco often seemed eager to insinuate his sexuality to Rodabaugh. The two were intimate friends, and Rocco alluded to homosociality in many of their correspondences. Rocco wrote Rodabaugh letters from every city he toured in the 1940s and sometimes called him from Bangkok, even after Rocco had grown distant from his own family. Rocco and Rodabaugh were close in ways and across barriers that surpassed any of Rocco's familial relationships, especially after the death of Rocco's mother. In his memoir, Rodabaugh relates a moment from the walks he and Rocco took together, in which Rocco told Rodabaugh that he trusted and needed him more than he ever could a wife:

Once, on one our walks, Maurice suddenly said, "When I die, I want you to see to it that I am buried beside my parents." When I replied, "By that time you'll have a wife, and she will be the proper person to take care of your funeral arrangements, or perhaps your children will do it," he answered that he felt that he could not trust any wife to make the arrangements that he desired. I then objected, "But I won't even know where you are! You could be in London, Paris, Hong Kong, or even Bangkok!" Rockhold replied, "<u>Bangkok</u>? Where is Bangkok? But, anyway, I don't know <u>how</u> you'll know where and when I die, but I know that you will know!" I then promised.[36]

In 1980, Rodabaugh was interviewed for a posthumous oral history about Rocco, broadcast on WMUB, an Oxford, Ohio, radio station. He recalled Rocco telling him: "Anybody ought to be able to like anybody they want to. You wanna know how everybody oughta act? Yeah, how. Heck, it's simple. First of all of course, everybody oughta love . . . well, you know, god. And then in god's name they oughta let people love other people. Any other people. *All* other people."[37] Rodabaugh repeats the same quote at the end of the interview and cries.

The emotional intimacy of Rodabaugh's reflections seem to gesture in some unknown and perhaps unknowable way toward awareness of Rocco's sexuality. Rocco might have succeeded in making Rodabaugh aware of his desires, after which his friend preserved his privacy. I don't know. Or Rodabaugh might have stubbornly missed the signs for years. Or any number of other possibilities, lived or expressed in private, perhaps under clouds of self-doubt or pressure. Once again the archive does not yield an answer. But the specter of homophobia surely figured somewhere in Rocco's calculation to leave.

In the United States, Rocco experienced a mixture of hypervisibility and invisibility. On one hand, because of his nonnormative identity he was potentially very visible and thus subject to insults and physical risk. On the other, his humanity as well as his professional achievements were invisible or underrecognized. He was seen by turns too much and too little. Moving out of the country might have been an attempt to reverse this. In other places, Blackness and queerness would not register within the same codes of hierarchy, belonging, and being that so limited him here. Rocco could be less marked by his skin and by his desire, while professionally he might appear like he had in Australia in 1955, as a venerable icon of jazz rather than a faded star. If the Harlem Blackbirds tour was any indication, elsewhere his talent might be better recognized and compensated. "*Something else* was never listed as one of the reasons people left home," writes Hartman of Black migrants in the early twentieth century. "The inchoate, what you wanted but couldn't name, the resolute, stubborn desire for an elsewhere and an otherwise that had yet to emerge clearly, a notion of the possible whose outlines were fuzzy and amorphous, exerted a force no less powerful and tenacious."[38] This uncertain promise seems to have been Rocco's gambit in leaving for Europe.

Rocco began his expatriate phase in 1959 on a three-month tour of the United Kingdom, playing with high tenor Bill Kenny, formerly of the vocal quartet the Ink Spots. Rocco and the Ink Spots had played together many times in the United States. In the UK they performed at the Finsbury Park Empire Theatre in London, the Hippodrome in Manchester, and the Empire Theatre in Edinburgh, among other prominent spots. London's *New Musical Express* praised Rocco, noting that he had "all of the verve—but none of the gimmicks—of Jerry Lee Lewis."[39] If nothing else, he had already shed the novelty tag. US newspapers neglected to report on the tour. Within weeks Rocco was reviving his career beyond the view of American media.

After his final UK show in July, Rocco disappeared from newspaper stories in any country until December 1959, when *Die Tat* reported that he was a "huge success" in Zurich.[40] He played four shows in Switzerland that month. The preceding fall, his name had not been mentioned in any major French, Swiss, German, Dutch, or UK press source, although he was certainly living or traveling in one or several of those countries. Here the trail goes cold. Rocco was later reported to have owned a home in Switzerland, which if true he may have purchased during those opaque, unreported months. But Swiss privacy laws make it difficult to know, even now, what he was doing or where his assets were parked.[41] The Swiss archival assemblage famously offers inviting gaps for those who want to safeguard their money and information, making the country an excellent place to establish a business with sensitive data, of whatever legitimacy. Switzerland is famous for offering privacy, which Rocco was afforded on a personal level. Perhaps with some intrepid archival labor—finding someone who worked with him in Zurich, for example—the facts of Rocco's time in Switzerland could be illuminated at least partially. Nothing has emerged so far. But perhaps the most salient point about this moment is that Rocco was actively trying to work and live out of the limelight.

Throughout the next year, 1960, Rocco played primarily in the Netherlands, with occasional bookings back in Switzerland. He had a two-week engagement at a venue called Taveerne Tastevin in the Hague in May, and he played on Dutch public television station AVRO's *The Weekend Show*.[b] Rocco's appearances were reviewed with some frequency in the Dutch papers. The stories focused on his physicality and standing pianism and praised him universally, even while noting his skin color as if it were a quirk.

In 1961 and 1962 he remained mostly in Switzerland, with a handful of appearances in France and the Netherlands. The July 19, 1961, issue of *Provinciale Zeeuwse Courant* shows him standing at the piano on the set of the TV show *Muziek mozaiek*. In that episode, he backed Dutch jazz guitarist Wim Overgauw and bassist Ruud Jacobs. According to the article, Rocco was not visible in the broadcast, only audible on the soundtrack. But he does appear in the newspaper story photograph.

b ACKNOWLEDGMENT: Thanks to Dr. Meredith Schweig (Emory University) for help translating and interpreting materials from Dutch archives.

FIGURE 3.1. Maurice Rocco (*right, rear*) plays the piano in a jazz combo on the Dutch television show *Muziek mozaiek*. *Provinciale Zeeuwse Courant*, July 1961.

The photograph from *Muziek mozaiek*, as I read it, is a document of distance. By the time it was taken, Rocco was two years into an expatriate journey, renewing his career at great remove. The American press and audiences had turned elsewhere. In Europe, language and media barriers meant that Rocco was now seen through the lens of jazz fanhood on the continent, far from the United States not just in miles but also culturally. In the Netherlands there was no stigma in being shunned by rock and roll. In fact, playing prewar jazz was an asset, more or less the reverse of how rock and jazz were respectively heard in the United States in the early 1960s.

Rocco was widely praised in Europe, described with words like *exquisite*. But his Blackness was also the subject of uncomfortable fantasies. One article from *De Telegraaf* devised some overt biographical myths: "The star of the evening is by far the upright pianist Maurice Rocco. Born in New York, he learned to appreciate the harmonies of the piano at a very young age. His mother was a piano teacher in Harlem. At the age of 10 he would perform for the first time in a nightclub in Chicago. The little black boy was then somewhat lost in a crowded nightclub. There was no stool behind the piano. It had been forgotten or it was lost in the hustle and bustle."[42] Rocco's mother lived in Ohio, not New York, but Harlem was so closely linked with Black America in the European imagination that the reference slipped in anyway. In addition, Rocco never played in Chicago when he was ten, much less got lost in a crowded nightclub there. Like a game of telephone, the already apocryphal story about the origin of Rocco's standing style was transmuted by the author into an even more fictive tale from Rocco's youth. A life that had long been subject to exaggeration by the media was distorted in yet another fun-house mirror. The story used racist tropes, including Rocco's early adultification (gigging in a city far from home at the age of ten) and the spontaneous (as opposed to intentional and studied) development of his standing technique. Although these tropes were also common in the United States, the description as a whole situated Rocco squarely in an exoticist European racial epistemology, an order of knowledge different from anything he had been subjected to before.

Rocco also *looks* distant in the picture. He sits behind and apart from the other musicians in the combo. He is nearly fifty years old, visibly adrift from any career identity. His slumped shoulders and expectant face seem to pine for a lost self-assurance, a fame that might still be smoldering somewhere. He looks out toward a horizon of recognition, the kind once easily at hand. He had broken from an earlier life but not yet found a new one. It showed in the photograph. Like Molly Malone, his Dublin counterpart of song, he now wheeled the barrow through streets wide and narrow.

Then from August 1962 until July 1964 he is almost nowhere, at least in the archive. I cannot tell you much about his life during these two years in a conventional biographical sense, except by conjecture or with the thinnest of evidence. Rocco once told *Bangkok Post* nightlife reporter Harry Rolnick that he spent time in Singapore, but Rolnick is not sure when that might have happened. Singaporean archives turn up no mentions of Rocco's name or any known pseudonym. Meanwhile one of Rocco's drummers at the Bamboo Bar, Mongkorn Pikaew, remembers that Rocco might have been in Laos before coming to Thailand, but he could offer no further specifics. There are vague trails leading to Hong Kong but little evidence. There are also unverified suggestions that he may have toured the Middle East. Impresario Harry Wren might have slotted him into the Starnight Roof tour in Sydney in 1963, perhaps the most likely possibility. He appears to have been in Australia in August 1963, but it is unclear how long he stayed. After a spring and summer gigging at Swiss casinos in 1962, there are barely any inscriptions or memories until an obituary for his sister Geneva ran in an Ohio paper in June 1964. The obit said Rocco was in Switzerland, though that may have drawn on old information—no one in Rocco's family would have known his whereabouts by that point.

For two full years, Rocco dwelled in gaps, living in places and doing things that we may never know. The next phase of his career is better documented, but I would suggest that his years of archival absence are important traces of a tendency to disappear into intimate private layers formed by the shifting sediments

FIGURE 3.2. The first advertisement in the *Bangkok Post* to feature Maurice Rocco announced the beginning of his nightly residency at the Bamboo Bar on July 1, 1964.

of history. I suggest that the deepest truths we can draw from these disappearances are not latent in some detail yet to be found but are composed of the disappearances themselves. These absences suggest Rocco's wish to be away, somewhere else, even if we from the outside cannot always glimpse the interior of that elsewhere. For Rocco, that was often the point. His absences are not necessarily for us.

Then on July 1, 1964, with no prior notice, Rocco reemerged when an ad appeared in the *Bangkok Post*. The troubles that he had faced since 1950 led him at last to a rebirth in Bangkok. In that city he would encounter a peculiar new assemblage of documentary absence and presence, and a certain order of visibility, that would suit him well. In the Bamboo Bar, the venue that Germaine Krull had developed in the 1940s and 1950s, just two miles from New Phetchaburi Road, and exactly one month before the Gulf of Tonkin Resolution gave the American war in Vietnam a degree of formal authority, Rocco debuted in the city that would become a platform for his second act starting in July 1964.

In Bangkok Americans could hide—which is exactly what Rocco did, right out in the open.

4

INTIMATE NEOCOLONIAL

NIGHTLIFE

There are two American social phenomena that the army drags in its wake—pop music and drugs. —CLAUDE JOHNER, liner notes to *Good Morning Vietnam* (1972)

His countrymen pretending to be warrior-gods mean[t] good business. —PITCHAYA SUDBANTHAD, *Bangkok Wakes to Rain* (2019, referring to Clyde Alston, the fictional Maurice Rocco)

Bangkok had everything. —AIR AMERICA CAPTAIN TONY DURIZZI (interviewed in 2001)

Between 1965 and 1975, the decade of the American war in Vietnam, scenes of cosmopolitan music and nightlife exploded in Thailand. After years of dancing around each other, of fledgling overtures, of paving the way, the United States and Thailand became intimately engaged at almost every conceivable level.

This era saw the intermingling of souls first introduced in this book's opening pages. By 1965, Maurice Rocco and the freshly built spaces of Thai nightlife had finally come together.

So far I have referred to this historical period as the "American era," Benedict Anderson's term for the long arc of the US military presence in Thailand. But Thai speakers mostly use a different term. They call this period *yúk jii ay*, or the GI era. Soldiers in that era were a uniquely visible presence, so it makes sense that Thai people would emphasize not just Americans but the American military. Given this chapter's temporal frame, and the local terminology, this chapter will thus refer to the GI era rather than the American era.

Those who are old enough remember the GI era as a time of worldliness. Besides Maurice Rocco and Doris Duke, hundreds of thousands, perhaps millions, of other foreigners made Thailand a home or tourist destination over the course of a single decade. These visitors seemed to be everywhere. Anthropologist Pattana Kitiarsa notes that the GI era was not the first time that Siam/ Thailand had experienced significant global contact or development. But it was the first time that westerners engaged not only Thai elites but also working-class Thais at scale—as customers, lovers, colleagues, bandmates, and fellow soldiers.[1] This deep, sustained intimacy threw Thai culture and identity into flux. Transnational intimacy disturbed ardent nationalists and Buddhist conservatives, but it opened entrepreneurial and social opportunities for many other people. The cultural matrix into which Maurice Rocco settled beginning in July 1964 grew from a series of dynamic encounters between Thais, Thailand, and international visitors. This chapter is about these encounters within spaces of nightlife and the enduring social realities to which they have given rise.

War casts a long shadow over this story. One week after Doris Duke recorded Rocco at the Bamboo Bar, the encounter described in this book's introduction, US president Lyndon Johnson launched Operation Flaming Dart, America's first major bombing campaign against North Vietnam. Most of the planes on that mission flew from American bases in Thailand. As the conflict careened toward war, a troop surge raised the number of Americans in Vietnam from just 23,300 the previous year to 184,300 in 1965. The American presence in Thailand swelled in tandem. Rocco's second act dovetailed with this escalation and thus also with the growing number of soldiers stationed in or visiting the country. One of the epigraphs to this chapter rang particularly true for Rocco: "His countrymen pretending to be warrior-gods mean[t] good business."[2] Rocco's career revival was directly enabled by foreign military personnel stationed abroad. They would make up much of his audience.

In this chapter I draw on primary sources and interviews to explore the cosmopolitan nightlife scene during the GI era in Bangkok, among other Thai cities, and namely its physical growth; its class, ethnic, and gender hierarchies; and the ways that it still resonates today. The developmental work undertaken in Thailand in the 1950s, described in chapter 2, was a boon to many international musicians and nightlife workers. The development of the Bamboo Bar and New Phetchaburi Road (among other places) was at last cashed out, as global encounters found space to grow and grow profitable within them.

In addition, each section of this chapter considers the role of language and listening in engagements between westerners and Thais. Language and listening were negotiated in intimate neocolonial spaces in ways that reveal power differentials as well as processes of social change. Rather than claim that Thai and western practices were simply hybridized, which would presume two discrete, stable cultures shuffled together like a deck of cards, I argue that the GI era was neocolonial at its core and that neocolonial subjects and their de facto colonizers heard each other asymmetrically. Close readings of music and interviews with musicians suggest this especially, but the politics of listening were apparent in every dimension of public life. Nightlife in particular was noisy and always thick with overtones.

Nightlife's Milieu: *Farang* Privilege and Cold War Orientalism

Rocco thrived professionally in Thailand. He had steady gigs, not only at the Oriental but also at Bangkok's Windsor Coffee House, Napoleon Lounge, Stork Club, President Hotel, and Cesar Supperclub. Like most nightlife acts, he moved from gig to gig, but he had no trouble finding work. He left Thailand for about a year, from July 1965 until the same month in 1966, to play in Hong Kong and then London. But he returned thereafter to Bangkok, where he continued getting choice opportunities. In fact he was in such high demand that one might reasonably believe an unconfirmed anecdote that Rocco played at a Pattaya resort with Thai king Bhumibol Adulyadej in the 1960s. "Back at the clubhouse the king would often form part of an impromptu quartet in which he played the saxophone accompanied by Maurice Rocco," wrote the resort's historian in a 2018 newsletter.[3] In addition to possible royal jam sessions, Rocco was visited by American jazz luminaries such as Louis Jordan as well as friends from Oxford. His earnings were substantial, and his money went further than it had in the United States. Doris Duke was not the only person who heard Rocco as a star in his adopted country. Like many Americans then and now, Rocco had

FIGURE 4.1. Advertisement for Maurice Rocco at the Windsor Coffee House, Bangkok, in 1970.

exceptional status in Thailand. As a *farang*, he could do many things that would have been impossible at home.

But what is a *farang*? And what is their/our privileged status? Finally, what kind of *farang* was Rocco as a Black American? Most broadly, a *farang* is a foreigner. The word is derived from the Germanic demonym *Frank*, from which it was routed through Persian to various Asian languages. *Farang* referred to outsiders in Siam during the late nineteenth century, when the country was "increasingly part of a colonial economy but not a colonial subject dominated by a single master."[4] Classifying foreign visitors was an instrument for survival and integrity.

In the twentieth century, *farang* increasingly became something like the polar opposite of Thai identity. Pattana explains that *farang* eventually grew to function as an Occidental "Other," a "superior but suspicious" figure who cast Thai identity into relief.[5] *Farang* gradually became a foil to Thainess. This inverts the colonialist dynamic of Orientalism by situating westerners in relation to a Thai identity system rather than the other way around. Yet *farang* are rarely seen as a threat. Instead, they are a desirable link to all things modern, cosmopolitan, and financially valuable. Often this link is recursive. For example, when Maurice Rocco played at the Bamboo Bar, his repertoire was heard as modern chiefly because it was played by an inherently modern person, an American. Almost anything that *farang* do, by virtue of their proximity to wealth and the West, confers prestige. As vectors of cultural and economic value, *farang* have possessed special status for many decades. Although this status has shifted in recent years, especially with increased Chinese influence throughout Southeast Asia, it remains largely intact. Yet *farang* privilege likely crested during the Cold War. In the GI era, the word *macan*, a shortening of the word *American*, was common slang meaning "cool." Everyone wanted *farang* things.

Despite their desirability, *farang* are not always venerated in Thailand. They are commonly caricatured in Thai media, especially soap operas, as culturally oblivious clowns. As in many parts of the world, westerners in Thailand are stereotyped (not without cause) as boorish, loud, aggressive know-nothings. These stereotypes bind histories of entitled colonial incursion to mundane individual behavior, making *farang* visible in constraining ways. Along similar lines, it is usually impossible for westerners to rise above middle tiers in professional contexts in Thailand. Certain jobs and social roles are seen as ill-suited to those who lack *kwampenthai*, or essentialized Thainess. Political conservatives are the most likely to be so protectionist, but the Thai political Left has also periodically resisted the American presence, including during the GI era. At that time, the Left considered Americans an occupying force. Both ethnic propriety and anti-imperialist attitudes have long limited the social mobility of *farang* who visit or live in Thailand.

The category of *farang* is also notably colorist, and as a result its privileges are not fully available to everyone. Dipesh Chakrabarty refers to the "privileged supra-legal status that white colonials enjoy" as a kind of racialized extraterritoriality.[6] In Thailand this means that darker-skinned people, including those from the West, may be called *khèek*, which translates as "visitor" and can be derogatory. Black-skinned people, no matter their nationality, may be categorized as *khon phǐw dam* (people with black skin) or *farang dam* (black *farang*), terms that carry moderately racist implications. For now, in order to situate Rocco in the complex field of Thai colorism, it should be noted simply that as a black-skinned person his *farang* status was socially significant but ultimately only partial.

Regardless of skin color, however, all American *farang* have experienced some degree of structural privilege in Thailand since the 1960s simply because of the money they/we spend or generate. The exuberant reflections of Americans stationed in Thailand in the 1960s make this clear. "The Thai people were fabulous," recalls former navy engineman Bill McCollum, who served in Vietnam from 1968 to 1969. "They were all friendly, they all came across as, 'Welcome to my country.' I took as many sightseeing trips to Bangkok as I could."[7] Air America (i.e., CIA) agent Sandra McRainey, stationed in Bangkok from 1966 to 1970, remembers that "the Thais were very, very, very friendly people. There was no problem, none at all. . . . Bangkok was a very cosmopolitan city. I mean there was any type of food that you wanted and wonderful restaurants and hotels and nightclubs and everything. . . . You could buy whatever you wanted in the markets."[8] Most Americans who passed through Thailand during the war have described the country with similar enthusiasm, as a place of geniality, comfort, and convenience. Soldiers and CIA agents were not necessarily in Thailand to jet-set, but their experiences were often indistinguishable from the opulent fantasies of tourists. Rocco, playing his nightly gig at the Oriental, earning a high salary, and hobnobbing with elites, enjoyed a genuine taste of this privilege.

The conditions that favored *farang* were, of course, neither the consequence of a natural Thai affability nor a mere reflection of the US-Thai military alliance. They were the result of material efforts made by the government, military, and private sector to indulge and flatter Americans. Chapter 2 historicized Thailand's courting of not only America as ally but Americans as tourists around 1959 and 1960. This courtship escalated in the early 1960s, as visiting soldiers

FIGURE 4.2. "Thai Charm at New Ambassador" describes the opening of the new Ambassador Club in Bangkok, complete with adventure-travel language: "You look around and you notice that this place is somehow different from the other night clubs. . . . You feel again the elegance of your surroundings." The night club dancer in the photograph worked under the aegis of the Thai government's Department of Fine Arts, underscoring the link between the government and private tourism. *Bangkok Post*, November 2, 1963.

and civil servants spent massive amounts of money on tourism even before the war. Well aware of the potential long-term revenue these visitors promised, Prime Minister Sarit Thanarat's newly created Tourist Organization of Thailand (TOT) began a successful push to advertise the country to Americans in particular as a world-class vacation destination.[9] The satisfaction of tourists became a common concern. The Thai-language newspaper *Phim Thai*, for instance, published a lengthy editorial in 1964 demanding that the TOT "protect" tourists from variable or unequal prices when they shopped.[10]

At the same time, Sarit aggressively privatized the economy and relaxed rules for foreign investment, with direct consequences for nightlife. One result of privatization was a building boom for internationally owned hotels in the early 1960s. Another was new bars and restaurants, many backed by "a consortium of international investors, including the Bank of America Corporation, the Chase Manhattan Corporation, the International Finance Corporation, and

TABLE 4.1. US Military Personnel in Thailand, 1964–68

Year	Total US Military Personnel
1964	6,300
1965	13,700
1966	34,000
1967	43,669
1968	43,994

Source: Symington Subcommittee Hearings. Referenced in Surachat,
"United States Foreign Policy and Thai Military Rule, 1947–77," 151.

the Deutsche Bank AG," which collectively loaned $4 million to the Thai government to develop sections of Bangkok that would soon be patronized by GIs.[11] This financial infusion made the hedonistic jags of rest and recuperation (R&R) possible, catalyzing the construction of spaces where *farang* privilege could be fully enjoyed. New buildings and attention to everyday experiences of tourism created safe, pleasurable, modern enclaves in Bangkok for people like Bill McCollum and Sandra McRainey. This approach to development was savvy and profitable. By 1963, new hotels were opening at a rapid clip, and the TOT had a mandate to market Thai culture to westerners, a watershed in the creation of Thailand's intimate economies.

At the dawn of these efforts in 1960, the American Automobile Association forecast a boom in American visits to Thailand. Aided by the war and Sarit's attention to tourism, its forecast proved accurate. The number of tourists in Thailand increased from 81,340 annually in 1960 to 1.45 million by 1976. Total tourism revenues increased from about $6.5 million to roughly $130 million annually over the same period.[12] In the five years between 1965 and 1970, Thailand's hotel capacity tripled.[13] GIs were integral to this growth. The total number of US military personnel in Thailand increased through the mid-1960s (table 4.1).

Over the course of the war, American servicemen on leave or stationed in Thailand injected an estimated $850 million into the local economy.[14] This money did not flow equally in all directions, and in fact much of it landed in the pockets of elites. Still, the impact on the national economy was staggering. Among other things, Maurice Rocco's 1965 Bamboo Bar performance owed its success to this economic surge. The audience who came to hear him did not arrive by accident but because of a concerted economic push that had been ramping up for years.

R&R was enabled by a Thai economic program that regarded privatization, military alliance, and tourism as integrated concerns. Throughout the 1960s, military and private contracting grew symbiotically with the economy in general and the tourism sector in particular. Beginning in 1961, the United States built seven large military bases throughout Thailand. These bases, informally leased to the United States as airfields and radar stations, became the nexus of operations for nearly all American air missions flown into Vietnam. It is commonly estimated that about 80 percent of American bombing sorties between 1965 and 1975 originated from bases in Thailand. But these bases were significant not only for war. They also catalyzed the development of business and social life in their surroundings. "About 19.3% of the service industries in 1966 (nightclubs, bars, drinking places with prostitute and massage services) were located in Udarn, Ubon, Karat, Nakorn Phanom, Khonkaen [sic], all sites of U.S. bases."[15] Nightlife in those five cities catered almost exclusively to servicemen. Given the diffusion of bases throughout the country, nearly every part of Thailand was impacted by the American military. Previously sleepy fishing villages or rice farming areas like Pattaya and Ubon Ratchathani became, in the course of a year or two, epicenters of hospitality and nightlife, infused with wealth and arch-modern material culture unimaginable just a few years earlier. "The formula for getting rich in a town with Americans," mused Rong Wongsawan, "was nothing more than bars, nightclubs, curry restaurants, prostitutes, *mia chao* [rented wives], houses for rent, bungalows, and knick-knack shops."[16] The disruption was dramatic and sudden.

The bases meanwhile created what might be called a permission structure for international development, by giving the (not altogether accurate) impression that Thailand was fortified against violence and communism. Simply put, the presence of the military made global investors comfortable. "The number of U.S. firms in Thailand jumped from eighty-eight in 1965 to two hundred and forty in 1971."[17] US Army and government publications commended Thailand's stability, calling it ripe for trade partnership with wealthy countries. *Air Force* magazine noted in 1973 that "the strategic center of gravity in Southeast Asia has shifted westward to Thailand. Its pro-Western political orientation makes Thailand a friendly enclave surrounded by hostile, envious, or politically and militarily weak countries with Communist-fed insurrections of their own. Its tradition of independence and its relative political stability are a combination unique in Southeast Asia. . . . At stake is not just a country or even a region. It is the insurance of continued access to the Indian Ocean, and materials needed for American industry—the basis of our national existence and the American way of life."[18] Or, as Lieutenant Colonel Jerry A. Singleton put it, "Boy, I wanted to clean up those dirty communists and make the world safe for Coca-Cola, as we used to say."[19] Military involvement intensified, and Thailand was increasingly seen as a beacon of political stability and capitalism in an otherwise mercurial region. The country thus attracted enormous private investment, especially from Japan, Europe, and the United States, including for new entertainment districts to be patronized by troops. Militarism justified development that further served militarism, leaving tourist infrastructures as a lasting by-product. This was the way of the military-industrial-touristic complex.

This permission structure also extended to nightlife intimacies. A series of legal instruments ensured that westerners—especially young, white, heterosexual men—could act with near impunity while vacationing in Thailand. Meredith Lair describes the noncombat parts of the war in Vietnam as a "massive recreation program" in which American troops "found themselves empowered by American guns and dollars, yet without the behavioral restraints imposed by family, religion, and law."[20] Thailand empowered troops on R&R in precisely these ways, through agreements that codified *farang* privilege inside the tinted-window spaces of Bangkok after dark. *Farang* were granted a kind of soft diplomatic immunity.

One crucial instrument to this end was Thailand's Entertainment Places Act (sometimes translated as "Service Places Act") of 1966.[21] This act required night spots that hosted drinking and dancing, including many venues on New Phetchaburi Road, to obtain government licenses. Women were surveilled in the process: "The Thai interior Ministry directly participated in the Petchaburi Road [*sic*] extension, registering the women working in bars and mandating regular health checkups."[22] Superficially, the act seemed like mere oversight, but the devil was in the details. The act's language used highly subjective requirements for compliance, such as that the owner of a given establishment should "not have disgraceful behavior or lack morality."[23] This gave the police broad leeway to decide whether a venue should be raided or left alone. As a result, venues where sexual services were offered fell under a de facto police protection racket, since the police alone were empowered to decide whose behavior was "disgraceful." In the eyes of the law, ironically, only nightclubs that paid off the cops were in the moral clear. As Kristen Kelley writes, the act "created a situation in which it was legal to both run establishments that promoted commercial sex as well as to purchase sex, yet sex work was still illegal. This meant that every player in the commercial sex industry was immune from legal penalization, except for the sex worker."[24] Indeed, the fine for failing to abide by the act's provisions was minimal for the venue (the equivalent of about seventy dollars for employing an underage hostess, for example) and nonexistent for customers. The act did not refer explicitly to sex work. Instead it used thinly euphemistic language like "a comfort woman looking after a customer" (ผู้บำเรอสำหรับปรนนิบัติลูกค้า) to avoid the awkward fact that prostitution was illegal. The Entertainment Places Act thus allowed the police to profit from sex work while legally sheltering the industry's patrons. In other words, the Thai government promoted sex work while extending no protections whatsoever to sex workers. Indeed, the government's primary goal was to make westerners safe and comfortable, a situation much bemoaned by Thais. For many Thai people, women's sexual disempowerment relative to *farang* stood in for more general anxieties about a perceived loss of national autonomy.[25] Despite these concerns, the labor and legal vulnerability of sex workers gave Thai nightlife an enormous boost.

Also in 1966, the United States and Thailand began discussing two new agreements that would spur the R&R program. The first was the Treaty of Amity and Economic Relations, ratified over the course of 1967 and 1968. This treaty was an update of the first bilateral agreement ever signed between the two countries in 1833. Its main Cold War alteration was a blanket allowance for American entities, the US military among them, to receive the same benefits and legal protections that Thai companies enjoyed when owning or operating businesses on Thai soil. The same privilege was extended to Thais who opened businesses in the United States, though more Americans than Thais took advantage of this reciprocity. US citizens now had the right to own 100 percent of a business in Thailand, a privilege that no other foreign nationals possessed.[26] In towns like Pattaya, near which U-Tapao air base had recently opened in 1966, the revised Treaty of Amity fostered development of bars, restaurants, and massage parlors operated by Americans as well as by organs of the US government.[27] This eased the way for greater American control over R&R, as well as profit from it.

The second agreement, an especially fascinating document, is usually referred to in scholarly histories as "the R&R treaty." But it was not in fact a treaty, or even a formal agreement, but a memorandum of understanding (MoU). Its specifics underscore the perversely close relationship between military, government, and tourism. The R&R MoU was negotiated in backroom fashion—deliberately out of view of Congress—by US ambassador Graham Martin and Thai air chief marshal Dawee Chullasapya along with his aide air vice-marshal Srisakdi Sutcharitham.[28] This kind of secretive diplomatic practice was not at all uncommon. Even high-level Thai-US agreements under Ambassador Martin tended to be made off the record; only one of seven large US military bases in Thailand ever had its legal status defined in writing, for example.[29] This may have been part of a perfunctory effort to keep the bases out of the press, but more likely the ambassador wanted to avoid scrutiny from American politicians. One foreign service officer recalled the routine lack of documentation: "This was an enormously permissive relationship. The Thai let us do just about whatever we wanted to do, as long as it was within reason. You know, they wouldn't let us bomb Beijing from Utapao, or anything like that. However, this arrangement drove the Pentagon nuts, because none of it was written down. It was all on the basis of Memoranda of Conversations. There were desultory negotiations for a base rights agreement, which were never completed. And there were desultory negotiations for a status of forces agreement, which were never completed."[30] The so-called R&R treaty was, in reality, little more than a private discussion between Martin and Dawee, the details of which were only ever loosely summarized by the R&R MoU.[31] That summary sketch is all that the US Congress ever saw.

Perhaps the most remarkable part of the R&R MoU is that it was made between individuals rather than governments. Although Dawee was a high-ranking officer in the Thai air force, he brokered the MoU *on behalf of his own company*. Before entering negotiations, Dawee created a new corporation called Tommie's Tourist Agency.[32] The MoU named Tommie's the "single chosen tourist agency" for R&R, the lone company that the US military would hire for its R&R needs despite the fact that it was not yet in active operation. Moreover, Tommie's was the only Thai entity named as a negotiating party in the MoU; the Thai government itself was not involved. The MoU stated as much directly: "The purpose of this document is to summarize working arrangements that have been mutually developed between the R&R detachment, USMACTHAI/JUSMAG [US Military Assistance Command Thailand/Joint US Military Advisory Group] and the Directors of Tommies Tourist Agency in connection with the operation of the R&R program in Bangkok. These items have been formulated in a series of weekly meetings during Jan-Feb 1967 in an effort to establish policies and guidelines in the administration of the increased R&R program."[33]

The finer details of these "working arrangements" were not published in the MoU, or written down anywhere else, as was Ambassador Martin's practice. However, even the summary makes clear that Tommie's, a company in name only at that point, was being handed a monopoly.[34] The fact that Tommie's was owned by Dawee, who as a government figure was granting himself a personal monopoly, reveals the extent of self-dealing in Thailand's budding tourism industry. The Thai military was active in the tourism business, and Dawee used his position in the former to profit from the latter. According to Thanh-Đam Truong, Dawee also encouraged his own circle of associates to build physical infrastructure in neighborhoods that the MoU had earmarked for R&R, which if accurate would mean Dawee was a real estate kingmaker as well.

For all of the development money coming into Thailand, most of it flowed upstream to men of privilege like Dawee—dubbed "America's man" by Martin—who were already powerful and connected. It was around this time in history that in Thailand "the military officer elite became somewhat like a ruling caste."[35] Given the outsized role that companies like Tommie's played in R&R, it is no stretch to suggest that Thai military elites were the historical godfathers of western pleasure tourism in Thailand, with a knowing assist from the US government. Just as importantly for this book, Tommie's fostered the network of nightclubs that hosted much of the live music described throughout this chapter. Cronyism and jobbery underwrote the development of Bangkok's intimate cosmopolitan nightlife scene. The venues where Maurice Rocco and other international musicians played to international crowds owed their existence to untethered political corruption in Thailand.

Perhaps to avoid uncomfortable optics, Dawee did not run Tommie's himself. Instead, he delegated its daily operations to Tommy Clift, a Burmese former air force commander in chief who fled to Thailand in 1963, and to the wife of Air Vice-Marshal Srisakdi. Dawee and his team devised a commission-based network for moving GIs through R&R, ensuring that soldiers could have everything they wanted at bargain prices, from sight-seeing to hotel accommodations, from Coca-Cola and music to sex.[36] Each entity in the network paid a kickback to Tommie's in return for referrals. The agency reported earnings over $150,000 a month from currency exchange, bus fares, and other aboveboard operations.[37] However, its full earnings were undisclosed and certainly ran much higher. Tommie's held so much sway that hotels and nightclubs were built from the ground up with features meant to satisfy its standards. The Thai and American militaries, Military Assistance Command Thailand (MACTHAI), and the TOT all worked closely with Tommie's to ensure that visiting GIs could spend their money without trouble, within protected enclaves such as the American Strip along New Phetchaburi Road. In this arrangement the Thai legal system was plainly complicit with developers, the Thai and American militaries, and international capital.

As the head of a civilian agency, Ambassador Martin was wary of allowing the American military presence in Thailand to become too visible on the ground. For this reason, he initially limited the number of US troops in-country on R&R to four hundred at a time, further specifying that they could not wear uniforms while on leave. But that limit was soon raised to one thousand soldiers, and

FIGURE 4.3. "Dawee Chullasapya, Air Chief Marshal and Deputy Minister of Defense, Thailand (*center*), meets with Secretary of Defense Robert S. McNamara (*right*) at the Pentagon," 1965. Dawee, a key architect of Bangkok's intimate nightlife, visited with American presidents (John F. Kennedy, Lyndon B. Johnson, and Richard Nixon among them), cabinet officials, and media figures like Bob Hope, all of whom knew exactly what he was up to. Photograph: National Archives, Washington, DC.

after the R&R agreement it may have been lifted altogether. Anthropologist Patcharin Lapanun estimates that there may have been six thousand R&R visitors at a time in Thailand at the program's peak.[38] Other credible estimates have run as high as ten thousand soldiers at a time. Although the exact arrangements summarized by the MoU were never published, the agreement established the terms for Bangkok to function as a primary R&R site during the American war in Vietnam. The scenario that Martin had feared, with young American soldiers running rampant in the country and creating the appearance of a military occupation through their revelry, had come to pass. The best that could be done was to confine soldiers to specific neighborhoods and to minimize their legal exposure when they misbehaved. "JUSMAG built all of these bars down there. . . . They did not want them doing terrible things with Thai maidens, so they built all these massage parlors and bars."[39]

This is when New Phetchaburi Road, just isolated enough from the busiest parts of Bangkok, became a choice development site given the needs of both the Thai government and the US military. The MoU helped create isolated enclaves for R&R. Very soon, New Phetchaburi Road would become "a garish strip of cheap nightclubs and massage parlors that for sheer iniquity possibly surpass[es] anything to be found elsewhere in modern Asia."[40] But all that mattered was that it was a garish strip separated from the rest of the city. One former GI remembered that "there was this place called Petberry Road [*sic*] where there must have been a hundred bars. . . . At nighttime it was just packed with GIs."[41] Martin and Dawee's negotiations had ensured that nightly episodes of drunken revelry would not result in arrests or expulsions. Unsightly or embarrassing after-dark situations, out of sight of most Bangkokians, could be handled discreetly by American military police.

In tandem with the Entertainment Places Act and the Treaty of Amity, the R&R MoU allowed GIs to get away with almost anything. According to one foreign service officer, "The number of jurisdictional cases that we had was, for all practical purposes, insignificant. It was just incredible. I think that we ended up with one American airman going into a Thai jail—for having killed somebody!"[42] Formal and informal agreements enshrined "Thai friendliness" into law and practice for the benefit of *farang*, whose raucous presence had become its own kind of quagmire.

Their pockets full of combat pay, American soldiers were indulged by nearly everyone with power in Thailand. The need to grant privilege to *farang* aligned international business with the American and Thai militaries as well as local officials. As a result, GIs caroused with very little risk. To return to one veteran's remarks from the introduction to this book, what happened on R&R stayed there. One GI recalled that the military "took you to the R&R center and the first thing that they told you, you can do just about anything you want to, but don't raise much Cain, that will get you in trouble. Well, as we first walked in the door there, they handed us a glass of beer and a wet washcloth and they told us first off, don't find some girl, fall in love, and get married. . . . It was just party time." In other words, the military sanctioned indulgence in the most unrestrained activities of R&R, frowning only on relationships that might become more permanent, an approach that notably parallels the United States' own fear of commitment to Southeast Asia.

Meanwhile, the new apparatus of *farang* privilege relied at every level on the subjugation and uncompensated labor of women. Sex work in Thailand is a knotty topic and the focus of many active debates. Moreover, sex work was well established in Thailand long before the GI era, and Thai men remained its primary clients throughout the Cold War. But Thai women were exploited in new ways by the military-industrial-touristic complex, arguably even serving as its foundation. The R&R program and the nightlife scenes that it sustained were predicated on the sexual availability of these women. Thus, even though the GI era did not introduce paid sex to Thailand, it did compel the sex trade to grow and internationalize without labor protections and under an Orientalist gaze. As American soldiers never tire of pointing out, sometimes with excitement and sometimes embarrassment, cheap and unrestricted sex was Bangkok's signature commodity. The legacy of that entitlement has long outlasted the 1960s.[43] Pahole Sookkasikon writes of an enduring "Orientalism manifested through economies of the flesh" and of Thailand's reputation as "a place of sexual excess for the insatiable thirsts of predominantly white male tourists."[44] Though not all sex workers were women, the legal abandonment of sex workers by the Entertainment Places Act and other new legislation overwhelmingly affected female-identified people. Sex workers had next to no legal protections during the GI era, even as their labor was the basis of Thailand's dramatic growth as a tourist destination.

Ultimately, it was not only women sex workers but *all* women who were leveraged by wartime development. While treaties and agreements created an exploitative context for sex work, touristic advertising depicted Thai women as the primary avatars of local hospitality.[45] "Thai women have come to bear the burden of signifying Thainess," writes Penny Van Esterik.[46] Anthropologist Alexandra Dalferro details how the Thai state advertised its budding silk industry by linking silk with femininity.[47] One 1976 Thai Airways ad declared, "It's almost uncanny. The remarkable timing of the Thai hostess. It seems she knows what you want before you know it yourself. A drink, a snack, or simply a little peace and quiet. Taking care of businessmen. It's an art that comes naturally to the girls of Thai." No matter the setting, female servitude was presumed. Advertising materials, including the cover of the 1968 brochure from which this book takes its title, almost all showed young women at the front lines of hospitality work. In such ads, women tended to be dressed in "traditional" clothing, such as *phâa nûng* wrapped around their chests and shoulders, implying the beauty and cultural depth of the place they represent. But their sexual availability was still bluntly implied, as in the words blared across the cover of the brochure *Bangkok After Dark!!!!* This juxtaposition was also present in tourist advertising for other Asian countries, drawing on long-standing Orientalist constructions of female subjection. Culture was a respectable veneer over white men's sovereign right to pleasure. American soldiers had no trouble with the subtext.

In discussing Thai artists and performers who have grappled with these stultifying gender roles in recent decades, Pahole explains that the legacies of GI-era exploitation have left enduring impressions. Generations of Thai women and queer and gender-nonconforming people, from drag performer Pattaya

FIGURE 4.4. The cover of the 1968 edition of the tourist guide *Bangkok After Dark!!!!* alludes in its imagery and design to the sovereign right to pleasure possessed by *farang*.

Hart to *luk thung* icon Pumpuang Duangjan, have reframed colonial legacies of gender and sex. Thai performance artist Korakrit Arunanondchai positions the GI era in much of his work as the beginning of a decades-long Thai reckoning with identity and the body. These artistic projects typify efforts by Thai people to confront the "conflation of sex with violence" that resulted from imperialism's lascivious force.[48] Asian and Asian-presenting women continue to be categorized and coercively marketed, well into the twenty-first century, as servile and without rights in a system of heteropatriarchy. This is of course true for Asian-presenting women not only in Thailand but throughout the world.[49] It is therefore no surprise that so much creative work in Thailand that has wrestled with legacies of sexual hierarchy has been not only feminist but queer. *Farang* privilege is ultimately not just a colorist privilege but also in many ways a heteronormative one. White heterosexual *farang* men were uniquely privileged in Thailand during the American war in Vietnam.

Impunity, as theorized by Tyrell Haberkorn in the Thai context, may be the clearest way to summarize this privilege. Impunity is a lack of accountability. It is the capacity to behave in ways that are illegal by the letter (often dramatically so) yet not be prosecuted, as routinely happened with GIs visiting Thailand on R&R. For Haberkorn, impunity is fundamental to the structure of Thai politics and its human hierarchies. Inequity is often justified by reference to Buddhist notions of tiered human valuation. In Haberkorn's reading, acts of impunity not only reflect this unequal order but reinforce it. The more visible an act of impunity, the more natural that impunity becomes. Haberkorn's case studies, however, deal mostly with elite Thai figures, such as the police, politicians like Sarit, and those with royal blood.

One might ask how *farang* would fit into Haberkorn's theory of impunity. Around 1960, when westerners began arriving in Thailand in substantial numbers, *farang* had to be folded into the Thai social system more deeply than ever before. Thais needed to make sense of *farang* proximity and status. In Pattana's framework, *farang* are an Occidental "Other." Yet in the everyday experience of Thai people, westerners were a regular presence, not an abstract psychoanalytic force. Their high status had to be managed at the bar, in the nightclub, and in a variety of other intimate commercial encounters. There was no ready way to explain their privilege in these settings. For example, *farang* were not meritorious. In fact they had no standing within Buddhism at all. Nor did they occupy any position in a royal lineage or possess *baarámii* (a Thai measure of accumulated charisma), *amnâat* (formal power), or *itthíphon* (unofficial influence). In lieu of these, *farang* wielded what might best be described as commodified impunity—a form of sovereignty derived not from principles of royal or Buddhist status but from the money in their pockets. Their privilege was inscribed in new laws and international agreements like the R&R MoU. This privilege sometimes invited backlash, but it proved very difficult to resist. *Farang* privilege appeared in Thailand in the 1960s as something like a runoff from modern development, a potentially toxic burden that required special forms of waste management. Americans, especially white men, could flaunt impunity, even when their bad behavior occurred in plain view or affected others directly. In the Thai nightlife scenes of the Cold War, *farang* spent their time and money under the protection of a system of special benefits and privilege that had the weight of law and economic power. *Farang* privilege was a key dimension of the new Thai nightlife milieu that emerged around 1965. Thailand's cosmopolitan music and nightlife cannot be understood without acknowledging the force of this privilege. And Maurice Rocco's flush years in Thailand depended on his access to this very *farang* privilege, partial and temporary as it was for him.

Alongside *farang* privilege, a second key dimension of Thailand's new nightlife milieu was that of "Cold War Orientalism," the titular concept in a 2002 book by historian Christina Klein.[50] Klein's study begins in 1945, when international news made Americans increasingly aware of Asia as both place and idea. Middlebrow media products such as the Rodgers and Hammerstein musicals *South Pacific*, *Flower Drum Song*, and *The King and I* not only showed colorful Asian settings but created opportunities for middle-class Americans to imagine connections with Asian people. Klein argues that these connections allowed Americans to humanize their government's increasingly Asia-focused foreign policy—in a sense, to get to know the focus of this policy intimately. Yet the texts of musicals, books, and travel diaries from the period reveal that even these humanistic engagements were tinged with imperialism, albeit in a form more paternalistic than hawkish. On these fraught terms, middle-class Americans were learning about Asia.

Thailand was among the nations viewed by Americans through a Cold War Orientalist lens. This also owed to the increasing political attention paid to the country by Presidents Harry Truman and Dwight Eisenhower over the course of the 1950s. In the two years after *The King and I* debuted on Broadway in 1956, US military aid to Thailand increased from $4.5 million to $56 million.[51] Klein's analysis ends in 1961, when the war in Vietnam began to narrow American interest in the region to Southeast Asia. Without a doubt, consciousness of Thailand intensified in the 1960s, when a significant number of Americans not only read news or watched movies about the country but went there in person. A booming commercial aviation industry made international travel affordable and convenient even before the war began.[52] Klein's concept of

Cold War Orientalism describes the worldview that soldiers and other Americans carried with them when they went to Thailand for work, war, or leisure.

Maps, as Klein describes, played a vital and overtly ideological role in explaining global relationships to Americans during the 1950s. As with a Mercator projection, or more recently a CIA map, the entire world could be easily viewed from a god's-eye vantage. A cartographic logic lay at the heart of Cold War Orientalism. Thongchai Winichakul famously argues that maps were central to building the modern Thai nation, under duress from colonial powers like Great Britain.[53] The ways that maps depicted Thailand in relation to the rest of the world, and conceived of its internal jurisdictions, had radically transformed local conceptions of power and space in Southeast Asia in the nineteenth century. This shift had far-reaching implications for governance as well as for Siam's understanding of itself as a place. Thongchai's history is set at a time when cartographic logics were just beginning to permeate the Siamese bureaucracy. These logics were then reinforced in the twentieth century, especially by Thai king Bhumibol Adulyadej, who was often depicted in state propaganda wading through impoverished rural fields, poring over maps that symbolized the kind of rational development that allegedly only he could supervise. Caring for remote parts of the country with the aid of modern geospatial knowledge was a hallmark of Bhumibol's reign. Not incidentally, the scholarly framework of area studies also used maps in a Cold War Orientalist fashion, sorting spheres of disciplinary knowledge according to their global position.[54] Suddenly, a scholar was classified as an Asianist, an Americanist, or an Africanist, for example. Academics, development-minded monarchs, and imperial governments, not to mention middle-class Americans learning about Asia for the first time during the early Cold War, all used maps to manage and understand global difference.

Thai nightlife was also understood by visitors in the GI era, including American soldiers, through the ideological metaphor of maps. Klein calls this perspective a "global imaginary," a framework that "creates an imaginary coherence out of the contradictions and disjunctures of real relations, and thereby provides a stable sense of individual and national identity."[55] In other words, the global imaginary reduced vast, complex networks of belief, power, conflict, and perpetual change to a static blueprint that could be unfurled on the table and examined, as if everything and everyone in the world stood still over time. This had the effect of reducing culture to kitsch. The global imaginary suggested that the world order was inert, that certain places and people had unassailable qualities. Most of the time these qualities were little more than racist assumptions. Nevertheless, the mapping of culture became an aid to a new kind of transnational consumerism, including in nightlife, which promised pleasure through the sampling of global wares.

On R&R, a global imaginary not only mapped where in the world things belonged but also served as a menu of what an informed soldier/consumer might want to buy in a cosmopolitan marketplace. For *farang*, exotic food, global music, and sexual pleasure were each available in a variety of ethnic flavors. "The commercialization of diversity . . . was an extractive practice, in which signifiers of difference—national, cultural, linguistic, religious, racial, sexual, gendered—were isolated and amplified for commercial gain."[56] Much of what made a city like Bangkok so appealing at that moment was its capacity to stage maplike representations of the world along its streets and in its nightlife. A visiting soldier/tourist could eat, listen, and have sex like a sophisticate. Savvy consumers were those with the resources and knowledge to appreciate what was on offer—to get, in the words of bell hooks, "a bit of the Other."[57] Or, in this case, Others. "We set a goal to eat at a different nationality restaurant every night," remembers one serviceman of the time he was stationed in Bangkok.[58] The resulting tastes and consumption practices exemplified "cosmopolitan kitsch."[59]

Although Bangkok was the stage for such adventurous consumption, it was not only experiences of Thai or Asian culture that were exoticized. Advertisements in the *Bangkok Post* showed off a world of new consumerist possibilities. There were relatively few advertisements for nationally coded music, food, or sexual services until about 1963, at which point the phenomenon quickly expanded. On a single page of ads from the August 20, 1964, issue of the *Bangkok Post*, for example, Miss Keiki Minami was the "Sensational Exotic dancer from the land of cherry blossoms" (Japan), performing two shows nightly at the New Champagne Room. To her immediate right, a restaurant promised "Shanghai food, our specialty," by "expert cooks from Hong Kong." Below that, Happy Garden advertised its Saba Show, "a traditional Thai game for joyous occasions." A great range of "ethnic" things could be experienced in a single bar crawl. The Sani Chateau nightclub, run by a Japanese proprietor, rotated through different international acts every few weeks, always with a distinct, nationalized angle. Some acts featured at Sani in 1964 included Olga y Curró's "fury of Flamenco dance" from Spain; Miss Toko from Tokyo; the 3 Hot Shots, a group of "sensational acrobatic comedy dancers from Manila"; and Belgin Sayar, the "exotic dancer from Turkey."

Aside from flesh itself, global exoticism was the most important selling point for these acts. And it was full of racist caricature. National identity was linked with simplified forms of vernacular music and dance, while stereotypical

FIGURE 4.5. An advertisement for acts at the Sani Chateau, with each performer clearly identified by their national identity and style. *Bangkok Post*, July 2, 1964.

national temperaments were invoked for good measure, an extreme and deeply kitschy manifestation of what Jim Sykes calls the "music and identity episteme."[60] Spanish dancers thus exhibited "fury" while Korean women ("baby dolls") were passive and childlike. Racist stereotypes became hallmarks of the new nightlife milieu. Performers, in turn, exaggerated these stereotypes onstage, which gave the global imaginary exactly what it expected—and exactly what its customers wanted to spend money on.

Rocco had a place within the Cold War Orientalist framework as well. Even in a venue as elite as the Bamboo Bar, he was exoticized as a Black American musician, plotted on the map as a figure of old-fashioned American sophistication. This resembled how he had appeared in the film *Incendiary Blonde*, and just like in that film the role carried laudatory as well as uncomfortable implications. But in Thailand, importantly, the value of jazz was under little or no pressure from the ascent of rock and roll. In Thailand's local version of Cold War Orientalism, jazz was a timelessly upmarket genre. In this parallel modernity, jazz and rock and roll were not competing for the same customers. While young privates preferred rock bands, jazz was considered a better fit for officers and diplomats. Tsitsi Ella Jaji describes jazz in a similar frame around the same time in Senegal, where state elites celebrated Ellingtonian jazz, not contemporary styles like bebop, as core symbols of pan-Africanism.[61] Outside the United States, it was often older jazz, the kind that Rocco played, that carried the highest value. This revisionism of jazz's older forms in many respects gave the music more cachet than rock in Bangkok. Jazz provided the de facto musical environment for venues catering to wealthy clientele. This was reflected in the Oriental Hotel's marketing strategy, which exaggerated Rocco's elite bona fides in rather extreme ways. In one ad, the hotel fabricated that Rocco had "played for Queen Elizabeth 3 times at the Buckingham Palace," an engagement for which no evidence appears to exist, but which was apparently credible enough to print.[62] Onstage in Thailand, Rocco played the role of an opulent character from jazz's mythical gilded age. For cosmopolitan audiences in Asia, this was a believable and appealing story.

Rocco was not infantilized along lines of ethnicity and gender as the Korean baby dolls were. Nevertheless, the hyperbole around his celebrity clouded his past. The depth and breadth of Rocco's life, from his upbringing amid racism in southern Ohio to the craft of standing at the piano, from queer performativity to his abuse of Santha—the beautiful and the abhorrent alike—were obscured by a set of simplified ideas about the position of Black jazz on a Cold War Orientalist world map. Rocco's interconnections with other kinds of music were also obscured. The ways that he had helped establish a template for rock and roll, or the fact that jazz and other forms of Black music had influenced Thai musicians for several decades, were invisible. In brief, any history of circulation or global encounter was simply too dynamic to be represented on a map, but *farang* pursuing pleasure along a cosmopolitan bar strip knew no other way of seeing the world.

The Oriental Hotel's embellishments told a story in which jazz was strictly nonnative, an exotic new import. Thanks to this story, Rocco's performances were marketed with great success. But his story was flattened in the process. Exoticism as a marketing angle was only possible when histories of musical circulation were left untold. Jazz had in fact been present in Thailand since at least the 1930s, but in the 1960s the Cold War global imaginary presented jazz as if it had been alien to Southeast Asia until now. This erasure also goes some way toward explaining how Rocco's life in Thailand could be so thoroughly cleaved from his life in the United States. The two places were imagined as worlds apart. As jazz was remapped in Asia, Rocco retreated into the shelter of these powerful myths.

Cold War Orientalism was realized in the physical space of Bangkok, which presented the Cold War global imaginary in miniature. Different establishments represented the range of global fare that could be sampled. To shop, relax, eat, get drunk, or have sex in this field was also an educational opportunity, a way of knowing the world from a position of privilege.[a] Some parts of town were distinguished by their diversity, and thus by a range of global choices, while others hosted concentrations of one specific nationality or another. Notably, New Phetchaburi had the most venues with American and British themes. While the massage parlors on the American Strip often implied narratives of global sexual variety, such as Turkish massages, the bars and restaurants played to soldiers' nostalgia for the cuisine of their home country, most often steak and cheeseburgers. Other parts of the city, like Patpong and Sukhumvit, were growth areas accessible to soldiers but usually more compelling for nonmilitary tourists in search of treats like Brazilian steak or Peking duck. Rocco was one of many flags on this miniature map, his life and art reduced to a one-dimensional identity marker, a pale distillation of Black American jazz legible within the Cold War global imaginary.

The Poetics of Nightlife Intimacy

What was nightlife labor? Who did the work that made nightlife possible, how did these laborers understand themselves, and what were the industry's short- and long-term consequences for Thailand? To begin, the sheer scope of nightlife work that first appeared during the GI era must be acknowledged. By reputation, and perhaps by volume as well, the most prominent jobs were sexual services for international clients. In the middle of the twentieth century,

---

a ACKNOWLEDGMENT: A paid research assistant, Mare Knaupp, helped aggregate a significant collection of data to plot the location of establishments in Bangkok (bars, clubs, restaurants, massage parlors) with explicitly national themes (Mexican, Chinese, Spanish, English) between 1967 and 1972. In some cases this meant the cuisine that was served. For others it signaled the nationality of the house band or the theme of the venue itself (Florida Bar, Las Vegas Bar, Brit Club). Not every venue had a national marketing angle, but many did. Mapping these locales enabled us to see how different parts of the city manifested different parts of the Cold War global imaginary. I am happy to share this data with curious readers and researchers. Knaupp also assisted with many other aspects of this project.

sex work trailed only farming as a livelihood for Thai women.[63] Paid sex carried stigma for those who offered it, and workers typically hoped their commitments would be temporary. Scholarship on the tourism industry in Thailand during the Cold War has frequently focused on sex work because of its economic impact as well as its myriad sociopolitical controversies.[64] However, the varieties of labor introduced or expanded during the GI era were broader than sex work alone. Makeshift towns oriented to soldiers stationed at bases supported all kinds of labor. "A cluster of shanty towns sprang up around the base, offering servicemen everything from souvenirs to prostitutes."[65] By one estimate, 150,000 Thai people had "base-related jobs" during the war era, which added $250 million to the Thai economy annually.[66] Thai people worked in bars, clubs, and restaurants; merchants sold clothing, music albums, and electronics in informal markets; and musicians found lucrative opportunities. There were also many vocations that did not relate directly to nightlife but still depended on the American military presence. *Mèe bâan* (female maids) folded laundry and cleaned rooms, while mechanics repaired airplane parts. They were joined by bank tellers, construction workers, secretaries, translators, and many others. All these jobs depended on the infrastructural development historicized in chapter 2.

Intimate labor refers to the labor performed within intimate economies, which Ara Wilson defines as relations of exchange at "the intersection of market economies and intimate life."[67] Intimate labor is in some sense the work of directing traffic at this intersection. Thinking with intimate labor rather than "sex work" as an analytical category is a way of acknowledging that paid sex is often difficult to distinguish from other kinds of intimate work. It was not uncommon, for example, for paid sexual encounters in war-era Thailand to become bridges to long-term relationships, including marriages. Nor was (or is!) it uncommon for marriages to continually involve financial patronage, especially in contexts of inequality. Thus, intimate laborers are people who worked or continue to work in settings where intimacy is governed significantly by economic forces. In intimate labor, the boundaries between private life and the market may become blurry. Luise White's pioneering scholarship on prostitution in colonial Nairobi not only recognizes sex work as labor but usefully situates that labor within networks of agency, gender, family, economy, and coloniality that extend well beyond the private realm.[68] To the same point much earlier in history, Friedrich Engels wrote of late eighteenth-century France that "marriage itself remained, as before, the legally recognized form, the official cloak of prostitution."[69] In other words, it is not historically unusual for intimacy and labor to mix. During the GI era, capital governed not just sex but all manner of intimate human relationships. This part of the chapter is concerned with the intimate labor of such relationships, often conducted in spaces of nightlife.

Among the most remarkable intimate laborer roles in the GI-era economy was that of the *mia chao*, or "rented wife." *Mia chao* were temporary or periodic domestic partners of western servicemen.[70] In some cases they were hired for the duration of a short combat leave, with or without hope of continuing their partnerships in the future. In other cases they became long-term or even life partners of *farang*. In these instances they have more often been called *mia farang*, or "*farang* wife." The distinction between *mia chao* and *mia farang* is loose, and both identities have borne stigma. In the 1960s, many *mia chao/mia farang* were otherwise poor, displaced by development, or without meaningful life opportunities. They came overwhelmingly from rice-farming villages in northeastern Thailand. Most of these women and their families were saddled with significant debt, a widespread effect of the midcentury consolidation of farmland ownership. As a result, they had few or no chances to build wealth. Contact with American soldiers, who had money to spare, was therefore an alluring opportunity.

No small number of Thai women as well as some men therefore sought intimate relationships with *farang*, hoping to remain in Thailand with vastly higher incomes or else to move into privileged situations abroad. In a context of profound financial imbalance between neocolonial visitors and Thai people with few resources, *mia chao* are the result of a particularly disruptive encroachment of money into intimate relationships. Simply put, *farang* had so much wealth that a market for their companionship, an intimate economy, became almost inevitable.

Mia chao are not sex workers in any straightforward sense. Many develop long-term relationships in order to support their families (often including children from first marriages to Thai men), to whom they may send remittances from a foreign country where they live. Patcharin has examined this labor as a vital economic lifeline for many Thai families, up to the present.[71] From the GI era forward, *mia chao/mia farang* have been economically indispensable to northeastern Thailand in particular, working in roles that balance labor and intimacy. In addition to their economic importance, *mia chao* in the 1960s–'70s also worked at the front lines of Thai-American cultural relations and were in many ways the architects of a new communicative poetics.

By about 1967, *mia chao* were enough of a social fact that they began to appear as characters in novels, visual media, and music. One famous song, called

จดหมายรักจากเมียเช่า (Love letter from a rented wife), was released as part of a TV serial in the late 1960s.[72] The lyrics describe the precarity of being *mia chao* through the story of a woman callously abandoned by a fictional American GI. The song is in the genre of *luk thung*, a working-class tale of woe sung with ample melisma in call-and-response dialogue with slow, despondent horn lines. Thick with cosmopolitan influence, it resembles the lovesick chamber pop of western women crooners like Brenda Lee or Patsy Cline. One lyrical fragment of "Love letter," in which the singer delivers the line "*sâw kwaa* sad movie" (sadder than a sad movie), is a melodic and lyrical quotation of Sue Thompson's 1961 hit "Sad Movies (Make Me Cry)." "Love letter" may have been the first popular work of art in Thailand to convey the experiences of *mia chao* at all, let alone so richly.

In the song's narrative, a *farang* soldier named John has left his station in the Thai city of Udon Thani to return to Illinois. The lyrics are the lines of a forlorn letter addressed to John from the *mia chao* he has left behind. Trying to coax him back, she tells John that her loneliness is so profound that she will contract typhoid. She contemplates suicide in the face of his departure, the ensuing lack of money, and her own shame in being "thrown away." Notably, "Love letter" is not autobiographical. Its singer, Mani Maniwan, was an actress playing the role of a *mia chao* on television, while the lyricist, a well-known songwriter (and National Artist of Thailand) named Ajin Banjaporn, was a man. Nevertheless, the song is remembered in Thailand as an important document of the travails of *mia chao*. An entire 2015 episode of the Thai PBS television documentary show ข้างหลังเพลง (Behind the music) is devoted to the song's lasting influence. In that episode, major contemporary Thai pop singers like Bie the Star attest to the song's musical and cultural import. "Love Letter" remains a powerful emblem of the complexity of intimate labor in the GI era.

Although it plays as hyperbole, the song's references to death cannot be reduced to the tropes of tragic romantic balladry. The woman in the song's narrative is an adult with multiple material dependencies on her relationship, not a teenager hyperbolizing the pain of a breakup. This scenario was routine for *mia chao*, who had no assurances that the money that lifted them out of poverty would continue to flow. Indeed, as the war in Vietnam peaked and began to decline around 1969, the livelihoods of *mia chao* became precarious. When the American military finally left Thailand in the mid-1970s, rented wives staged public protests against the withdrawal, pitting them against anti-imperialist student groups who wanted American soldiers to leave. One day in 1975, "about 600 hired wives [*mia chao*] at Korat and Udorn also became activists, with 15 rented buses and loud speakers as equipment. They counter-protested the university students' efforts to make American servicemen leave the country. With the number of clients dwindling, the women had been distraught at the thought of returning to their lives before the influx of American servicemen."[73] The consequences of withdrawal or abandonment for intimate laborers cannot be understated. Each night at the bar, death loomed over American soldiers who would return to Vietnam in just a few days. But life and death were also at stake for Thai intimate laborers. Mani's dramatic lyrics were no exaggeration.

Journalist Weerawat Somnuek recently interviewed a former bargirl named Banjong Boonkit, who in the 1960s worked in Udon Thani near the Ramasun radar station on the outskirts of town.[74] Ramasun employed hundreds of Americans, who monitored the Chinese military by day and lit out for bars and clubs in town at night. Banjong, from a farming family and with only a fourth-grade education, endeavored to make money in the ensuing nightlife scene. Her status there was characteristically ambiguous, especially as she tells the story now. Formally employed as a waitress, she pursued relationships with both Thai men and American soldiers. It is not clear where or whether she drew lines between money and intimacy. Banjong leaves gaps in her telling that stand as facts of history, and that perhaps were no clearer then than they are in the narratives she offers today. In any case, only one of Banjong's friends ever found a long-term *farang* partner. This woman moved to the United States with her partner in 1975, returning to Udon only after his death in the late 2010s. It was especially hard for Isaan women to find western partners in the GI era, since these women lacked education or status compared to women from Bangkok, so Banjong considered her friend very fortunate. Other *mia chao* found partners, only for them to die in Vietnam. Still others, like the fictional rented wife of GI John, were left behind when their partners finished military service and went home. Intimate labor offered little clarity or security.

In 2019, Thai music expert Peter Doolan and I traveled two hours south from Bangkok to the district of Sattahip to meet Karuna Chuangchan, a Thai woman then in her midsixties who worked during the 1970s as a translator for Thai women seeking *farang* partners. In that decade, Karuna was quite literally an author of love letters from rented wives. Like Banjong, Karuna grew up near U-Tapao, a US military base. Today she manages a bucolic guesthouse near the same former base, which is now a commercial airport. At U-Tapao, Karuna's father manufactured bombs for the US Air Force. With monied soldiers suddenly everywhere in town, teenaged Karuna made the canny decision to learn English. There were abundant work opportunities for those who could speak even a little bit of what had effectively become the local neocolonial language. Many Thai people studied English for personal or professional reasons.

But Karuna went a step further by starting a business translating letters from her female friends to *farang* with whom they hoped to connect romantically. She was not alone—singer Por Chalat Noi told me that rural towns with air bases swelled with Thai interpreters almost as soon as the GIs arrived. Karuna was sixteen years old in 1971 when she decided to become, in her own words, a matchmaker. She charged women twenty baht (about seventy cents) per translation. Karuna explained how she helped one friend deepen her relationship with a man she met at a bar in Sattahip. That couple eventually married and left Thailand:

> KARUNA: At that time we called them *mia chao*. Because the American soldier, they want to take the lady to America. Both of them went back. Some married, some not married. I write a letter for one lady. I remember her name now, her name is Mali Ratna. At that time she was a little bit of a hippie. And one day she come to me, "Phi Meow [Karuna's nickname], I have seen one man, I never know what his name." So I start writing letter to him.

> BEN: So you were trying to figure out what she wanted to express. What kinds of things did you say in those letters?

> KARUNA: When I see the lady I know how good she feels. And I can feel that in her, what she likes, her thinking ways. And some of them go together and get married.... Mali Ratna, I have found that she married one man. Maybe not American, but maybe Australian? I heard that she married and have a good life over there.[75]

Karuna proudly describes the work she did in those years as a craft. She not only translated letters but counseled her friends on how to express their own romantic feelings. In eliciting and representing these feelings, she invested everything in the quality of her prose. Karuna's job was a labor of poetics as much as translation. She retrospectively thinks about the work she did for *mia chao*, despite the financial mediation involved, as having helped them find authentic love. She further distinguishes this kind of love from, for example, the experiences of women like her friend Kwan, who moved to Bangkok in the early 1970s to do sex work and send money home to her ill mother. Karuna visited Kwan once and felt upset seeing her living conditions.

Where is the line between authentic love and labor? Sensing this tension in our discussion, I asked Karuna how she might define the term *love*. She responded with a laugh and said, "After my husband married me, he said, 'Karuna, I have nothing for you, but I will give you my life.' From that day until today, he only work and work and work and work and work and work and give everything to me." Karuna's definition of love, drawn from the experience of a forty-year marriage, centered the mutual dependency of labor. Love is work.

Karuna tells Mali Ratna's story in part as evidence that the love she brokered was authentic. But the distinction between employment and romance remains ambiguous, as it generally was for *mia chao*. As Patcharin writes with reference to *mia chao*, "Love and money are considered mutually exclusive [in the West], whereas in Thai society they overlap somewhat."[76] The figure of *mia chao* embodies a dialectical process: many kinds of intimate labor emerged across social categories in the GI era, and this labor in turn precipitated shifts in these categories, ultimately generating new categories.[77] In the spaces of nightlife where Banjong, Mali, and Karuna sought their livelihoods, social roles were in flux. These women experimented with new forms of agency, labor, access to money, and cosmopolitan knowledge.

As a translator, Karuna was among the earliest figures of a new communicative regime that granted Thai people access to the resources of Americans. This regime required new articulations of language and sound. Translating love letters was in this way part of a broader arbitration of language and communication. The opening pages of this book began with Maurice Rocco enmeshed in the strange work of mediating between different frames of soul/soulfulness. The same labor of mediation was common in many corners of nightlife at the time, and musicians as well as *mia chao* routinely performed it. Both groups used speech and sonic expression as instruments of intimate labor. In order to understand the intimacy of the Thai-American Cold War relationship, it is thus useful to understand how language and sound served as mediating forces within intimate relationships.

Under neocolonialism, listening was asymmetrical. Thai people like Karuna were compelled to spend far more time learning and translating the subtleties of English than Americans ever had to spend reckoning with Thai.[78] "They spoke English most of the places you had to go," said one American living in Bangkok in the late 1960s. "You didn't have to speak Thai."[79] Even beyond language, Americans were often dismissive of the sounds they heard in Southeast Asia. From music to speech to the din of everyday life, Southeast Asian sound was heard as nonsense, if not as a direct threat. "They played noisy, antagonizing sounds that were foreign to your ear just to throw you off-balance. They didn't do it on purpose, it was just there. I mean it was music to their ears, but it wasn't to ours," reflected former US soldier Larry Henry about the music he heard in Vietnam.[80] Local musical detail and symbols were beyond the ken of soldiers like Henry, who felt alienated by the sonic environment he encountered during his service. Recalled another soldier: "Some sailor had a radio playing, he was picking up this station out of Cambodia or Thailand somewhere with all that Oriental music, I can't describe that twicky, twangy, you know it when you hear it. I looked up and thought, I felt like a million miles away, like what am I doing here, just weird."[81] For this soldier, Cambodian and Thai music could scarcely be parsed beyond their menacing ambience. Ana María Ochoa Gautier's discussion of an earlier colonial contact zone, Europeans in nineteenth-century Colombia, rings familiar here. For Ochoa Gautier the "collapsed auditory regimes" of Europe and Colombia brought colonists into earshot of what they believed to be the precivilizational nature of Colombians.[82] In a similar fashion, local music and sound in war-era Thailand has been described by many American veterans as a meaningless affective presence, evidence of the bright line between advanced civilization and a pre-rational Other. Thai music was meaningless to these soldiers except as a reminder that they were far from home. Even US president Lyndon Johnson noted the alienation he felt when hearing Thai musical instruments on a trip to the country in 1966. "The American National Anthem was played with Thai musicians using Thai instruments which really gave our Anthem a rather foreign and weird sound," wrote the president in his diary.[83]

American efforts to domesticate weird-seeming sounds in Southeast Asia by assigning them analogical meaning were often crass. One soldier recalled hearing the incidentally foul-mouthed tokay gecko for the first time in Vietnam: "One of my drill instructors told us of a story about the 'fuck you' lizard in Vietnam. He said that was the sound it made. Yea, sure, right. While on lookout in the tower one night, I heard, 'fuck you, fuck you.' I couldn't believe it when I looked on the ground and saw five or ten lizards. I would not have ever believed it if I would not have seen or heard it myself."[84] Even the fauna of Southeast Asia was heard as vulgar and antagonistic.[85]

For many soldiers, western music was the most powerful antidote to the frightening, meaningless din of Southeast Asian sound environments. Rock and roll accomplished this most of the time, but any familiar style would do. "My tape recorder has come," wrote Marine David Petteys triumphantly in a letter home to his parents in late 1966. "It's so good to have GOOD music again. I'm currently listening to Beethoven's 3rd 'Eroica.' It's so inspirational and noble. Right now, we're recording tapes. We've borrowed an organ concerto from my hootch-mate, and I'm recording it while Paul plays it, then vice versa."[86] Western classical music was, for this soldier, a civilizing aural salve.

Thai words and sounds were incoherent to most American visitors, except a small number who studied Thai because they worked in intelligence or for volunteer programs. The American military did not prioritize teaching foreign languages, even to soldiers stationed in-country, unless those soldiers had a specific need to communicate in it. Meanwhile Americans did not generally encounter Thai music, except when it was staged for them in touristic spaces. In the rare instances when GIs spoke of Thai music approvingly, it was usually in reference to classical dance performances at restaurants or state-sponsored events. Notably, these performances were predominantly visual (Kodak was a regular sponsor of one concert series promoted by the TOT at the main branch of the National Museum), with ornate, "traditional" costumes that situated the events squarely in the Cold War global imaginary. It was only when music could be visualized according to the logics of this imaginary that *farang* could readily make sense of it. Klein notes that in *The King and I*, Siamese children only communicate with words after the point in the plot when they have learned English. Before that, their voices are represented symbolically by orchestral instruments.[87] Thai and other Southeast Asian speech, language, and music were simply meaningless to most American visitors.

By stark contrast, Thais learned English eagerly. Thai-language newspapers ran daily ads for language tutoring, along with regular features about the minutiae of English. A typical article from 1967 in *Siam Rath* headlined "ของฝรั่ง (มะริกัน)" (*Farang* things [American]) explained that in a place like Times Square in New York, or downtown Boston, one might hear someone ask, "'ว้อท ชะ กะน่า แฮฟ' (What Cha gona have=what are you going to have?)."[88] Informing the reader about not only vocabulary but also usage revealed a serious general interest in the nuances of the English language. Middle-class weekly magazines, recognizing high demand, rushed to include English language lessons. According to Sudina Paungpetch, "*Sakulthai* and *Satrisarn*, popular lady's magazines, published lyrics and translations of songs such as the Beatles' 'Hey Jude' and later Carole King's 'Will You Love Me Tomorrow?' to help readers sing along and figure out what they meant."[89] Karuna's love letter business is one of countless examples of the value of English competency as a professional skill for Thai people. Thais had incentive to be resourceful as well as autodidactic in learning it.

Further analysis of the song "Love letter from a rented wife" suggests how far this effort had come by 1967. "Love letter" is a prominent and early example of a phenomenon sometimes called *thai kham angkrit kham* (literally, "Thai words English words").[90] This term describes a form of code-mixing in which Thai speakers integrate English words into advertising, song lyrics, movie dialogue, names, and everyday speech. Some of these integrations are lightly modified adoptions, like the word for computer—คอมพิวเตอร์ or *khɔɔmphiwtəə*—that have entered the lexicon as loanwords. But in certain corpuses, such as the lyrics to "Love letter," the content is divided about halfway between two tongues. Such cases, where multiple English words are integrated into a Thai corpus, are examples of *thai kham angkrit kham*. This integration entails not only a poetic negotiation between languages but also creative practices of nativization. English words are pronounced differently, according to the mandates of Thai grammar, and at times the words are semantically altered. Below are the complete lyrics of "Love letter" as they are sung in the original recording by Mani Maniwan in *thai kham angkrit kham*, followed by an English translation:

I เขียน letter ถึงเธอ dear John
เขียนในแฟลตที่ you เคยนอน
จังหวัด อุดร ประเทศ Thailand
I broken heart you must understand
John จำ John dollar ขาดแคลน
เมีย second hand ของ you ยัง คอย
You ทิ้ง เมียเช่า หิ้วกระเป๋า go home
ทิ้ง รอยจูบลูบโลม
จน shape I โทรมเพราะ you enjoy
Forget your wife กลับ ไปอยู่ Illinois
I เสียใจจนเป็น typhoid
เอา Tiger Oil มาทากันตาย
โศกเศร้ากว่า sad movie
Oh John you make me cry!
I lonely เสียจนผอมผ่าย
อยากตาย why you ทิ้ง me
รอยน้ำตาหยด ที่รดบนลายเซ็น
หาซองใส่ จ่าหน้าไม่เป็น
โธ่ เวร เอ๋ย เวร who ช่วยเขียนที่
ฉีกทิ้ง letter หันไปเจอ DDT
Goodbye สวัสดี
Go meet กับ me ที่เมืองฮึง the end

I write a letter to you Dear John
Written in the flat where you once slept
In the province of Udon, Thailand
I broken heart you must understand
My John, John the dollars are running out

The secondhand wife that you once had
You threw away your rented wife, grabbed your bags, and went home
Threw away the kisses and soft caresses
Now I've lost my beautiful shape that you enjoyed
Forget your wife and go back to Illinois
I'm so sad I'll get typhoid
I'll drink Tiger Oil until I'm dead
Sadder than a sad movie
Oh John, you make me cry!
I'm so lonely I'll waste away
I want to die; why did you throw me away?
The lines of tears fall on my signature
As I search for an envelope; I don't have the address
Alas! Damn! Oh, damn! Who will help me write it?
I rip up the letter and toss it, turn and find some DDT
Goodbye, farewell
Go meet me at the end

The song features sophisticated code-mixing. The common Thai pronunciation of the English word *understand*, for example, employs /e/ as its final vowel sound. By rhyming this with the Thai word *khlɛɛn* (แคลน), Mani creates a smooth resonance between Thai and English. Meanwhile, rather than alternating lines of English and Thai, words mix organically within individual lines of the song's text. This mirrors the heteroglossia of Thai speech in the GI era, especially when Thais spoke to *farang*, as *mia chao* did all the time. Finally, the song applies Thai grammatical constructions to English, as in the line "I broken heart you must understand." The song does not make light of the *mia chao* character's informal grammar; rather, it reproduces certain nuances of actual *mia chao* speech. Although this and other examples of *thai kham angkrit kham* may have sounded superficially like an even split between languages—a hybridization—the labor of developing such poetics as a composite tongue fell almost entirely to Thai people, especially women. Perhaps no single group was more active in this than intimate laborers, who had the most personally consequential and certainly the most frequent interactions with foreign soldiers of anyone in Thailand at the time. In that respect, *thai kham angkrit kham* might be acknowledged as a singular poetic achievement of Thai intimate laborers, working under conditions of neocolonial power imbalance.

Scholars have often described Thai identity and expression, including language, as hybridized. But hybridity, a biological metaphor that indicates the mixing of two discrete organisms, is inadequate to explain the phenomenon of *thai kham angkrit kham*, just as it is inadequate to explain the milieu of the GI era and its effects. Thai and English ultimately mixed under a regime of asymmetrical power. By subtle poetic means, "Love letter from a rented wife" evokes the translational work that *mia chao* performed as a routine part of the division of labor within their intimate relationships. The combinatory mode called *thai kham angkrit kham* is best understood as a resonance or a colonial effect rather than a hybrid.

Throughout the 1960s, language-mixing began to occur more often—and more organically. *Luk thung* megastar Suraphon Sombatcharoen used the device several times, including in his well-known single "Snooker."[91] That song tells an understated and mostly literal story about how gambling on snooker is fun while you have the hot hand but humbling once your luck runs out. Suraphon sings entirely in Thai until the final line, when he switches to *thai kham angkrit kham* to deliver the song's parable in English: "*Farang* same same—no have money, go home." "Snooker" might be heard as a literal nightlife anecdote, making the simple point that *farang* have lucky streaks like anyone else. But it could also be interpreted as a commentary on the American presence in Thailand. While their war in Vietnam was escalating, Americans flooded Southeast Asia. But once their luck and money ran out, the American military would surely leave. That was beginning to appear likely in the late 1960s, when the song was recorded. "Snooker" thus potentially doubles as a parable about the precarity of Thailand's neocolonial cosmopolitanism. And it was written, with brilliant poetic touches, in *thai kham angkrit kham*, a combinatory idiom that originated within the very nightlife that it narrated.

Thai-English code-mixing is extremely common today in Thailand, including in popular music.[92] Weekly singing competition shows like *The Voice* feature performers switching deftly between Thai, English, and even Spanish. Code-mixing is not limited to music; Thai advertising leans heavily on English words and idioms as a token of modernity. Trips to the mall or on Bangkok's Skytrain, spaces of cosmopolitan consumption, are full of ads and announcements laced with English. This now-pervasive feature of the Thai sonic and communicative environment dates to the American war in Vietnam. And it owes its earliest poetics to intimate nightlife laborers, most of whom were poor women from the provinces.

Mia farang, like the phenomenon of *thai kham angkrit kham*, are now everywhere in Thailand.[93] "A 2004 government survey found just shy of 20,000 Isaan women married to foreigners, 87 percent of whom were westerners from Europe, North America, Australia or New Zealand," according to a 2017 article in *Khao Sod*. "90 percent of the slightly more than 27,000 foreigners living in the northeastern region were married to women from there."[94] These women sent a total of $44 million in remittances home annually to their families and villages as of 2004. In one small village in Udon Thani (the same city where the fictional GI John was stationed in "Love letter from a rented wife"), called Ban Na Dok Mai, there are now about five hundred *farang* married to local women. The subdistrict where these men are most densely concentrated, Non Wai, is informally called the "*farang* son-in-law district." Many other Thai-*farang* couples have moved abroad. The 2018 documentary *Heartbound* follows four Thai Danish couples negotiating the challenges of emigration, raising children remotely, and maintaining identity. The popular 1990 Thai novel ดีฉันไม่ใช่โสเภณี (I am not a whore) meanwhile makes powerful claims to the dignity of *mia farang* labor.[95] In sum, it is no longer unusual to find Thai-*farang* couples in Thailand.

Thai nationalists have long been anxious that language mixing will destroy the Thai language, a concern that sometimes rises to moral panic.[96] Almost in parallel, residual stigma is still directed at *mia farang* for their supposed role in the corruption of Thainess. But in the twenty-first century both anxieties have significantly receded. In fact, today the racial figure of the *lûuk khrûng* (literally, "half child") has become not only accepted but fashionable. Golfer Tiger Woods and US senator Ladda Tammy Duckworth are among those identified as *lûuk khrûng* in addition to many Thai celebrities whose mixed identities are considered an asset. Linguistic code-mixing and blended families are resonances of the neocolonial Cold War, and these have been woven into Thai social systems together. In significant ways, *mia chao/mia farang* were the most important early poets of *thai kham angkrit kham*, an expressive register that emerged in the intimate transnational context of Cold War nightlife in Thailand, and which now forms part of the bedrock of a globalized Thai society.

Musical Cosmopolitanism

Luk thung star Chatri Sichon recorded a response song to "Love letter from a rented wife" later in 1967. In the tradition of rhythm and blues and country music, จดหมายจากผัวฝรั่ง (Love letter from a *farang* husband) is John's answer to his *mia chao*'s anguished letter. The lyrics offer the perspective of the American husband, on the defensive about his departure. Less compelling musically or lyrically than the original, "Love letter from a *farang* husband" is no longer widely remembered in Thailand. But it contains one key detail that opens toward a discussion of musical cosmopolitanism in the GI era, the same sort of cosmopolitanism heard along New Phetchaburi Road and inside the Bamboo Bar.

Namely, the song's bridge includes the line "Where are the days that we used to know, roaming the hills and the shore?"—benign lyrics that hide a deep compositional story. The words are a direct quotation of American crooner Ed Ames's obscure 1967 B side "My Love Is Gone from Me." Ames's song only ever had modest commercial success in the United States. But it was an influential hit in Thailand and other parts of Southeast Asia in the late 1960s. Among those moved by it was a *mor lam* songwriter named Don Mod Daeng. Don was drawn to one particular melody in "My Love Is Gone from Me," a descending four-note violin part that repeats at several points in the song. *Mor lam* in the mid-1960s was moving toward orchestrations and song structures reminiscent of global pop music, and Don found this figure a useful device for modulating between keys. The musical figure that he borrowed from Ames became a kind of signature in his recordings.

It so happens that the figure Don chose for this purpose had been traveling the world for several centuries already. Sometimes called the Andalusian cadence or Chacona figure, it is a four-note pattern running stepwise downward, frequently in a lower register. Music critic Alex Ross (following a sweeping study by historian Ned Sublette) has written about the Chacona figure, which originated in South America as a stock chord progression in lively dances more than five hundred years ago.[97] From there the figure was adapted in Moorish music in Spain in the sixteenth century. The Chacona then became common across Europe in the baroque period as a symbol of lament, riffed on by Johann Sebastian Bach among others. In its first hundred years, the Chacona thus already had a remarkable history of circulation. But Ross details yet another phase in the Chacona's migration, this time to the United States in the twentieth century, where it became a staple of Delta blues, as well as blues-derived music like rhythm and blues and rock and roll. The Chacona figure can be heard, with the same sense of lament that it carried in the Baroque period, in the bass lines of Led Zeppelin's "Dazed and Confused," Ray Charles's "Hit the Road Jack," and countless other rock or soul songs. "My Love Is Gone from Me" is one example among hundreds of western pop tunes that have used the Chacona figure. But in Thailand, Ames's song was an unlikely hit, and it happens to be the recording that moved Don Mod Daeng to find a place for the Chacona figure in *mor lam*, where it became (and remains) a common gesture for songwriters. Thai *mor lam* is thus another node in the centuries-long migration of the Chacona figure that Ross and Sublette have described.

The peculiar fact that Ames's song was so influential in Thailand during the Cold War typifies the messy networks of cosmopolitanism that grew out of Thai-western musical contact zones. There are only overdetermined explanations for why Cliff Richard rivaled the Beatles in popularity in Southeast Asia, for example, or why Irish band The Cranberries' song "Zombie" was so popular that it topped Thailand's singles charts into the late 2000s, more than ten years after its original release. Akin to *thai kham angkrit kham*, these musical oddities occurred when Thai people listened closely to the expressive culture of a neocolonial occupier. Also like *thai kham angkrit kham*, the resulting objects of musical cosmopolitanism were often forged in and around nightlife, in this case by composers and musicians. Thai artists such as Chatri and Don Mod Daeng interpreted and interpolated global pop music in surprising ways.

To be sure, creative misinterpretation happens whenever music circulates. But in this historical case, tracing misinterpretation reveals just how far the significations of Euro-American music drifted when traveling through Thailand in the 1960s. The values of 1960s rock and psychedelic music (freedom, experimentation, antiwar leftism), for example, have been proclaimed so fervently in the West that it can be hard to imagine the music bearing any other meanings. Yet for Thai listeners these countercultural values barely registered. Thailand's fascination with the otherwise forgotten "My Love Is Gone from Me" is an object lesson in the unpredictable polysemy of musical circulation, the ways that one can never be sure how music will be heard, quoted, or recombined in a new place.

The Cold War was not the first context for musical exchange between Thailand and the West. Siamese music had been recorded as early as 1900 by Europeans and was included in the Berlin Phonogramm-Archiv, an important early archive for the discipline of comparative musicology.[98] Later, both during and after World War I, bands sponsored by the Siamese government played *phleeng săakon* (international music) to symbolize the country's modernity. *Luk thung* musicians heard and incorporated Afro-Latin musical ideas as early as the 1930s. American-style jazz was meanwhile used as a propaganda tool, most notably by the composer and saxophonist King Bhumibol Adulyadej. These are just some of the musical circulations involving Thailand and the west before the Cold War. Nevertheless, the war in Vietnam accelerated Thai interest in Euro-American sounds like never before. Nightlife became an incubator for advanced forms of intercultural exchange. During the Cold War, familiarity with *farang* musical idioms was becoming an immensely valuable skill for Thai musicians.

Thai listeners encountered international music during the Cold War in three principal ways: first, through the radio; second, through albums and cassettes sold at military base exchanges; and third, through live performances in nightlife venues. The era of elite, government-backed Thai big bands in the 1940s coincided with the construction of vast radio networks throughout the country. By 1957, Thailand had thirty-two radio stations reaching an estimated 10 million of the country's 22 million people.[99] Military-run stations played Tin Pan Alley and western classical music in addition to local styles. The American government, including the US Operations Mission (USOM) and the US Information Service, had a heavy hand in both developing infrastructure for national radio service and encouraging stations to program pro-western content.[100] Radio was a top-down, propagandistic technology from its very beginning. Its content reflected the Thai government's pro-American leanings. Meanwhile, post exchange stores inside US military bases sold western records as well as state-of-the-art playback technologies, including cassette tape players. An American soldier stationed or on leave in Bangkok could buy the newest stateside releases, along with late-model Japanese speakers, receivers, turntables, and tape machines, sometimes long before the same equipment was available in the United States. A robust secondary market for these goods quickly emerged, sometimes as a result of large-scale theft rings from post exchanges. Entrepreneurial Thais (often in collaboration with GIs) became both black market resellers as well as active consumers of the latest *farang* music. Finally, musicians like Maurice Rocco began to tour or even take on long-term residencies at nightlife venues where Thais among others could hear them in person. In these three ways, contemporary western music became well known to Thai listeners by the mid-1960s.

It would be reductive to say that Thai music changed as a result. More accurately, music in Thailand became something far more capacious than the nationally bounded term *Thai music* could any longer contain. This was a moment of syncretism. Cosmopolitanism was the order of the day, and Thai music grew into a more deeply layered social phenomenon. Within local styles like *mor lam ploen*, a quasi-psychedelic sound came into fashion. Many listeners in the West heard this sound as hollowly imitative. The same Orientalist presumptions have since led to *farang* hearing music from Thailand as either magically consonant with or tragically corrupted by the West. But the reality was more complex.

Certain styles that emanated from the West, including jazz, were in fact interpolated into a local version of the Cold War global imaginary. In this imaginary, Maurice Rocco's boogie-woogie was figured not as passé but as chic, a valuable token of Americana. As a result, Rocco floated above the roughest labor contexts, playing in more rarefied environments. Although he benefited from the nightlife situation made possible by the existence of New Phetchaburi

Road as an R&R enclave, he did not himself have to play the dive bars along that nightlife strip. As a jazz musician and a *farang*, he was called to a higher tier of entertainment, to places like the Bamboo Bar. He was fortunate in that regard. Jazz was quite literally the music of kings in Thailand, and its associations would carry him far. Every musician working in Thailand during the GI era navigated a particular order of cosmopolitan expectations. Some simply had it better than others.

The discussion below listens closely to some discrete historical moments within a layered order of intimate transnational nightlife, during a moment of transnational synthesis. The first such moment is the electrification of a Thai stringed instrument called the *phin*.

The Cosmopolitan Electric *Phin*

The *phin* was first electrified in 1970. A polymath named Noppadon Duangporn (born Narong Pongpap), a *mor lam* composer, singer, and bandleader from Ubon Ratchathani, had spent the prior several years experimenting with adding electric pickups to musical instruments, working primarily with the *phin* and a free-reed instrument called the *khɛɛn*. Noppadon did not plug in his instruments in public until 1970. But as soon as he did, he radically transformed *mor lam* as both a genre and a style of stagecraft. Noppadon would spend the rest of his life reminding people that he was the architect of this crucial sonic innovation. According to *phin* master Tongsai Thaptanon, Noppadon once even printed himself a "certificate of invention" to formally affirm his own original contributions.

Noppadon died in July 2019 at the age of seventy-seven. Peter Doolan and I happened to arrive in Thailand mere days later; we were too late to attend his funeral, but in the following weeks many of Noppadon's friends and associates assembled in Ubon, allowing us to meet and interview several major musical figures of twentieth-century *mor lam*, including Tongsai, Por Chalat Noi, Tinnakorn Attapaiboon, and Mae Banyen Rakkaen, largely thanks to the help of *mor lam* historian Yodh Warong. Both Por and Banyen have been named National Artists of Thailand, an honor akin to receiving a National Medal of Arts in the United States. I was given a copy of Noppadon's funeral book, an eighty-page collection created by his friends and family that narrates his entire life in elaborate, illustrated, and sometimes wonderfully tangential detail. This was an opportune moment to learn about the GI era—and the origins of a putatively psychedelic tonality in *mor lam*—from musicians whose careers began in that very era. According to his funeral book, Noppadon's electrification was bound to new broadcasting technologies: "In order to create a clear sound that would be considered his own original, he invented and established the electric *phin* with a specific vocabulary: the 'contact *phin*' and the 'floating mic *khɛɛn*.' This made Isaan music sound clearer. He brought his *phin/khɛɛn* band to play live on army radio station 11, which was channel 5 in Khon Kaen, and which presented programming from Ubon Ratchathani *phin/khɛɛn* bands for the first time throughout Isaan, popularizing the new sound."[101]

The first *mor lam* record to feature electrification was the debut album by the Phet Phin Tong band, a now legendary group that Noppadon assembled. Phet Phin Tong exemplifies the mature sound of *lam ploen*, a theatrical subgenre of *mor lam* that first appeared in the 1940s and 1950s. In the late 1960s, Noppadon hired some of the best singers and instrumentalists in Ubon to create a supergroup that could experiment with new forms and timbres grafted onto existing styles of *mor lam*. His band toured Isaan along highways freshly paved by the US government and its contractors. Phet Phin Tong combined an Ubon-specific *mor lam* sound with danceable rhythms and, of course, electric amplification. Their shows were massively popular, selling out theaters and large outdoor lots, contributing to a new nightlife context dominated by Thais rather than *farang*. And yet still their goal was to create something explicitly modern and cosmopolitan, and to gain an international profile in the process. Thus the name of the band's first album was *Mor lam banlɯɯ lôok* (Global *mor lam* party). *Lam ploen* musicians had used syncopated rhythms and aspired to performative virtuosity since the genre's inception; Phet Phin Tong signaled an advanced phase in that twenty-year development.

Electricity played a key symbolic role in the group's modern identity. Thai audiences were familiar with Euro-American psychedelic releases from the past few years, such as the Beatles' *Sgt. Pepper's Lonely Hearts Club Band*, Jimi Hendrix's *Are You Experienced?*, and Jefferson Airplane's *Surrealistic Pillow*, all of which appeared around the apex of psychedelic rock in 1967. These and other albums not only featured electric instruments but also drew the listener's attention to electrical networks—including their failures—through effects like feedback and distortion. Rather than using electricity for amplification alone, these tonal effects in Euro-American psychedelic music intentionally highlighted breakages, overloads, and disturbances in audio transmission systems. For most *farang*, this sonic aesthetic sounded a politics of social critique. The Beatles, Hendrix, and Jefferson Airplane were all readily known in Thailand from the radio, tapes and vinyl recordings purchased from military post exchange stores, and cover songs played live. Thai listeners thus heard feedback and distortion in popular music at more or less exactly the same time that most Americans did. For a group like Phet Phin Tong, electrification was a *farang* technology and thus a totem of modernity. But Phet Phin Tong and its Thai audiences did not hear electrified timbres according to the same semantic codes that *farang* did. Electricity coursed through Thailand along different circuits.

The story of electrification in the Thai provinces began in the early 1960s, a period when Noppadon worked with electrical networks as a technician in his hometown of Bang Ta Wang Hin, near Ubon. He claimed to have installed his village's first electrical wiring in 1964 and, further, that his own home was the first in the area to be connected to a central power grid. This experience, he said, was what gave him the technical prowess to tinker with electrifying his own musical instruments. Notably, national electrical networks in Isaan had been designed and built by the US government. As with roads, the greater purpose of these networks was to connect rural Thai provinces to the country's central government in order to surveil and restrict communist insurgency in marginal places. The earliest US-managed construction of electrical grids began in 1955, guided by USOM and carried out by the US Navy and JUSMAG. R. Sean Randolph quotes former USOM director Tracy Park, who in 1965 explained how rural development programs doubled as security projects: "Economic Development is, after all, one of the best counterinsurgency weapons we have. If we can develop among the rural people a friendship and loyalty toward their government, we shall have gone a long way toward making it possible for them to resist communist subversion attempts from outside."[102] Electrification in Thailand was thus, like networks of rural roads and schools, bound up with the neocolonial fight against communism.

Noppadon himself was an eager anti-communist. He described his own role in electrifying the village of Bang Ta Wang Hin as patriotic work that would serve "security, safety, and comfort," echoing the language that USOM and JUSMAG had long used to justify the same projects.[103] Noppadon similarly trumpeted his role as a pillar of community modernization. He volunteered to help advance sanitation and to "improve" the habits of Isaan people, for example by convincing rural Thais not to eat disease-causing raw fish. Such hygiene reform measures also tacked with an American vision for modernizing Thailand's rural areas. Noppadon's enthusiastic support for electrification was nested within the geopolitics of Cold War development. In short, he was no critic of the United States, or of capitalism or coloniality. There was very little about Noppadon personally or artistically that resonated with a psychedelic, leftist ethos aside from the sound of his instrument.

He was also ardently royalist. Phet Phin Tong took their name after playing a special show for the Thai king and queen in January 1971 at Khon Kaen University in Isaan. Following the well-received performance, Noppadon offered his own *phin* as a gift to the king. The king refused the gift, praising the instrument as "precious like a diamond" while telling Noppadon to keep and honor it. The king's description of the *phin* led Noppadon to name his band Phet Phin Tong, meaning something like "diamond-precious golden *phin*." This royal imprimatur was enormously important to Noppadon, as it securely linked his band to Buddhist piety and the rigidly anti-communist Thai monarchy.

Finally, Noppadon believed in conservative modes of individual action and gendered behavior. His funeral book enumerates the rules he established for his band, including prohibitions against drinking alcohol or using drugs, gambling, and wearing revealing clothes. Women band members in particular were required to dress modestly. These rules applied to Phet Phin Tong's members not only while performing but in every part of their lives. Noppadon was explicit that the band members could not shed their modesty after their shows ended. The musicians were expected to be models of conservative moral conduct, in no way aspiring to the libertine sensibilities of western psychedelic rock.

And yet sonically, Phet Phin Tong's psychedelic tonality is exactly what *farang* connoisseurs in the early twenty-first century hope to find when digging through crates for vintage Thai recordings. The band's music is in high demand now in an international market, enjoying a place of pride on many reissue compilations. Phet Phin Tong's sound is heavily syncopated, low fidelity, distorted, and full of deep grooves, yet just foreign enough to sound exotic. On their albums, the *phin* has a stark timbre created by a simple tube amplifier, which is tonally reminiscent of early rock and roll. The original albums are also hard to find, adding to their aura of mystique. Given all of this, western listeners have described Phet Phin Tong in predictable terms: "SE Asian pop drones that the John Cale–era Velvet Underground would be simpatico with," reads one record store blurb about a Phet Phin Tong track that appears on a popular vintage Thai music compilation. Electric studio effects famously sounded out the Beatles' increased political engagement. The Velvet Underground undertook gonzo research into drugs, queerness, and urban decay to the tune of electrical signals blasting beyond their circuits. While there is little doubt that Noppadon and his *phin* player Tongsai were tonally influenced by Euro-American psychedelic bands like these, the values of western psychedelia were not their values at all. While psychedelic rock's epistemologies of electrification mostly told a critical story about industrial society and postwar capitalism, Phet Phin Tong and their audience heard electrified *mor lam* with socially conservative pride. Noppadon's comfort with American developmental discourses as well as his steadfast commitment to temperate Buddhist conduct did not contradict his band's electrosonic experiments. In Thailand, a psychedelic sound simply meant something else.

Perhaps we should not be surprised. Multivalence and dynamism are normal in music. Styles combine and recombine, sliding between social and aesthetic spaces, lending a motive here or co-opting a concept there. The articulation of *lam ploen* with psychedelic rock is thus not so remarkable in itself. However, genres at specific moments and in specific contexts may be more primed for certain kinds of recombination than others, for reasons both formal and sociopolitical. For example, *lam ploen* was already steeped in rhythmic and performative ideas from the Black Atlantic, dating in Thailand to the years of groups like the jazz-influenced Suntaraporn band in the 1940s, if not earlier. Psychedelic rock meanwhile borrowed heavily from the blues, and thus psych and *mor lam* shared formal elements even before they met each other in the 1960s. John Garzoli makes a comparable point about articulations of *mor lam* and jazz in the twentieth century. Structural homologies in those two musics afforded creative combination. "Similarities in tuning and melodic style make *khɛɛn* phrases compatible with Western music so jazz elements can be brought into alignment with [*mor lam*] phrase length, melodic contour, and rhythm without contradicting established idiomatic practices."[104] But Garzoli is clear that in their synthesis, *mor lam* and jazz have ultimately failed to resolve certain "ethical contradictions," including in their very different approaches to improvisation. Improvisation in jazz is linked to Black American ideals of individual expression, whereas in Isaan improvising is understood as part of an entertaining live performance. This produces a condition where jazz–*mor lam* groups have found musical sympathies, often combining successfully. But in the resulting mixture the values of certain musical gestures remain ambiguous. This is precisely what happened with *lam ploen* and psychedelic rock amid Noppadon's electrical experiments. The two styles found ready partners in each other but did not necessarily resolve their ideological differences. Instead they produced something new: an ambiguous resonance between sound and space—jazz in a haunted sun-room. Souls mingled in dialectic rather than translation.

This intimate dialectic in many ways defined *lam ploen*, a subgenre of *mor lam* to which Noppadon was a key contributor. This music went largely unheard by *farang* in Thailand, but it was nevertheless an important and highly cosmopolitan musical presence in GI-era nightlife scenes.

Filipino Migrants

Back on New Phetchaburi Road, musicians who could play in a manner legible to *farang* flourished during the GI era. While *lam ploen* groups like Phet Phin Tong played for Thai audiences in Isaan, others gigged in Bangkok's nightlife venues, in areas like the capital's "golden mile," mainly for American soldiers. These bands were international in both repertoire and passport, with Filipino musicians best represented among them. The unique position of Filipino bands in GI-era nightlife offers another relevant story for understanding musical cosmopolitanism in Thailand during the Cold War.

Filipino bands succeeded in R&R circuits in part because they could rapidly learn new English-language songs, often almost as soon as those songs were available on record. There are obvious historical reasons for this. English was a colonial language widely spoken in the Philippines, making western rock lyrics relatively easy for musicians to pick up. Meanwhile cities like Manila and Cebu housed active cosmopolitan music scenes that had been centers of expertise in global popular styles, including music of the Black Atlantic, since the turn of the twentieth century, a history that Mary Talusan has examined.[105] Filipino musicians from those scenes were, in turn, among the first international artists ever to tour Thailand playing modern genres like jazz. Fritz Schenker relates an anecdote about a Filipino journalist who in 1921 asked a prince of Siam "if there were any Filipinos in Siam, to which the prince responded, 'Yes, sir, musicians, sir.'"[106] Unaware of this historical context, *farang* tended to hear Filipino musicians as spectacular but unthinking copycats. "Each one of the bars had a significant rock and roll that would mimic like, one would mimic the Beatles, another one do the Rolling Stones," remembers one former GI.[107] "Mostly they were Filipinos trying to be the Beatles or some other current rock group. They had memorized all their records," recalls another.[108] The colonial discourse of Filipinos as mimics draws on the racist trope that Asia can only hollowly imitate the West, including in art and culture.[109] Despite this Orientalist reception, Filipino artists found ample work in the livelier areas of GI nightlife like New Phetchaburi.

Concert listings during the GI era show Filipino artists with long-term residencies throughout Thailand, especially in Bangkok. Pianist Narcing Aguilar played at Domino; Tony Aguilar at the Garden Café; the Mabuhay Revue at Sani Chateau; the Mighty Pioneers at Monte Carlo; and an unnamed "Phillipine Band [*sic*]" nightly at the Peninsula Restaurant. Saxophonist Narding Aristorenas and trombonist Vic Luna were sidemen in numerous jazz ensembles.

Famous performers like Ollie Delfino and Katy de la Cruz went on brief tours of Bangkok. Maurice Rocco played with Filipino guitarist Mandy Satiago at the Bamboo Bar. Aside from Thais themselves, no other nationality was as well represented as Filipinos in the country's war-era nightlife entertainment scene.

The explanation for this begins at least sixty years earlier, during America's colonial occupation of the Philippines following the Spanish-American War.[110] In 1898 the United States began to assert what has been called "tutelary colonialism," prioritizing cultural assimilation over resource extraction. This approach was allegedly morally superior to the form of colonialism practiced by the Spanish in the years immediately prior. Filipinos were unmoved by the distinction, however, and violently revolted against the US occupation. This began a bloody process of decolonization that would not be legally complete until 1946. Forty-eight years of occupation led to colonial encounters of many kinds, including in music. Scores of Filipino performers gained expertise in styles like Dixieland jazz and ragtime, as well as in European marching band music. Among these was a Filipino multi-instrumentalist jazz phenom named Billy Flores, who anchored Thailand's Suntaraporn band in the 1940s. To some extent this knowledge of jazz and related genres was learned from Black American soldiers fighting in the Spanish-American War, some of whom defected to fight with Philippine guerillas against the United States. A number of these soldiers brought instruments on their military tours, with some performing in military bands. Black American lieutenant colonel Walter Loving notably conducted the Philippine Constabulary Band from 1902 until 1915.[111] Filipinos and African Americans had a ready affinity, given colonialism's outright disdain for what Richard Wright called the "underdogs of the human race"—Black and brown people. Black soldiers saw in the US military's racist violence against colonized Filipinos an echo of their own experience at home.[112] "The ways racist white soldiers lumped Blacks and Filipinos together allowed the two to see themselves as similar," observes Talusan.[113] Simultaneously, ragtime sheet music and recordings from Tin Pan Alley also circulated around the colonized world, including the Philippines.[114] In these ways the Philippines developed a deep relationship with Black Americans and their music as early as the 1910s, at least a decade before Shanghai became a center for jazz, indeed before any other Asian country adopted jazz at scale.

The US Army had once more dragged pop music in its wake. By the 1910s and 1920s, popular music was thriving in Philippine nightlife. Peter Keppy describes the remarkable career of Luis Borromeo, a Filipino entertainer who encountered jazz and vaudeville in Cebu in the first decade of the twentieth century, just as it was first taking hold there. Borromeo temporarily left the

Philippines to study piano in the United States, where he also performed in yellowface as a "Chinese" act on the West Coast from 1916 to 1921.[115] Upon returning to his home country, he effectively invented an entertainment style called *vad-o-vil* (or *badobil*), a riff on vaudeville with an emphasis on crowd-pleasing entertainment. Borromeo initially hoped to tour internationally in that style, but his show proved so popular in the Philippines that he never left. Borromeo's act in the 1920s was part of a cosmopolitan scene that predated comparable scenes in Bangkok by twenty or thirty years. Regionally, the Philippines was years ahead of other countries in its engagement with syncopated musics and skill with modern modes of live performance and sound recording. As a result, and also because so many Filipino musicians had already toured Thailand before the GI era, Filipino musicians were often first in line for nightclub jobs once the windfall of R&R arrived in Thailand.

For Filipino musicians like the multi-instrumentalist Jess Jocson, whom I interviewed in 2019, R&R in Thailand was the best opportunity in the world in the 1960s. A glut of musicians in the Philippines could not find enough gigs to support themselves at home. By contrast, Thailand offered steady work reasonably close by. Jocson was seventeen years old in 1963 when he was invited to join a new four-piece combo called the Mighty Pioneers. Before he had a legal passport, Jocson met the Pioneers in Hong Kong. They played there for about a year, then left for Bangkok in October 1964, just a few months after Maurice Rocco arrived. The bonanza of nightlife work drew musicians from all over the world. Jocson would sing and play lead guitar with the Mighty Pioneers for several years in Thailand, with long-term residencies at night spots like the Monte Carlo Club and a venue called Seeda on Rajdamnoen Road. The band covered Gary Puckett, the Monkees, the Rolling Stones, and other rock and pop groups, in addition to playing some original compositions. They performed for international audiences, especially Chinese, Japanese, Australian, American, and Thai, as Jocson recalls. Most of their shows were played in R&R-oriented venues where female hostesses were available for hire by male servicemen. Jocson thrived in the nightlife world built so rapaciously by Dawee and Tommie's Tourist Agency. He enjoyed years of steady work there, including as a drummer for an Australian rock band. The skills in global popular music honed by Filipinos over the first half of the twentieth century were suddenly very marketable. The windfall would last until the late 1960s, at which point the Pioneers left for Singapore.

Filipino musicians were talented, and they were also comparatively cheap to hire given the saturated labor market and low wages in their own country. This led to a system of racialized extraction. Jocson explained to me that "the way they look at Filipinos, Americans, the agents, the bookers, the cruise lines, they think we Filipinos will be the yes men for whatever they say. Because the Philippines are not that big, and salaries are not that good. Sometimes you don't even have a place to perform because there are too many musicians, competing with each other. What will you do if you're the owner? You'll get the cheapest one. That's what happened."[116] Just as vast income gaps created an economy of intimate companionship between *farang* and *mia chao*, Thailand became an attractive destination for Filipino bands seeking an audience with those same soldiers. In both cases, laborers were squeezed so that nightlife could be made more affordable for American soldier-tourists. Yet for Filipinos, playing abroad was still considered a lucky gig.

Jocson's elegy for his own exploitation speaks to a labor situation that continues. Filipino musicians are hired in the twenty-first century as underpaid global itinerants, a role that has drawn them into migration for more than 120 years. This role is a colonial effect. It began with a colonial intimacy that conferred skills in popular music, which were then captured and devalued by regimes of uneven global development in neocolonial times. These skills routed musicians into new diasporas, of which Thailand in the GI era was just one temporary node. The routes persist. In 2005 the owner of JS Contractors, a recruitment agency that manages international gigs for about forty Filipino bands, estimated in the *New York Times* that 120,000 Filipino musicians were working overseas or on cruise ships. Most often these artists are asked to play covers of western songs, just as they were in Thailand during the American war in Vietnam. "Why Filipinos are scattered?" mused Jocson. "Competition. We better go abroad." The COVID-19 pandemic of the early 2020s worsened the vulnerability that Filipino musicians have experienced in the global economy for over a century, threatening their industry (and thus their livelihood) as well as their health. The GI era in Thailand was a brief, fortunate moment in an ongoing history of colonial labor and extraction.

Musical Waste

Yet another layer of cosmopolitan musical engagement in the GI era involved Thai bands playing to *farang* audiences at US military bases. By contrast with Phet Phin Tong, the Thai bands that played these bases did not usually perform *mor lam* or other styles that originated in Southeast Asia. Rather, they specialized in overtly blues-based music like hard rock and "shadow music," an entire subgenre indebted to (and named after) British act Cliff Richard and the Shadows. Most of these bands used standard rock setups, including electric guitar, bass, and drum kits, with no regional instruments in the mix. In the late 1960s and early 1970s, these groups were largely unknown to Thai audiences, in part because their live shows were staged next to or even inside of American military installations. Sudina notes that guitarist Shor Onn Na Bangchang, for example, "regarded by some as the 'Thai Jimi Hendrix' . . . mastered his skills playing for the GI's near Utapao base," adding that "his American customers brought him records of songs they wanted him to try, showed him new techniques, and became his friends." Soldiers were Shor Onn's patrons. Meanwhile the guitarist Lam Morrison, "whose last name was given to him by American GIs impressed by his talent and appearance that reminded them of Jim Morrison of The Doors, was part of the 'V.I.P' band, famous around the bases in the northeast."[117] Shor Onn and Lam were part of a wave of Thai bands who toured the country along R&R circuits. Stylistically, they hewed close to what American and British rock bands of the time played, because that was what their patrons wanted. The V.I.P. Band performed and recorded covers of virtuosic, blues-based guitar songs like Mountain's "Roll Over Beethoven," Deep Purple's "Hard Road (Wring That Neck)," and later Yngwie Malmsteen's "Far beyond the Sun."

The V.I.P. Band at first bypassed Thai audiences entirely. They often sang in English, with no stylistic connections to *mor lam* or *luk thung*. Lam Morrison modeled his persona and appearance after early 1970s guitar icons like Duane Allman. His band's sound was much closer to blues rock or boogie rock than it was to the progressive experimentalism of Led Zeppelin or the sinister protometal of early Black Sabbath. The V.I.P. Band's audience was so narrowly confined to American soldiers that it made more sense for the group to play in remote cities with military bases, such as Korat or Ubon, than it would have to play in the far more populous city of Bangkok. As a result, and although their success depended almost entirely on the American military presence, these bands did not perform in spaces that were especially diverse. Instead, the V.I.P. Band made their name in military enclaves, playing almost entirely for *farang*.

Amnat Silaket and his friend Mii were about ten years old when the V.I.P. Band rose to prominence in the late 1960s. In those years, Amnat was an aspiring guitarist and Mii a drummer. Both lived in Ubon near the local US air base. The two friends idolized Lam Morrison, whom they now identify as the unrivaled "originator" (เป็นต้นกำเนิด) of Thai guitar rock. Amnat later made his career as a musician and producer, with expertise in the musical idioms he learned during the GI era. He now runs Pro Music Studios, a digital recording studio with active bookings by local bands in Ubon, where I met him in 2019. The studio walls are adorned with images and album covers from Albert Hammond, Elvis Presley, Thai shadow music band the Impossibles, Eric Clapton, Humble Pie,

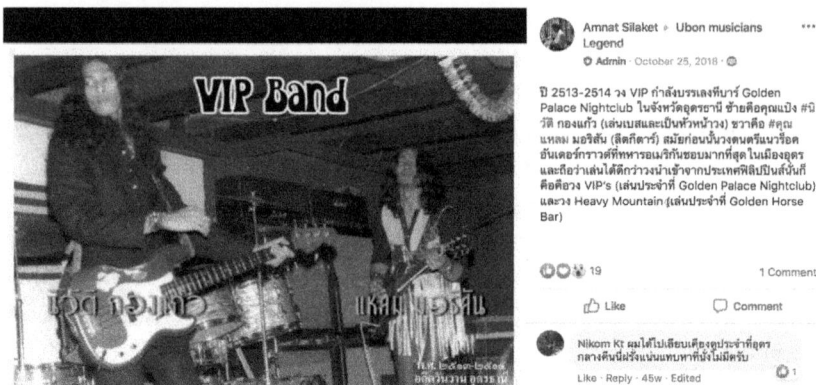

Amnat Silaket ▸ Ubon musicians
Legend
Admin · October 25, 2018 · 🌐

ปี 2513-2514 วง VIP กำลังบรรเลงที่บาร์ Golden
Palace Nightclub ในจังหวัดอุดรธานี ซ้ายคือคุณแป้ง #นิ
วัติ กองแก้ว (เล่นเบสและเป็นหัวหน้าวง) ขวาคือ #คุณ
แหลม มอริสัน (ลีดกีตาร์) สมัยก่อนนั้นวงดนตรีแนวร็อค
อันเดอร์กราวด์ที่ทหารอเมริกันชมชอบมากที่สุด ในเมืองอุดร
และถือว่าเล่นได้ดีกว่าวงนำเข้าจากประเทศฟิลิปปินส์นั้นก็
คือตีวง VIP's (เล่นประจำที่ Golden Palace Nightclub)
และวง Heavy Mountain (เล่นประจำที่ Golden Horse
Bar)

👍😍❤ 19   1 Comment

   👍 Like   💬 Comment

Nikom Kt ผมได้ไปเดียวเที่ยงดูประจำที่อุดร
กลางคืนนี่ผ่งรินนั่นแทบทุกที่นั่งไม่มีครับ
Like · Reply · 46w · Edited

FIGURE 4.6. Amnat Silaket captions this Facebook post: "In the year 1970–71, the V.I.P. Band played at the Golden Palace Nightclub in the province of Udon Thani. On the left is 'Bang' Niwit Gongaew (bass guitar and bandleader). On the right is Lam Morrison (lead guitar). In the past, underground rock bands that American soldiers liked the most in Udon, and who were considered the best, came from the Philippines. These images are of the V.I.P. Band (who played at the Golden Palace Nightclub) and Heavy Mountain (who played at the Golden Horse Bar)." Image courtesy of Amnat Silaket and the Ubon Musicians Legend Facebook page.

and a young King Bhumibol and Queen Sirikit. It is a uniquely Isaan gallery of musical reverence.

Just as significantly, Amnat moderates a Facebook group called Ubon Musicians Legend (UML). As of the early 2020s, this page hosts an active community, with both Thai and *farang* regulars—mostly men—posting news, videos, updates, and birthday wishes pertinent to music in Ubon or to the Ubon musical imaginary. The specific genealogies of blues-based hard rock that were introduced to the region by the R&R circuit figure centrally in this imaginary now. UML is a significant archive of Isaan musical history. Many of the older group members post personal photographs, annotating them with details and memories of specific shows or people.

The UML Facebook page also serves as an informal archive of the GI era in Ubon, hosting thousands of photographs and film clips.[b] The level of detail is remarkable. Minor bands that never recorded in a studio are featured alongside international acts. Members of UML tag onstage images with the names of each individual musician in a group. Wide street shots show the relative location

---

b ACKNOWLEDGMENT: SUNY Stony Brook PhD student Christine Pash assisted in sorting and tagging a large trove of these images.

FIGURE 4.7. Amnat's caption reads: "Women looking for *farang* visitors. The price of a Coke was 10 baht per bottle." Image courtesy of Amnat Silaket and the Ubon Musicians Legend Facebook page.

of different bars along central entertainment strips. The result is a substantial body of human and geographic knowledge. The archive also includes many nonmusical images of nightlife that reveal the mundane practices (as well as the tedium) of intimate labor. In a rare fashion, one sees the articulation of music and intimate labor in common nightlife spaces. UML is thus an important source of sociocultural detail about the GI era in Ubon and other northeastern provinces.

This digital archive testifies to the extraordinary effects of the GI era on the Thai provinces where US military bases were built. These effects were in many ways more pronounced in rural areas than in Bangkok. Although Bangkok was also changing rapidly, the capital had a history of cosmopolitanism, as well as an existing concentration of wealth. Places like Ubon and Korat, on the other hand, had been modernized from whole cloth. Subsistence rice farming gave way to massive and modern new industries, nearly all in service to the US military population. Local demand for entertainment emanated from American soldiers alone. This is how Lam Morrison and the V.I.P. Band came to learn blues rock and how the band found success touring in provincial areas. They played what American soldiers wanted to hear. This is likely also why Thai hard rock fandom in the twenty-first century remains concentrated in Northeast Thailand.

Yodh, Peter, and I visited Amnat and Mii at their studio in 2019. The two musicians described the economic and social shape of musical culture in the war era. They recalled that soldiers would ask musicians to learn the repertoire

FIGURE 4.8. A *farang* soldier listens, or does not. Image courtesy of Amnat Silaket and the Ubon Musicians Legend Facebook page.

from their favorite albums and then reproduce those songs onstage. Thai audiences at the time were not yet broadly familiar with hard rock, but certain Thai artists prospered by mediating this fantasy for soldiers. GIs thus steered local musical trends by paying for them. Lam Morrison learned the guitar parts to every Doors song, for example, and then performed them with requisite panache for *farang* crowds. His training and even his persona were governed by the tastes and desires of American soldiers.

Lam and his cohort were at the same time initiated into an American order of racial segregation. According to Amnat and Mii, the majority of soldiers dictating repertoire through record gifts were white. These soldiers became the V.I.P. Band's primary audience and, in effect, their patrons as well. "Famous bands didn't play in the Black bars," noted Mii. Music was racially coded and spatially sorted. For example, bands who played guitar solos were mostly found at white venues, while bands that specialized in what Mii called "funk rhythms" played at Black venues. These reductive codings assigned specific musical qualities—often quite arbitrarily—to racialized spaces. Just as in the historically segregated US music industry, there were more opportunities for bands whose music appealed to white crowds. Amnat and Mii remember that in Ubon, racial segregation was strict. Black soldiers often could not go into white bars at all, mirroring the racial segregation of American-oriented bars in Vietnam at the same time.[118] Between the neocolonial inroads of musical style, the growth of intimate labor, rapid commercial development, and the reproduction of American racial segregation, American consumer desires dictated nightlife in Isaan, creating a troubling simulacrum of home.

At the time of our visit to Amnat and Mii, I was interested in a term that I had heard northeasterners use often to describe the GI era—*thíng wáy*, meaning "to discard." The term carries a sense of negligent permanence, like a Styrofoam cup casually tossed away, only to clog an ecosystem for centuries. *Thíng wáy* is invoked frequently in conversations about the repercussions of war. Singing as a *mia chao*, Mani Maniwan asks her *farang* husband John, "Why you *thíng* me?" A recent thread on a popular Thai-language message board is titled "สมัยสงครามเวียดนาม อเมริกันมาตั้งฐาน+สร้างสนามบิน อะไรทิ้งไว้ที่อีสาน บ้างครับ" (In the Vietnam War era, Americans built bases and airports; what did they leave behind [*thíng wáy*] in Isaan?).[119] The thread accrued more than seven hundred posts. Some people answered the question earnestly; others were sardonic. To cite both serious and wry examples, posters responded that Americans had *thíng wáy* half-Thai children, bombs, prosperity, satellites, machinery, disorder, estrangement from Isaan, and so on. Clearly the term resonates. I asked Amnat what he himself felt the GIs had *thíng wáy* in Ubon. He responded immediately, as if he had considered the question before: "Civilization." Amnat clarified that the waste of "civilization" was inherently neither good nor bad. It was rather an unassimilable material that future generations in Isaan had been left to manage.[120]

"Discarded civilization" is a powerful articulation of the ways that Isaan experienced the GI era and its aftermath. Here Lam Morrison's career after the war is instructive. Once the American military had completed its withdrawal from Thailand in July 1976, Lam and the V.I.P. Band no longer had a ready audience in the provinces, so they relocated to Bangkok and the newly developed nearby resort area of Pattaya. By that time, Lam's talent had become more apparent to Thais, and hard rock was reasonably well known in the country. Within a few years Lam was an enduring national icon. However, he and the V.I.P. Band have remained persistently absent from subsequent western repackagings of Thai music. Of the many reissue compilations of vintage Thai music released by labels like Sublime Frequencies, Finders Keepers, Light in the Attic, and ZuDrangMa, none have included even a single song by Lam or the V.I.P. Band. The Thai band that was indisputably the most in demand among GIs, and that is now remembered by Ubon residents like Amnat and Mii as the most impressive and important figure in early Thai hard rock, has been cast aside as the West rewrites the history of Thai music at festivals and through reissue albums. The Thai hard rock scene was used by US soldiers in the 1970s, and then it was discarded, *thíng wáy*.

There are a few possible reasons for this. First, the heavily curated world music market does not value electric blues-rock, which today is heard by elite Euro-American listeners as middlebrow and formulaic.[121] The V.I.P. Band's work is therefore out of fashion compared with more soul- or funk-oriented groups like Phet Phin Tong. But second and just as important, it is possible that the V.I.P Band learned hard rock a bit *too well*. Their covers were often faithful to the point of emulation. In the marketplace of world music 2.0, covers have little value, because western listeners suspect them of offering imitation without originality. This deprecatory attitude toward covers is simply not shared by many Southeast Asian musical communities.[122] Indeed, Mii's insistence that Lam Morrison was an "originator" distinguishes him from western listeners who are more likely to hear Lam's covers as merely imitative. The lone exception to this occurs when a cover strongly implies cultural difference. For example, Thai band the Cat's cover of "Hit the Road Jack" has been reissued on several recent compilations by western labels. The Cat's lead singer has a strong accent, which seems to affirm her exotic remove from the milieu of American soul music. Similarly, Sroeng Santi's "Mai rak yar rak" interpolates Tony Iommi's iconic guitar riff from the Black Sabbath song "Supernaut." Sroeng's piece is in many ways reminiscent of *mor lam*, with Thai-language lyrics, a Thai drum, and a looping form rather than a verse-chorus structure. "Mai rak yar rak" thus also suggests exotic distance and difference, with just a dash of the familiar provided by the lead guitar part. That is an ideal formula for the marketplace of world music 2.0, and it makes Sroeng's song an excellent candidate for reissue.

By contrast, Lam Morrison could shred at the level of a guitarist like Deep Purple's Ritchie Blackmore. Because of his virtuosity, Lam's playing suggests no cultural distance at all. Such advanced skill risks serving as a reminder of historical intimacy between the West and Thailand, which the contemporary world music industry strongly prefers to ignore or minimize. Lam's work was valued and utilized during the GI era, but western listeners have since turned away from him. Thai hard rock musicians, like other intimate laborers from Isaan whose work in the service of neocolonial nightlife may take centuries to biodegrade, have been *thíng wáy*.

Rocco's Urbane Company

Where, amid all this, was Maurice Rocco? The examples of musical cosmopolitanism discussed so far—electric *lam ploen*, Filipino bar bands in Bangkok, and Thai hard rockers at military bases—were all set in contexts of low-level wage labor. Compared to them, Rocco played in an elevated tier. For most of his time in Thailand he faced little precarity and earned plenty of money. He lived and performed in physical proximity to bands like the Mighty Pioneers and to venues on New Phetchaburi Road, at times as close as one kilometer away. But as a *farang dam* whose music was coded as sophisticated, he was an artist of higher status.

Rocco's friends remember that he was professionally and personally satisfied. "Bangkok had everything he desired, and he seemed awfully comfortable," said Harry Rolnick, a longtime nightlife reporter for the *Bangkok Post* and a friend of Rocco's.[123] Rafael Ortiz was a soldier stationed in Bangkok when he came to know the pianist: "We would sometimes go out with a group that included various musicians and bar owners, but Maurice would always be the center of attention," Ortiz remembers. "His tip jar was always full. The customers loved him and were generous with tips. He lived in an apartment and was always well dressed, so he was more than just getting by."[124] Added Charles Teckman, a Miami University professor and administrator who spent time with Rocco in Bangkok in 1972: "He was not a man of poverty. When I saw him he was working first-class nightclubs."[125]

Rolnick lived in Bangkok from 1965 until 1976, working at the *Post* almost the entire time. He was among the urbane company Rocco kept. In a series of interviews, Rolnick told me stories about hosting visitors including Philip Roth, Tennessee Williams, Jayne Mansfield, and Rosemary Clooney and escorting them through Bangkok nightlife. Rolnick had been a musician and composer of off-Broadway shows before joining the Merchant Marines and eventually landing in Thailand for reasons not dissimilar from those that motivated Rocco or Jess Jocson: because he could find work there. His literati friends typified the crowd that gathered at the Bamboo Bar and other venues where Rocco played. After a show, Rolnick might take his visitors to New Phetchaburi Road as a curiosity, leaving them to seedier things in the hours after the Bamboo Bar closed, as they wished. Their options were abundant. But the respectable part of an evening for international travelers often involved catching a Maurice Rocco set.

Both Rolnick and Ortiz remember details from his shows. "He knew anything ever written by everybody, all the way back to ragtime," said Rolnick. "He knew the words perfectly. He was known as the standup pianist because he never sat down. His technique was not that of an Art Tatum but the technique of someone who played unbelievably perfect pop music. He didn't roll things around like a jazz pianist, but he never made a mistake in harmony at all." Ortiz remembers that he "went to the club one night and Maurice Rocco was playing. He was playing an upright piano disguised as a baby grand, where the customers could sit down and be right in front of the musicians. I expected a crazy boogie player a la Jerry Lee Lewis, but to my surprise Maurice was playing standards and singing. (The jazz and boogie would come later)."

Both men noted his fame as well as his appeal to elite audiences. Rolnick marveled that "when Duke Ellington came to Bangkok about four months before he died, I was interviewing him and he said, 'By the way, do you know Maurice Rocco?' I said yes. He said, 'What's he doing in Bangkok?' I said, 'He's playing the piano, like he does everywhere else.' He says, 'Where can I see him?' I said, 'You can go to this place tonight where he's playing.' I mean that's how well known he was." Ortiz recalled seeing him once "in a classical music hall where they were giving lectures on jazz. The main attraction was trumpeter Dizzy Gillespie. Maurice opened for him." According to Ortiz, at bars and clubs where Rocco played, "the crowd was composed mainly of expats from the US and Australia, mainly white, and mainly late thirties and early forties. At that time I was the only military regular that would visit this club. . . . This was still Beatles time, so most of the GIs would seek clubs playing rock. However there was (to my surprise) a substantial niche group who preferred a cooler atmosphere." In Thailand Rocco entertained high-end crowds. Teckman asked Rocco when he would come back to the United States, and Rocco told him "when my music comes back in style there," effectively meaning never.[126]

These rose-colored remembrances reveal the stratification of Bangkok's war-era nightlife. Given his stylistic specialties in boogie-woogie and swing, which were not at all out of fashion in Thailand, Rocco had the privilege of playing for officers, diplomats, and other elites. By contrast, Filipino bands played workaday venues in areas like New Phetchaburi Road for carousing soldiers, Lam Morrison played inside military bases, and Phet Phin Tong played in rural movie theaters, at local festivals, and in unpaved outdoor lots. Rocco's experience of Cold War Bangkok nightlife was closer to that of Germaine Krull's globe-trotting entrepreneurs than it was to the average Thai person or even the average American. This difference was a manifestation of new social layers that situated and hierarchized human beings in a cosmopolitan moment. Nightlife was mapped according to a Cold War Orientalist imaginary that reorganized status and human worth. Each layer involved cosmopolitan engagement, while also suggesting the emergence of new social systems in which *farang* privilege was a powerful force.

Within these systems, Rocco could both prosper and hide. Just as he found support in Thailand's local matrix of musical meaning and human valuation, nondocumentation also liberated him. But none of this would last. As the GI era wore on, the status of Black and queer people in Thailand shifted significantly. The next chapter examines Blackness and queerness over the long arc of the GI era, bringing the story of Thai-American intimate nightlife encounters to its stormy conclusion.

5

RICE OUTSIDE

THE FIELD

Wherever there are Americans, there are thieves. —RONG WONGSAWAN, สัตหีบ: ยังไม่มี ลาก่อน (Sattahip: There's no goodbye yet) (2009)

The GI era transformed and broadened the scope of Thai identity. These changes were rarely addressed in state rhetoric, which preferred to project a unified national subject. But in literary and musical representations of everyday life in Thailand, transformed subjects were everywhere. Janit Feangfu, for example, finds in Thai fiction of the 1970s an "evolving, alive, dynamic, and pluralistic" landscape of self-definition that was far more complex and unsettled than the largely homogeneous notion of "Thainess" advanced by the government.[1] Young, middle-class Thais traveled abroad and came of age as cosmopolitans, while poor women sought economic mobility in the fluctuations of development. These and other Thais felt the globalizing effects of cheap air travel, Cold

War–era geographic mobility, and mass communication. Amid the changes, many people discovered new subjectivities.

Luk thung singer Phloen Phromden's mid-1960s single "ตะลุยบางกอก" (Heading into Bangkok) narrates a train trip from the provinces to the capital to meet women in spaces of nightlife. When he arrives, Phloen finds beautiful people—professionally ambitious, fashionable, light-skinned—whom he cannot easily situate within familiar categories of Thai identity. In the song's lyrics, people dress in strange new ways, and dance to ultramodern "shadow music." One woman "doesn't chew betel nut but smokes a mysterious herb," a succinct pharmacology of the rural/urban divide. The women even dance and mingle with *farang*. Phloen is surprised and curious. His final lyrical foray is into a nightclub, where the money "never stops stacking." The song is both a cautionary tale about the excesses of modernity and a report, in the singer's *lam ploen*–adjacent style, about the variety of Thai subjects who have emerged in a milieu of global capital. Whether syncretic, antagonistic, or libidinal, these new subjectivities all developed in reference to the American presence.

Two particular categories of identity—Blackness and sex/gender alterity—were much discussed and negotiated during the GI era. These were among the many new categories that became legible in Thailand during the war. Thais spent more than a decade debating and refining how such new identities could be reconciled with older ones. This final chapter of *Bangkok after Dark* will consider how Blackness and sex/gender alterity were codified and experienced in the intimate neocolonial contact zone of nightlife. Maurice Rocco, being Black and queer, had an experience abroad that was substantially shaped by emerging identity conceptions in Thailand. These also shaped the discourse around his murder, the event that concludes this chapter and brings the main thread of the book's story to an end.

The Wages of Lightness

The most important fictional work about Blackness in Thailand during the GI era was a 1973 novel called *Khâaw nɔ̀ɔk naa* (Rice outside the field).[2] The novel is a continuing source of fascination in Thailand. It has been adapted into many films and television series over the past five decades. The plot involves the diverging stories of two sisters—Deuan, who is half-Thai, half-white, and Dam, who is half-Thai, half-Black. In the Thai racial imaginary, whiteness is not unmarked. Thus each sister's particular hybridity is a visible component of her identity. Both girls are born to the same *mia chao* (rented wife) Thai mother, but they have different and differently colored *farang* fathers. Deuan's life is therefore

charmed, while Dam's is ill-fated. In some sense, the novel is rather straightfor-
wardly about the abject position of dark-skinned people in Thailand.

A closer look at the story's details, however, reveals a distinction between dark
skin and Blackness, as well as how different global ideologies regarding skin color
had to be reconciled in transnational contexts during the war era. Dark-skinned
people in Thailand have long been subject to colorism. But Thai colorism has a
different basis and character from the "deep structure" of western white supremacy.[3] Jan Weisman argues that the conceptions of status and color most strongly
at play in "Rice outside the field" must be understood beyond a western racial
frame. Specifically, the characters in the novel regard dark skin as a karmic
punishment—a "phenotypical expression of accumulated religious merit."[4]
These characters put forward the notion of accumulated merit from past lives
to explain why certain people are privileged and others are not. Guided by selective readings of Buddhist scriptures, many Thais indeed understood dark skin
to be a consequence of karmic deficits.[5] This prejudice, still frequently held,
is most often brought to bear on the comparatively dark people of Isaan. The
poverty of Isaan farmers is routinely explained by skin color. The term *nâa laaw*
(Lao face), for example, is an anti-northeastern insult used to justify exclusion
from political power.[6] In the vicious circle of Thai colorism, it is repulsive to
let one's skin darken out in the rice fields, just as it is also surely deserved. This
is plainly ideological, a bulwark erected by middle-class central Thais against
their own loss of status. Especially in the 1960s–'70s, concerned with a rising
petite bourgeoisie, the urban middle class doubled down on antiprovincial colorism. As a result the subordination of dark-skinned Thais has been continually
held as a matter of fate rather than politics. The sins of past lives can never be
absolved by civil rights.

Black Americans entered this scene of colorism obliquely in the 1960s.
Blackness in the United States was very different from the Thai conceptions of darkness described above. Indeed most Thai people had little or no
understanding of either cultural Blackness or anti-Black racism, and little or
no experience with Black Americans. Nevertheless, the concept of Blackness
superficially resembled the existing liminal category of dark-skinned rural-
ity, which Thais understood very well. The novel "Rice outside the field" can
thus be read as an account of how Blackness acquired symbolic meaning in
Thailand not under the aegis of scientific racism or legacies of enslavement,
as in the United States and Europe, but in resonant combination with existing prejudices against dark-skinned Thais. The result was a dialectic between a
quasi-Buddhist colorism and the anti-Blackness of America. The two systems
of racial coding found many points of agreement, even as neither could be fully

reduced to the other. Thus the figure of the *farang* was divided into at least two subcategories, which were hierarchized according to color: "Part-White Amerasians carry the potential of being viewed as especially moral individuals—or at least as having conducted their lives particularly virtuously in past incarnations," suggests Weisman, "while part-Black Amerasians may be viewed as products of immorality."[7] This hierarchy was naturalized by logics of colorism that found support (however flimsy) in religious texts. A conversation between two characters in "Rice outside the field" dramatizes how these ideas sounded in ordinary conversation:

> "Why aren't all people born equal?" Pranorm gave one of those facile replies, which express the general feelings and beliefs of the average Thai Buddhist: "We didn't make merit equally and so we can't all be born equal, of course. Those who made a lot of merit in former lives become the children of millionaires, or Miss Thailand or at the very least beautiful people. We didn't make much merit and so we are born at this level.... So you be diligent and make a lot of merit, Dam, and in your next life you'll be born all white and beautiful."[8]

The US military was meanwhile a structurally racist institution, a microcosm of its government and country. "One could leave the United States, but one couldn't leave its racial heritage behind," notes historian Gerald F. Goodwin about the war in Vietnam.[9] Black veteran Horace Coleman is quoted in Doug Bradley and Craig Werner's *We Gotta Get Out of This Place*: "The longer I was home, the more I saw and thought the way the United States is run really wasn't that different from how the war was run."[10] Black troops were underrepresented in the officer corps by a factor of five yet overrepresented among casualties. According to one soldier quoted by Goodwin, "'There were two promotion lists on base, one for blacks and one for whites,' and those on the white list were always given preference."[11] Wallace Terry's oral history *Bloods*, as well as his 1972 interview-album *Guess Who's Coming Home: Black Fighting Men Recorded Live in Vietnam*, offer firsthand accounts of Black soldiers serving in Vietnam. Their narratives tend to foreground structural racism. "The racial incidents didn't happen in the field. Just when we went to the back," said Richard J. Ford III of the Twenty-Fifth Infantry Division, referring to the offices and bureaucratic spaces where the war was managed.[12] "We felt we were being taken advantage of, 'cause it seemed like more blacks in the field than in the rear." Ford is correct: Black soldiers comprised about 10 percent of the overall military force but 20 percent of its active combat troops. Black soldiers recognized that racism emanated less from personal prejudice among soldiers than from the military as an institution. In other words, foxholes could make interracial allies of individuals, but the US military still reflected the racial hierarchies of its homeland.

Nightlife was one space where Thai antidark colorism and the anti-Black racism introduced by American neocolonialism happened to resonate. Thai nightlife venues oriented toward *farang* reproduced the de facto segregation and inequity that were ingrained habits of American entities during the war. In *Bloods*, Harold Bryant of the First Cavalry Division describes spending time in racially designated "soul bars" while on shore leave in Vietnam.[13] Staff Sergeant Don F. Browne recalls an area of Tan Son Nhut called Soul Alley where Cambodian women sought to pass as Black and where there was at least one restaurant run by a Black air force soldier that served soul food.[14] The *New York Times* reported in 1972 that in Nakhon Phanom Province in Isaan, "those establishments that wish to do business with blacks say so, with signs describing the places as 'soul' establishments."[15] These venues were welcomed by many Black soldiers as affinity spaces. But Amnat Silaket and his friend Mii remember that bars catering to soldiers in Isaan were in fact strictly segregated, and that "Black people could not visit white bars."[16] There were a handful of soul bars on Bangkok's New Phetchaburi Road, including Jack's American Star Bar, Whiskey Jazz, Le Fee, and Soul Sister, but these were located at the far end of the GI strip, at a remove from its main district. Jack's, for instance, sat at the corner of New Phetchaburi Road and Soi Ekkamai, roughly a mile from the central nightlife area in what was then a mostly undeveloped section of the city.

In Jack's and other Black bars, Thai hostesses wore their hair in imitation of Afros. Journalist Ron Chepesiuk quotes Black former Drug Enforcement Administration agent Pete Davis, who was based in Bangkok in the early 1970s: "The bars were strictly segregated by music. You would have country music in one bar and soul music in another. If you were Black and wanted to go into a country music bar, even the girls would give you attitude. They would look at you as if to say—what are you doing here?"[17] When non-*farang* bands played in GI areas, they learned to perform in racially coded styles suited to the venue. For example, Jess Jocson recalls how his all-Filipino band learned American country songs as well as a specific repertoire of vintage Black rock and roll, which white noncommissioned officers enjoyed. To some degree, racialized styles could mix, as Amnat Silaket noted, but people mostly could not. Amnat reflected on how guitar solos and certain rhythms were among the musical signifiers of race that customers expected to hear in the respective environments of white and Black clubs. Music helped to divide nightlife racially, and those divisions in turn reiterated familiar hierarchies. The position of Black soldiers in both war and wartime leisure in Southeast Asia thus came to echo the segregation of the United States. Thai people were incentivized to work in nightlife by money that never stopped stacking, and in the process they were also compelled to learn the symbols and practices of American racial capitalism. This was true despite a lack of local knowledge about racial violence or American anti-Black ideology. Racism was, rather, a neocolonial technology integral to new frontiers of capitalism that primarily served white American customers. "The music of people of color was seen as lower class in Thailand," writes Kamontam Kuabutr, "while the music of white people was classic, and considered high-class."[18] Racial difference governed nightlife work in Thailand, and intimate laborers had to know how it was ordered, including in music.

A number of scholars have argued that in Thailand, class is a more fundamental concern than race or gender. This is certainly worth bearing in mind when considering identity dynamics such as the status of Thai Chinese people or the disruptions brought about by women's economic mobility, both of which have been convincingly described through frameworks of class.[19] But the GI era complicated any neat division between class and race. Under the crushing weight of American patronage, Thailand was pressured to reproduce US-style racial hierarchy in many parts of its own public life.[20] By the mid-1960s it was no longer clear whether anti-Blackness in Thailand was an analogy for class-based, Buddhistic colorism or an obliging extension of white supremacy.

Meanwhile, light skin was increasingly associated with modernity, a link that encouraged the veneration of white *farang*. Soon enough lightness was not only a symbol of local class standing but also a totem of Thailand's global aspirations. Weisman suggests that in the GI era, whiteness became a visual surrogate for ideals of national development, while Blackness (not simply dark skin) was increasingly "taken to represent the degraded conditions away from which Thai development should tend."[21] By the end of the war, Thai anti-Blackness was neither a strictly local phenomenon nor an importation. Rather, this particular mode of racial bias was a resonance, yet another colonial effect. By the time the next famous novel about Blackness in Thailand was published in 1981—Botan's ผู้หญิงคนนั้นชื่อบุญรอด (That woman is called Bunrot)—the figure of the *farang* was clearly divided between white and nonwhite. "Many people who saw [the dark-skinned Bunrot] noted that she was foreign, but not a *farang*," wrote Botan.[22] During the course of the war, the figure of the *farang* became racially binarized.

There is a further wrinkle in the story of Dam, the half-Black sister in "Rice outside the field," and indeed one quite relevant to Maurice Rocco: Dam has

FIGURE 5.1. Advertisement for Jack's American Star Bar, January 1965. Image courtesy of Norman Smith.

musical talent. Some adults discover that, as a child, the dark-skinned girl is a gifted singer. This immediately and dramatically recasts her identity. During moments in her life when Dam is regarded as a hybridized Black Thai person, she is not only abject but considered a direct threat to the integrity of the nation. To be Black *and* Thai was an alarming impurity. But after her agent decides to help her pass as African American, she flourishes. This marketing move raises her status by removing her from the field of local identity entirely. Suddenly, "Dam's success as a singer is due to her genetic 'other'-ness. Her talent is carried, as it were, in her Black American 'blood,' and her career blooms only after her employer passes her off as a Black American."[23]

This narrative reveals a gap between dark-skinned or half-Black Thais and Black Americans in the emergent system of Thai racial coding. While Black Thais in particular were seen as a risk, Black Americans were generally external to Thai social concerns. Thus when Dam is staged through her musicality as *essentially* Black American, "Americans—not Thais or Thai society—are responsible for what happens to her."[24] Gender plays a role here, too. Dark women were supposed to be poor, and according to Weisman the ascendant working class of the GI era threatened a patriarchal order in which women could be kept by rich Thai men as minor wives or else be solicited for commercial sex by poorer Thai men. As long as Dam was seen as merely dark skinned, Thais of conservative sensibility insisted that she be socially immobile. But once she was viewed as essentially American, she could no longer threaten the local patriarchy, and she was free to become socially and economically mobile. This is because America was understood as a world apart, with its own distinct politics. Racial hybridity disrupted ethnonationalist ideals of Thainess. But certain identities stood outside that field, and these external identities were not a threat. They might even be admired. Notably, Dam was granted this exemption because she could sing like an American, recasting the meaning of her skin color. Musicality made her Black.

This speaks to a critical nuance in Maurice Rocco's life. Rocco in Thailand occupied precisely the exalted, exceptional social position that Dam's character took on when people learned that she could sing. As a Black American, Rocco was happily exempted from the Thai social field. But as a Black *musician*, he stood further outside of it still. Ironically, this was enabled by the racist notion of essentialism, the idea that as a Black American, his musical ability must have been inherent. But Rocco's supposedly natural musicality, which implied "genetic other-ness," granted him release from the kind of opprobrium that a half-Black, half-Thai person was liable to receive. He could be read as a living ideal rather than a hybrid. The additional fact that he was a very good musician, whose skill in an older vintage of jazz symbolized prestige among cosmopolitan moderns, excused him from the de facto segregation of the New Phetchaburi bar scene. All of this was true even before considering the implications of his sexuality. In large part because of his intersectional position as a Black American musician, Rocco was spared certain everyday judgments and risks. He had the privilege of prestige and relative safety. But the roots of this privilege were different from the *farang* privilege held by white-identified soldiers and tourists. He

FIGURE 5.2. The cover of *luk thung* singer Pong Prida's single "Pua negro" (Black husband), recorded in the 1970s, depicts a Thai woman with a well-off Black American partner. Pong lived in Udon, a city with an American air force base and a significant military presence during the war. His morality tale scolds the woman for her materialism in partnering with a wealthy *farang*. Pong wrote several songs with similar themes bemoaning Black-Thai relationships, and his attitude exemplifies a conservative attitude toward mixed relationships that always reserved its harshest judgments for women. Image courtesy of Peter Doolan.

was a social exception. And yet still he remained vulnerable in consequential ways. He was, for both better and worse, an outsider in Thailand.

These ethnoracial conditions remain intact. Non-Black Thai actors playing Black characters still wear blackface, including the Thai actress who played Dam in the most recent TV serialization of "Rice outside the field" in 2013. Household products routinely use cartoon images of Black Americans in their branding. Caricature is broadly acceptable, and darkness remains unfashionable. Skin-whitening products are popular, as they are in many parts of Asia. Advertisements use lightness as a symbol of beauty. These effects simultaneously reveal an association of light skin with Euro-American modernity and "a common perception . . . that those who have lighter skin come from higher social strata, while those with darker complexions hail from the country's poorer, rural regions."[25] The self-serving language of past-life meritocracy as it applies to skin color is still invoked whenever complexions are implicitly or explicitly ranked. In other words, race and class cannot be fully separated.

Younger Black or dark non-Thai people living in Thailand have lately reflected publicly on their experience of skin-tone politics in the country. Thai Malian TikTok star Natthawadee "Suzie" Waikalo has discussed her experience of racial discrimination in multiple videos and public talks. She has described being fired from a job because of her black skin, as well as everyday aggressions such as people moving away from her on the bus. For the most part the colorism of these aggressions is undisguised. Thai beauty pageant winner Patcharaporn Chantarapadit, who has dark skin, was subjected to racist insults online after she voiced support for pro-democracy protests in 2020. Many of the insults against her invoked Blackness or Africanness, although she is from Southern Thailand and was born to two Thai parents. In Suzie and Patcharaporn's cases, different ethnic contexts of dark skin are collapsed into a single degraded category that threatens to hybridize an imagined Thai ethnic purity. For many dark-skinned people living in Thailand now, such racism creates fear, stress, and constraint, despite being underwritten by different anxieties and hierarchies than in the West. The partial escape hatch, for Rocco and Dam in the GI era and for others today, is to be read as American and thus as an exception.

Stephan Turner, a Black American theater artist who runs the Gate Theater in Chiang Mai, explained to me: "I am not bound by [Thai colorist] racism because the maldistribution of wealth and resources doesn't affect me personally. What some foreigners or Thais may think of the color of my skin is none of my business unless it's presented to me. In which case we can either have a conversation or have something else. However, as I've said, there's never been a problem with Thais. Only minor comments and fleeting provocations with ignorant westerners."[26] Kendrix Thomas, a photographer living in central Thailand, wrote similarly in a blog post in 2014 that as a Black American in Thailand in the twenty-first century, "it's like I get a pass for being black because I'm an American."[27] The contemporary regime of Thai colorism, which grants this pass, was shaped significantly by the colonial effects of the 1960s and 1970s.

Coupled Shadows

There are parallels as well as junctures between Thai conceptions of Blackness and sex/gender alterity in the GI era. Both were transformed in the contact zones of neocolonialism. As with American Blackness, Thais regarded certain nonnormative gender or sexual identities in the early part of the war as wholly foreign. Local frameworks of alterity only passingly overlapped with American codes of sex and gender. But by the end of the war, after more than a decade of intimate engagement, sex/gender identity in Thailand had vastly expanded.[28] This expansion was grounded in local "genderscapes," even as it also accommodated certain American frameworks, including queerphobia.[29] The shift in local sex/gender systems was profound during the GI era, but until recently there has been limited scholarship on the topic. Below, I revisit an earlier generation of writing on Thai sex/gender histories of the war period, including the work of Peter Jackson and Rosalind Morris, considering these alongside primary sources as well as recent scholarship by Dredge Byung'chu Käng', Amporn Jirattikorn, Visisya Pinthongvijayakul, Nattapol Wisuttipat, and others.

Like this chapter's earlier reflections on Blackness, the following pages will examine a colonial effect: the field of sex and gender identity that emerged in Thailand during the GI era. The role of queer Black people like Rocco in this emergent field of sex/gender draws our attention both to the ways that Thailand was never exempt from discourses about race in the twentieth century and to how these discourses were invariably linked to sex/gender. These intersections matter for understanding Black queerness in diaspora. Omise'eke Natasha Tinsley calls for "tracing as carefully as possible the particular, specific, always marked contours, the contested beachscapes of African diaspora histories of gender and sexuality."[30] Although Rocco's story cannot by itself account for this complex history, his Black diasporic presence in Thai queer life can open a number of conversations that have been mostly absent in Thai studies.

The culture of the military forms a backdrop to this discussion. The US military formally excluded queer people from service during the war in Vietnam, as it had done since the eighteenth century. Although enforcement of this exclusion was less strict during Vietnam than World War II due to higher demand for soldiers, those caught having same-sex intercourse or cross-dressing could still receive an undesirable discharge. Lives that had recently been medicalized were now instead criminalized. Allan Bérubé quotes a Naval Training Center manual from 1952: "Homosexuality . . . is an offense to all decent and law-abiding people, and it is not to be condoned on grounds of 'mental illness' any more than other crime."[31] Those who were discharged risked being outed as well as losing hard-earned military benefits. And yet in practice, the most potent manifestation of the military's homophobia was silence. Queerness was not supposed to be acknowledged.

This expectation carried over to queer life for *farang* stationed or taking leave in Thailand. Gay nightlife venues operated discreetly, often in basements, and queer relationships or identities were not publicized. In fact sexual alterity was much more taboo for Americans in Thailand than it was for Thais themselves, for a combination of moralistic and political reasons. English-language newspapers scarcely mentioned gay life. When they did, it was generally described in terms of scandal or mental illness and always handled delicately. A 1976 *Bangkok Post* article called "Girls Who Like Girls" profiled a Thai woman named Nittiya who dated and had sex with women.[32] The piece drips with shame ("I know that it is wrong and I always feel guilty about it afterwards"), while the anonymous journalist carefully avoids direct terminology. It is an article about queerness that *does not mention queerness*. In this case the shock was compounded by the fact that the subject of the profile was a woman; nonnormative female sexuality was especially taboo. The piece on one hand reveals a discomfort with queer female sexuality among both Thais and Americans. But it also shows how reticent the English-language press was when covering queerness of any sort. Sexual alterity went unmentioned, following the norms of the military and the United States more broadly.

Extensive searches of English-language newspapers during the GI era turn up no printed mentions of openly gay venues in mainstream papers until April 1976, when at last a small ad appears for Bar Charles, a "very secluded gay bar in Patpong."[33] Gay bars for men were the first among various kinds of queer establishments to appear in such a public fashion, around the mid-1970s. Benedict Anderson's personal papers, archived at Cornell University after his death, make clear that gay life became fairly open in the 1980s, although it was still cis male focused and in many ways *farang* centered. Anderson collected copies of Thai magazines like *Morakot* (มรกต), which debuted in that decade with glossy spreads of male or *kathoey* models along with advertisements for bars and clubs. *Mithuna* then launched as the first Thai-language queer magazine in 1987. The first gay nightlife guides began to appear in the same year. After more than two decades of sub-rosa connections between Thais and *farang*, a combination of economic imperatives and liberalized attitudes created more open spaces for nonnormative sexual cultures.

But before the 1980s, especially during the war in Vietnam, English-language tourist guides such as *Bangkok After Dark!!!!* acknowledged only straight, cis male customers. During the 1960s and early 1970s, in emerging spaces of tourism and global business, the presumed subject of commerce was always a straight man. Want ads asked for "very attractive lady applicants" for retail work.[34] Thailand's National Statistical Office reported in 1965 that "Bangkok women are one of the chief attractions of the city. The visitor is struck by her physical beauty and grace, her small build and modest manner."[35] Just like queer people in the military, queer worlds in Thailand existed, but by custom and especially in English-language sources they could not be acknowledged. This silence of course generated archival gaps. There is little evidence to shed light on Maurice Rocco's experiences as a gay man in Thailand in the 1960s and 1970s, for example. Different ways of narrating history will be necessary. *To that end, the services of a ghost guide will be enlisted soon.*

In one notable study of the earliest encounters between structures of Thai and *farang* sexual alterity, Peter Jackson revisits the murder in Bangkok of a prominent white American journalist named Darrell Berrigan. A longtime expatriate in Bangkok, Berrigan was founder and editor of the daily newspaper *Bangkok World*. Berrigan was gay, but his high-level diplomatic connections insulated him from political trouble. Yet the world of nightlife offered no such protection. Berrigan was found dead in his car from multiple gunshot wounds one morning in October 1965. The killer was widely assumed to be his hired male sexual partner. English-language newspapers mostly avoided reference to Berrigan's sexuality when they reported the story, as once again silence was the norm for western readers, but Thai papers discussed the matter with open curiosity. Who was Berrigan's partner? What kind of relationship did the two men have? How did *farang* and Thai men relate to one another in matters of love and sex? In 1965, the beginning of the GI era and of Maurice Rocco's time in Thailand, these were new and fascinating questions. Indeed, Berrigan's murder marked the beginning of what Jackson calls a "discursive shift" around nonnormative sexuality among Thais.[36] Prior to that event and the discussions it provoked, there was in effect no such thing as "gay" identity in Thailand.[37] Much like Thai colorism, male homoerotic relations between Thais had previously been organized around class status and imbued with a strongly heteronormative character. Thus the role of the man (*phûu chaay*) in a given coupling mapped onto masculinized power and status, while his *kathoey* partner belonged to a feminized underclass.

The figure of the *kathoey* is particularly complex. Prior to the twentieth century, *kathoey* was a capacious category that could potentially encompass what might now be called trans, intersex, and gay people, among others. With the advent of the Cold War, *kathoey* came to be regarded as a naturalized third sex, a kin of male being with special access to the feminine spiritual realm. *Kathoey* identity was by turns physical and transcendental, expressed outwardly through dress but simultaneously marking a spiritual mobility from the male to the female realm. The word *kathoey* is borrowed from the Khmer language, and the concept is described in Buddhist texts dating back thousands of years. But in the twentieth century the category assumed different meanings than it had in Buddhist canons. Cold War–era *kathoey*ness reduced to one very general concept what had once been multiple subtypes of sex and gender alterity, described in a clerical code called the Vinaya. These once-canonical subtypes included men who performed oral sex on men, people with a preference for voyeurism, people who lacked genitals entirely, "people who become sexually aroused in parallel with the phases of the moon," and many more.[38] Notably, the Vinaya sorts identity according to desire in some cases and anatomy in others, without distinguishing them into categories that align clearly with sex/gender or phenotype/genotype. The Cold War–era word *kathoey* thus reduced a range of differences into a rather amorphous category of alterity, marked by appearance rather than practice. In the process, alterity was also increasingly subjected to legal oversight.[39] Morris argues that one must "look [beyond the specular] for an understanding of sex/gender systems—to the entire range of sexual practices and identities available within a particular social formation."[40] In other words, in twentieth-century Thailand, under an order of specularity that conformed with capitalist modernity, there *appeared* to be fewer identity categories than in the past, even if this was not the case in practice. One gay *farang* man recalled in a message board post that in 1971, "the dictionary translated a homosexual as a *kathoey*, so that's what I told people I was."[41] For most people the term was an overly general translation, perhaps an artifact of transnational ambiguities. In the GI era it lacked nuance. When considering *kathoey* in history, it is crucial to offer this degree of semantic context. In addition to encompassing many different beings, *kathoey* has also signified differently at different moments.[42] As Käng notes, "The lines between *tom*: woman: *kathoey*: *gay*: man are neither clear nor fixed," and further, "the terrain of the Thai sex/gender system is indigenized and becomes local in the tension between the autochthonous and the global."[43] The local interpretation of Berrigan's murder is important precisely because sex/gender alterity and the definition of *kathoey* were in the process of shifting in a manner strongly influenced by intimate contact with the West: something new was coming.

At the beginning of the GI era, the Thai gender system—at least at a public level—continued to reflect the homogenizing and binarizing effects of the cultural edicts issued by former field marshal Phibun Songkram in the 1940s. Phibun, in an effort to create the appearance of modernness before a western gaze, prescribed universal modes of dress for men and women. This codified a gender binary at the level of the state.[44] Although the notion of the *kathoey* is broadly accepted in Thai Buddhism, Phibun's edicts pointedly neglected to acknowledge nonbinary people as a category of everyday Thai subjects. The images of properly modern Thais that accompanied his edicts showed only conventionally dressed and styled "men" and "women." Even after those edicts lost their legal authority, they maintained a lasting cultural influence, especially in wealthier urban areas. In places like Bangkok, particularly in professional settings, *kathoey* were left largely on the margins of Cold War modernity. Perhaps partly as a consequence, while *kathoey* have long faced less risk of violence in Thailand than, for example, trans people do in the West, they are nevertheless seen as improper to spaces of political or economic power. For example, the first openly gender-nonconforming member of the Thai parliament, Tanwarin Sukkhapisit, was not elected until 2019 (and then promptly removed from power in 2020). *Kathoey* instead often work in malls or spaces of nightlife, which can be spaces of refuge. And while they generally inspire compassion rather than rage or antipathy from middle-class Thais, *kathoey* are still excluded from many arenas of public life, especially spaces that confer power.

The umbrella category of *kathoey* itself perhaps reflects an ingrained patriarchal order. During the early Cold War, before confirmation surgeries were available, *kathoey* had penises ipso facto. *Lam ploen* singer Sonthaya Kalasin, who transitioned in the 1970s and had gender confirmation surgery in the 1990s, explained to me that she identifies as *khâamphêet*, a loose equivalent of *trans*, rather than as *kathoey*. For Sonthaya, *khon khâamphêet* must be postoperative, whereas *kathoey* are "people with male bodies who dress as women" because they are inhabited by female spirits.[45] Thai *kathoey* may not be understood as people whose own identifications determine their gender (as gender is typically defined in the West) but instead as men who have been granted special access to spiritual femininity. Thus, as Morris and others have noted, the historical definition of *kathoey* may be said to retain a patriarchal character. "Female crossdressers had no special designation until quite recently, when borrowings from the English language created a taxonomy of female sexual deviance."[46] Similarly, lesbian desire may be expressed safely in spiritual contexts, rendering it exterior to mainstream spaces of sexuality. Visisya asserts that, commonly, "non-normative female sexual desire is enacted, performed, and endorsed . . . through mediumship," rendering the role of the Thai lesbian medium a parallel to that of the requisitely penised *kathoey*; both delimit alterity by confining it to spiritual contexts.[47]

This parsing of *kathoey* identity at a particular moment in history could be elaborated further still. However, Amporn and others have aptly described the term *kathoey* as ultimately "not fully translatable."[48] The term has no permanent essence or definition, and in fact the untranslatability of *kathoey* is crucial for understanding the sediments of sex and gender identity that preceded the arrival of gayness and its discursive shifts in Thailand. At the particular time of Berrigan's murder, *kathoey* were defined by reference to a strongly binary and heteronormative system and were primarily understood as feminized partners within male homosexual relationships. But the circumstances around Berrigan's murder were part of an intimate neocolonial encounter that began to interrupt this understanding.

Jackson suggests that as of 1965, the word and identity called *gay* was a novel and in fact quite elite way of figuring male sexual relationships. Gayness implied a degree of equality not found in *phûu chaay–kathoey* couplings. Berrigan's murder was not disruptive because it revealed two men in a sexual relationship—that was fine—but because the two men had engaged each other as social equals. That part was astonishing, and difficult to assimilate. "The gay form of male prostitution and homosexuality was shocking because of its perceived breach of class as well as gender norms."[49] Berrigan's murder brought to light a disruptive new mode of same-sex sexuality that was neither structured by heteronormativity nor ordered by class status. Up to that point homosexual worlds had been little known to most Thai people. Homosexuality, though moderately stigmatized, was neither violently policed nor criminalized under Thai law. It was merely something in the background, perhaps considered immoral but hardly a threat to the social order. But at the moment (and partly because) of Berrigan's murder, gayness was seen to unsettle an established class hierarchy. *Kathoey* and men were supposed to be class opposites. Gay relationships scrambled those roles. The figure of the gay in Thailand was thus something of a hybrid of *kathoey* and *phûu chaay*, not an untouched importation from the West. "Thai men appropriated the term 'gay' to relabel an existing indigenous category, the 'masculine kathoey' [kathoey phu-chai], rather than to mark a new phenomenon," notes Jackson.[50] The existing category of *kathoey* was destabilized by the figure of the gay, as well as by the specter of *kathoey* sex work as an equitable mediation between Thais and homosexual *farang*. This change mattered enormously not only for Maurice Rocco's life in Thailand but also for the eventual interpretation of his murder.

Meanwhile, however vehement homophobia may have been in American domestic politics, it was not a priority for the United States in international affairs. Homophobia was often promulgated for show by the American government rather than because of deep-seated queerphobia among bureaucrats. Thus it was possible for gay nightlife venues to function safely in Thailand, and even to serve Americans, as long as they were not too visible. Doug Sanders suggests that the first gay bar in Bangkok may have been Twilight, in 1965 or 1966, "opened by a drag queen named Kun Yosawadee, who had previously opened a house with boys in the early 1960s."[51] That bar eventually gave its

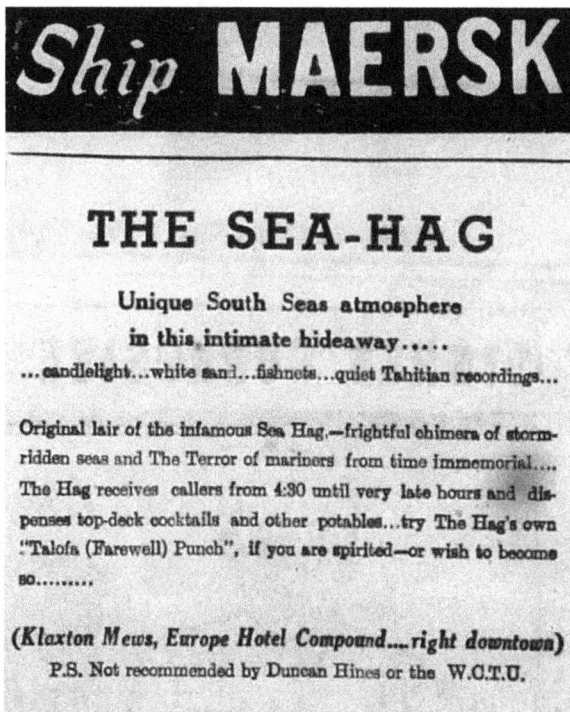

FIGURE 5.3. A February 1956 advertisement for the Sea Hag in the *Bangkok Post*. The language of the copy, from its sense of camp to its insinuations and its wry humor (WCTU stands for Women's Christian Temperance Union), signaled to queer clientele with the same tacit surety as Maurice Rocco's fluttering eyelashes.

name to Soi Twilight, a street near Patpong that housed one of Bangkok's first gay nightlife areas. Others have suggested that the first such bar was the Sea Hag, a former seaman's saloon on Silom Road that was probably gay friendly as early as the 1950s and became an openly gay bar in the mid-1960s.

Regardless, in the next several years many more such venues would open, including the Star Night Club, Lonely Boy, Two Vikings Bar, Mitsui Bar, Playboy Bar, Rome Club Disco, and Tulip Bar. Others simultaneously began operating in the newly developed resort town of Pattaya. At first none of these advertised as gay venues in mainstream print publications, or left many traces otherwise, given the American imperative for queer silence. I learned about them from scattered sources—interviews, blog posts, dim memories of ancient weekends. But the venues were common enough, along with oft-mentioned cruising spots like Ratchaprasong intersection. These were the spaces where gay Thais and *farang* met. These spaces also scaled up, serving as transnational contact zones for different systems of sex and gender alterity.

What was Maurice Rocco's experience of these contact zones? They were, for some time in the 1960s and '70s, relatively safe for him. Perhaps that is all we need to know. Rocco's sex life at this time was lived beyond the visible social field, in places that could not be advertised, falling outside the archive and within categories only beginning to acquire names. *Kathoey* was in discursive flux; *gay* was not yet clarified. Gay bars nestled modestly where neocolonial unspeakability met local liminality, a place (as it happened) of white sand and quiet Tahitian recordings. In these bars one could find precisely the ambiguity, the unsettledness, the space of archival absence that suited Rocco, that made his life livable. "During the day he'd ride the buses, he'd pick up a [young man], bring him back, and then at night he would play the piano. It was a nice situation for him, quite perfect," recalled Rocco's friend Harry Rolnick.[52] Even many of his closest associates were unaware. "In all the time I knew Maurice I had not an inkling that he was gay or bi," Rafael Ortiz told me.[53] "He was gay," remembers Mongkorn Pikaew, "but if you weren't close with him, you wouldn't have known. I once brought him to Patpong. . . . I know that he had a young boyfriend, because the boyfriend came to the Bamboo Bar to eat and drink."[54] Whoever the young man drinking his gimlet and watching Rocco play was, no one asked, or knew, or perhaps had the language to describe. In the destabilized gaps of Thai-*farang* intimate encounter, with identities up in the air, Rocco could quietly be. The white ants feast forever on our urge to know more.

"He hails a tuk-tuk and tells the driver to turn right when he says so at the intersection of Sukhumvit and a minor soi," writes Pitchaya Sudbanthad about Clyde Alston, the fictional Rocco.

> They make more turns, past storefronts and stalls. . . . This hour, away from the tourist roads and the baited hotels and massage parlors, dark swaths of the city sometimes get so quiet he can hear the whole animal breathe. He tells the driver to stop at a nondescript building with black-filmed windows and framed by a strip of Christmas lights. Stepping inside, he counts maybe two dozen men, some settled into rounded grottoes carved into the wall, others at the bar, lips whispering by ears, arms resting on willing shoulders. Coupled shadows shuffle on the floor to tinny bossa nova. He plops himself on a barstool.
>
> It takes less than five minutes before a young Thai approaches him from across the room. The man has a pale, heart-shaped face, and in the

dim light of the club he could be a crane striding past water buffalos in a rice field.

"Louis Armstrong alone tonight? Handsome man doesn't have to be."[55]

Withdrawal Symptoms

Thailand was volatile from the early 1970s until the full US withdrawal of troops from Southeast Asia in 1976. Then it combusted in ways that were tragic for many people, including Maurice Rocco. The flows of capital and development that began with a trickle of speculation after World War II, and which grew steadily throughout the 1950s and 1960s, placing Thailand among the fastest-growing economies in the Third World, began to recede around 1970. Turbulence followed. *Time* magazine wrote in 1971 that "[Thailand] profited from the war to the tune of $600 million in foreign exchange over the past five years, and 100,000 jobs at U.S. bases. At present, the U.S. is reducing its 48,000-man force by nearly a third. Among the many losers: Tommy Tours Agency."[56] That is the same Tommy (Tommie) Tours that had run Bangkok's rest and recuperation (R&R) operations since the late 1960s. The likely eventual consequences of withdrawal were obvious, including the potential for the Thai military to return to power. "If the military feels critically threatened by the withdrawal, angered by American inability to deliver previous aid promises, and suspicious of the new government's inclination to reduce their power, they may retaliate and seize power once again," predicted a report from one US think tank in 1975.[57] Within a year, the report was proven correct.

But the results of withdrawal were in fact even more dramatic than that. Regional economies throughout Thailand deflated in a matter of months, as the expectations of permanent wealth that had come with neocolonial intimacy were revealed as illusory. "U.S. military spending did not create a significant redistribution of income in the country," notes Surachat Bamrungsuk, in part because that spending was concentrated in urban areas and in towns with military bases.[58] And even in those places the long-term effect of the bases was not higher quality of life but pockets of inflation that caused local economies to crash when the bases closed. "A few months ago a village that grew out of almost nothing near a United States Army camp in Sakhon Nakhon province was a thriving community of 3,000 people. But now that the 809th Engineering Battalion (Construction) has gone, the shutters are creaking down and the girls have left and there is only the ghost of prosperity," lamented the *Bangkok Post*.[59] Jittima Juajai's 1976 *luk krung* single "Phetchaburi Tat Mai" (New

Phetchaburi Road) bids a sentimental goodbye to New Phetchaburi's GI-era economy, which despite its seediness had provided livelihoods to many Thais. The song even fondly recalls the numbers pinned to women's chests, which allowed *farang* men to choose among them for sexual services. It is notable that the song's lyrics were composed by a man, and that Jittima herself graduated from Thailand's most elite university; neither singer nor composer knew intimate labor firsthand. Nevertheless, there was nostalgia for US troops as soon as the notional riches of the war years began crumbling to dust. Long before the withdrawal was complete, the American presence had shocked the Thai economy, giving way to political crisis.

Some of this crisis opened doors to reform. Leftist movements throughout the country grew larger and more ambitious in the late 1960s. At the apex of those movements, an emboldened student coalition successfully overthrew the military government in October 1973, replacing it for several years with a democratic alternative. The conditions for this uprising included a dramatic recent rise in university students, itself an effect of a growing middle class and expanded educational system.[60] Much of the organizing that led to the 1973 uprising occurred on campuses, among upwardly mobile students who were the first in their families to attend college. The Communist Party of Thailand became a robust national operation, anti-colonialism was a widespread cause, and farmers agitated for land reform and rent control. Critical outlets such as activist Sulak Sivaraksa's *Social Science Review* (as it was generally called) helped circulate leftist ideas nationally in print, including strong critiques of American neocolonialism. Progressives were energized and the United States was a target of increasing national ire.

This book has not discussed leftist movements in detail, focusing instead on spaces of cosmopolitan nightlife where political consciousness, when it appeared, had different manifestations than on campuses. Leftism in Thailand arguably had its heyday in the early 1970s, as political upheaval gave radical ideas wider berth than in the past. It might also be noted that leftist movements were accompanied by plenty of music, including the radical folk genre "songs for life" (*phleeng phûa chiiwít*). "Songs for life" is just beyond the frame of this book's concerns. But the vibrancy of the Left was one hopeful effect of the time, and it was well represented in art.

Still, an ascendant Left could not outrun the havoc of the American withdrawal. Nor could it ultimately counter the military or far Right, who lay in wait after 1973, returning first through scattershot acts of violence and then more forcefully in 1976. Right-wing nationalist movements were undergirded by a nearly impregnable combination of royal, military, and popular support.

These movements organized themselves in the first half of the 1970s, often in the guise of pro-state, quasi-fascist Buddhist youth groups. When instability turned to open disorder in 1975 and especially 1976, these groups were well positioned to fight on behalf of religious and pro-state forces. Large coteries of disaffected young men became foot soldiers. On a Wednesday morning in October 1976, in the depths of a power vacuum left by the American withdrawal, the Thai military seized the reins of government from would-be republicans, fomenting a deadly massacre of leftist students at Bangkok's Thammasat University as they stormed back to authoritarian rule. The Thammasat massacre, during which paramilitary fighters mutilated the bodies of students who they imagined were demons (and thus killable without sin), has been described by Thongchai Winichakul as "the most heinous event in modern Thai history."[61] And yet Thongchai, a scholar and former student activist, recalls that the violence was not spontaneous. It was a counterresponse after years of leftist advances. Anderson famously described this upheaval as a set of "withdrawal symptoms," a metaphor for the convulsive effects in the body politic that followed the departure of American troops.

Before the dramatic events of October 1976, Bangkok had endured at least two years of persistent violence. Street protests were routine, and the Right attacked students and laborers who critiqued the American presence and lack of a constitution. Sometimes the disorder was political. At other moments it seemed merely part of the fabric of contemporary life in contentious times. The young leader of Thailand's Socialist Party was assassinated in February 1976. A grenade exploded in Siam Square in March 1976 during a protest against American troops, killing at least four students. Gunfire was reported at Thammasat University the very same day. Political assassinations became common, as both para–state militants and conservative elites sought to undermine leftist movements by any means at their disposal. Although precise statistics are difficult to come by, newspaper coverage suggests that petty crime involving weapons also rose. Reports of tourist robberies increased. One French tourist was robbed of cash and a suitcase by a man who came to his hotel room posing as a telephone technician in April 1976. Thailand in the mid-1970s was beset by crime and conflict that spread beyond politics and into daily life. The spring of 1976 was, in short, a dangerous time.

The increasing unrest and conflict certainly impacted the life of a gay, Black *farang* musician. Cross-cultural engagement, where Rocco had once found refuge as a social exception, was now a context of vulnerability and even danger. Facing a confluence of leftist, nationalist, and reformist critics, Americans lost much of their former privilege. *Farang* were not only visible in the mid-1970s but increasingly marked, no matter their skin color. But Rocco was almost sixty years old and ensconced in a comfortable life. Where else could he go?

Ghost Guide

The narrator of a 1975 short story collection called ตะลุยเกย์คลับ (Heading into a gay club) was a so-called ghost guide (ไกด์ผี), a freelancer unaffiliated with a tourist agency.[a] The ghost guide stories were written by Ta Tha-It, a pseudonymous author known for his documentary writing style.[62] Ta wrote with studied journalistic (even ethnographic!) attention, and the ghost guide was his trusty narrator. The stories in "Heading into a gay club" offer perspective on the lives of young Thai bourgeoisie in the late GI era—not the political Left per se but people coming of age amid expanded subjective fields of gender and sexuality and in the tumult of the American withdrawal.[63] The ghost guide's friends had money and time. With rich *farang* as a springboard, they could experiment with relationships, identities, and labor opportunities beyond what earlier generations had known. The ghost guide's reports from the cosmopolitan worlds where he came of age lend detail to the context in which Maurice Rocco's life was taken.

As a narrator, the ghost guide brought Thai readers to hidden corners where Thais and *farang* engaged one another intimately. As Thailand was increasingly unsettled by colonial effects, the ghost guide offered valuable insights, "reintroduc[ing] Thailand's tourist attractions to the Thai reader, who consequently learn[ed] about little-known places in her/his own country."[64] The narrator explained salacious things in a just-so fashion. In this voice, Ta wrote vividly about the worlds of *farang* in Thailand, a topic both strange and thrilling to his readers. In the trendy manner of *thai kham angkrit kham*, he often mixed English and Thai words in his prose.[65] Ta's narrator brought readers into off-limits social areas at a moment when cosmopolitan life was often invisible or at least unknown to many Thais. Just as the ghost guide promised Thais insights about veiled people and places at the time the stories were published, today the same stories bring historians into areas that most archives cannot, about which records have not been kept.[66]

Among those areas is sexual alterity. One of Ta's stories, ไกด์กะเทย (*Kathoey* guide) describes *kathoey* seeking intimate relationships with *farang*. The story was published in 1975, on the cusp of the following year's military-led counter-

a ACKNOWLEDGMENT: SUNY Stony Brook doctor of musical arts student Duangka-mon Wattanasak helped me better understand the context as well as the period dialect of these short stories.

revolution. Ta observes *kathoey* during an active discursive shift. He writes about identity and desire, authenticity and opportunity. For the first half of the story the narrator muses about *kathoey* fashion and selfhood, addressing questions about bodies, clothing, and self-identity that surely fascinated his readers. In the second half he relates an anecdote about his own *kathoey* roommate, whose desires and relationships unsettle gender binaries in profound and playful ways. The ghost guide reckons, as his readers must have done, with categories in flux. It is clear in the story that *kathoey* were not singular at all. Some had begun to identify with western gayness; others had not. Some were sincerely attracted to *farang*; others discovered that they could assert power over them. The ambiguous meeting of love and labor was similar to what *mia chao* experienced in the same years. Neocolonial power imbalance made it so. The details of these relationships were unknown to most middle-class Thais, and the ghost guide stories provided them a rare vantage.

"Heading into a gay club" is fictional, but ghost guiding was a real job. These guides' services were solicited by *farang* seeking informal pleasures off the main touristic grid, such as finding *kathoey* intimate partners. These experiences were rendered silent by normative American queerphobia, but they otherwise ran parallel to the mainstream tourist economies that had been marketed to westerners for more than twenty years. These informal economies needed clandestine chaperones for gay tourists, people whom the state could rely on as financial intermediaries and yet publicly disavow. From this position, the ghost guide spoke of topics that the public transcript could or would not. As Lawrence Chua observes, "Ta's stories are the lurid shadows of the paradise that the [Tourist Organization of Thailand] sought to narrate."[67] But by 1975 the shadows were more than lurid; they were also vulnerable and marginal thanks to the indifference of the law, opportunistic violence, and the compulsory homophobia of an American neocolonial gaze. This is precisely when and how Rocco's formerly hidden corners became places of risk. The silence that had once made queer shadows a redoubt now left them exposed and unprotected. This vulnerability was one tragic synthesis of the GI era in Thailand, by the mid-1970s in its waning days.

The words of the ghost guide now join with other voices to announce, in intimate tones, what I offer as the conclusion to a belated funeral book for Maurice Rocco. In the tragic last moments of Rocco's life, souls resonated with violent finality. By the end of the GI era, which is also the end of Rocco's story, it had become difficult to distinguish the being that Rocco embodied in the United States from the being he became abroad, just as it was difficult to distinguish American worlds from Thai ones. The contact zone where Rocco rekindled his career and found refuge was more than the sum of its national parts, more than one system of social and aesthetic categorization added to another. Thailand was defined by its transnational intimacies. And everyone in it, no matter their nationality, was now part of the resulting synthesis. Rocco's life ended under an order of knowledge that could only be understood as part of this synthesis. Rocco died as he had lived in Thailand, as a medium for encounters between unsettled spirits, resonating together.

"I jumped into the work of being a ghost guide when I was sixteen. I saw young *kathoey* with shaggy-haired *farang*. At that time I would involve myself more than I do now, because the police weren't so strict back when the tourism industry was at its height. *Farang* swarmed Thailand."[68] The ghost guide alludes to a bygone pinnacle of Thai-*farang* gay relationships since muddled by mutual suspicion and the temptation of stickups. Rocco knew it.

"Maybe he feared something might happen to him, because he told me that he had two plane tickets leaving Thailand. One going east to Hawaii and one going west to Europe," said Ortiz. "One time I was broke and I borrowed one hundred baht from him. One hundred baht was the equivalent of five US dollars. When I went to pay him back I took out a hundred-baht note but he noticed that I also had a five-dollar bill. He asked if I needed that 'ace.' I didn't know what an ace was so he told me that it was a five-dollar bill. I gave him the 'ace.' Apparently he was already stocking up on US currency."[69]

Rocco continued his routine, walking between the Ambassador Club on Ratchadamri Road, where he led his trio, the Bamboo Bar in the Oriental Hotel, the buses where *kathoey* cruised, and his apartment on Soi Chit Lom. He was a person of habit.

"He stood," said Mongkorn. "Every night. He stood to play. He never sat. . . . He liked to play his favorite songs."[70]

But "it was a dangerous time to be gay in Bangkok," remembers Rolnick, "with a lot of these boys coming down from the villages, and they saw a way to make quick money not only to be paid but to look around people's apartments to see if they had any money which could be stolen."[71]

Specifically, trade (men hired for sex by gay men) had once come from Phayao Province in the North, but now with air base closures they migrated more often from Isaan, according to Charnvit Kasetsiri, one of Thailand's most prominent historians and a gay man who lived through the period. Bangkok brokers preferred to hire northerners because they had light skin. But things were changing.

"Lots of gay men were murdered around that time," remembers Charnvit.[72]

Rocco began collecting bladed weapons.

"I asked my *kathoey* friend Jed how it goes down," said the ghost guide. "Jed told me: I enter the room with the man. I walk in and he carries me gently onto the bed. He kisses the tip of my ear. It makes my hair stand on end, all over my body. He pours me a drink with a loving, supple touch. Then we embrace and bind our bodies delicately. If he can take care of me, I want to stay with him."[73]

Rocco renewed his passport in 1975.

"A lot of gay celebrities would come there, and I would interview them and they would say, 'Do you know where we can get gay sex?'" said Rolnick. "And I would tell them where they could go and I would give them the rules, the rules being don't keep anything valuable in your apartment."[74]

Rocco had many debts.

The ghost guide is neutral about *kathoey* who make their living from *farang*. The balance of opportunity between the provinces and capital was shifting on the cusp of the US withdrawal. Rural people were displaced from farms or forced to seek work away from shuttered air bases. Their children were part of a wave of internal migration. Bangkok was morally bankrupt, but it was rich. Not every opportunity would yield merit. Your desire doesn't figure anyway. It's a gig.

"Wallets stick to their hands when they hug, as the *farang* leaves for his own hotel," reports the ghost guide about *kathoey* pickpockets. "The really skilled ones simply vanish. By the time the *farang* realizes his money is gone, he doesn't know what to do. Some of them file reports, but in many cases they keep it quiet because they're ashamed. The police often have to sweep the thieves out."[75]

Rocco cruised in the afternoon and played the piano at night. Nightlife— leisure—that was the work. Days of the week are important heralds of fortune in Thailand. It is therefore crucial to note that it was on Wednesday, March 24, 1976, in the late afternoon, that Rocco met two young men and invited them to his apartment in the Court Piyatam building near the British embassy.

"Well, Maurice played the dangerous game," said Rolnick. "He was very nice with the boys he was with. And he was just a very sweet person, but he did it the wrong way, that was all it was."[76]

Ladda Uddasang was Court Piyatam's *mêɛ bâan*. She saw the two young men inside the apartment talking to Rocco when she arrived that day with a carpenter to fix a broken mosquito screen. Rocco wore pink silk pants and a blue shirt. Pink is astrologically unlucky on Wednesdays in the daytime. It was 4:30 p.m. The boys left one hour later.

Ladda returned to clean Rocco's apartment the next day around 1:30 p.m. She found his corpse naked on the bed. She ran to tell the building manager, who called the police.

"Rocco was stabbed with a Malaysian kris he owned shortly after two youths visited his room," reported the *Bangkok Post*.[77] His trachea was slashed. The knife was dropped in the bathroom basin. The killers knew that the *farang* would never know. "Bad people searched for things [to steal] from the room," reported *Thai Rath*.[78] "But they didn't find anything. It's understood that they killed him then."

"He died on a Wednesday," remembered Mongkorn accurately of a day forty years in the past. "I know because the Bamboo Bar was closed on Mondays. On Tuesday we went to work. On Wednesday he didn't come, and we knew something bad had happened."[79]

Ladda told the police that Rocco often hosted young *kathoey*. She described the two who visited that day as young with long hair. She had seen others like them but never those two.

Rocco died ambiguously, between worlds. His body was cremated at a nearby *wát*. His most recent birth had been on June 26, 1915, a Saturday.

The Transmigration of Soul

In death, life was illuminated. There would be no new secrets, and some old ones were forced into the light of acknowledgment. The privileges of treading quietly in unsettled worlds ended with his murder. But it became clear in the subsequent weeks just how precarious that privilege had been. In particular, homophobia and anti-Black racism emerged from every part of the police investigation, news coverage, gossip mill, and logistics of repatriation.

Rolnick heard the news of his friend's death from a colleague in the newsroom. "One of the girls in the *Bangkok Post*, a nice society Thai girl, said, 'Harry, did you know the negro Maurice Rocco?' I said, 'Yes, I know Maurice.' She said, 'Oh, he's dead.'"[80] The term she used to describe Rocco, although common in the mid-1970s, was in this case imbued with racist intent. Rolnick was floored by the news but noticed what his colleague implied by her nonchalance: "He was only a negro, so he didn't mean that much to her."

The police asked Rolnick to identify his friend's body, and he did. This began the process of establishing not so much the motive or the identity of the killers (neither was ever determined) but of posthumously judging the value of Rocco's existence. Rolnick entered Rocco's apartment where the police were investigating the gruesome scene on Thursday. "There were about four police laughing and giggling because they'd seen a lot of pictures that Maurice had taken of the naked boys."[81] In the aftermath, Rolnick bore witness to the racism and homophobia that would govern the response to Rocco's death.

The cremation took place the following Saturday, but the *Post* did not print an announcement. Everyone at the paper, save Rolnick, claimed to be too busy to attend. No one from the Oriental Hotel paid their respects. Rolnick called Kurt Wachtveitl, the manager of the Oriental, who scoffed that he would not attend because Rocco still owed him twenty-five dollars. Vicious attitudes were suddenly out in the open. "The racism was always latent, it was always there. No matter where they went it was always there. You read any of James Baldwin's essays. It was always there."[82]

Rocco's death was reported in both English- and Thai-language newspapers.[83] Much like coverage of Darrell Berrigan's murder in 1965, Anglophone papers were circumspect about Rocco's sexuality, while Thai papers did not hesitate to address it. The top line of the front page of *Thai Rath* two days after Rocco was killed read, "Two young men sodomize and kill an ink-skinned singer," using the moderately homophobic term *thŭa dam* (ถั่วดำ) to refer to the sex act.[84] The most overtly homophobic statement in the article is a quote from the police captain, who told a reporter that he felt "Rocco was sick with sexual perversion." His quote had a markedly more homophobic tone from the curiosity that marked the response to Berrigan's death twelve years earlier. The reference to queerness as illness is particularly striking.

Thai Rath's coverage was typically sensationalist, including a photograph of Rocco's corpse. Thai newspapers, even today, can read like turn-of-the-century New York scandal rags, brimming with lurid details. Drawing morbid interest is and was undoubtedly a motivating factor for papers in both countries. But Thai newspaper coverage of violence is governed by different principles, which are unfamiliar to most American readers, including a Buddhistic ethics of witnessing death as a means of increasing awareness of one's own mortality.[85] Thai journalists meanwhile may print the birthdays and home addresses of individuals in crime articles, details that in the United States would be considered irrelevant or inappropriate, but which are centrally important to Thai readers. Is the *Thai Rath* article an example of Rocco being exposed abjectly in death under an American neocolonial order of racial violence and queerphobia? Or is it characteristic of how Thai newspapers reflect ethically on death? There is no single answer. It is difficult and perhaps impossible to know which ethical system should organize the telling of Rocco's life story, including his murder. The *Thai Rath* article exemplifies what Pattana calls an "ambiguous intimacy," an unresolved Thai-American relationship that yielded a relational third space of enunciation.

In "*Kathoey* Guide," the ghost guide explains that mental illness had recently become a common explanation for nonnormative desire among Thais.

Switching to English, he quotes Sigmund Freud at length in discussing how some educated Thais felt that being *kathoey* was a disorder stemming from issues with a child's relationship to his mother. The guide's use of English, and his references to European psychoanalysis, give this explanation a veneer of erudite modernity. The facile citation of Freud notwithstanding, this part of the story demonstrates how middle-class Thais could now express homophobia through western clinical diagnoses, a move that would have been unlikely a decade earlier. The police captain's reference to gayness as mental illness likewise mirrored American rhetoric, including that of the anti-queer military. Observes Morris: "Reformations in the sexual domain are at least partly the result of transnational gazes and of the discourses that Orientalizing and self-Orientalizing desire produces."[86] Whether the policeman felt political pressure to offer his assessment or whether he had internalized homophobic sentiments is impossible to know. Regardless, Thai elites were now conversant in a discourse of homophobia that aligned with that of the West.

In the ensuing days, English-language newspapers covered Rocco's death more extensively than Thai papers. This owed to Rocco's upper-class, cosmopolitan, and predominantly *farang* audience. Working-class Thai readers knew little about him or his music. As described earlier, he was a social exception as well as a perpetual visitor. His music was unfamiliar because of the rarefied social worlds in which he had played. In the English-language *Bangkok Post*, Harry Rolnick covered his friend's life and death extensively, penning several detailed obituaries. Still Rolnick's retrospectives never mentioned Rocco's sexuality.

About two weeks after the murder, the *Post* ran two final stories. An April 8 article stated that the police had arrested a suspect, but the April 9 follow-up clarified that the investigation was still ongoing, with no arrests so far. There would be no further coverage of Rocco's murder or the investigation after April 9, in the *Post* or any other paper. The investigation appears to have ended without further evidence, let alone arrests. Absent political pressure to pursue the matter, the case was quietly dropped. The tone of the final two articles may offer some insight into the implicit rationale for this: gay men were responsible for whatever harm came to them. Queer Thai nightlife's back alleys were unsafe, the articles implied, and Rocco should have known it. Both articles linked queerness implicitly to crime: "Police last night combed haunts catering to known homosexuals and arrested a suspect in the killing of American jazz pianist Maurice Rocco."[87] These final days of coverage made clear that the police considered Rocco's sexuality primary to their investigation. Indeed, the reporting suggested that Rocco had invited trouble by hanging out in secretive corners. The language of "homosexual haunts" placed queer spaces—the spaces described by the ghost guide, the scenes that the Tourist Organization of Thailand needed commercially but would not name, let alone protect, and the dark swaths of the city so quiet where Louis Armstrong did not have to be alone—under the hard glare of police lights.

In death Rocco had no more privacy, no more privilege. In the context of a murder investigation, everything about his identity militated against an exhaustive inquiry by the Thai police. "The fact that Maurice was not an official, the fact that he was a private citizen, the fact he was a Black person, they didn't take it that seriously," Rolnick told me. Rocco's color, sexuality, and status had granted him space to live throughout his years in Thailand; in death these things made him ungrievable.

A small handful of obituaries for Rocco appeared in North American publications, most prominently in *Variety* magazine, in late March and early April 1976. But Rocco had by then been in Bangkok for nearly twelve years. He had not lived in or even visited the United States since 1959. By the late 1950s he was largely forgotten in the country of his birth. Over the course of seventeen years as an expatriate, he disappeared more fully and had been forgotten more completely.

Secretary of State Henry Kissinger sent two signed telegrams to the US embassy in Thailand arranging for the repatriation of Rocco's remains. The closest next of kin were his remaining siblings, who lived in Illinois, and a former agent in New York City. The cremation and transportation of his ashes to Oxford, Ohio, would cost $800. No one among Rocco's known contacts was willing or able to pay that amount. As an American murdered abroad, Rocco mattered to the State Department, as suggested by Kissinger's personal involvement in the repatriation effort.[88] But apparently not enough for the State Department to cover $800 in fees.

Louis Rodabaugh claims to have learned about Rocco's death by accident. "I happened to be in a restaurant in Canton [Ohio] at precisely the right time to hear the following one-sentence news report on radio," remembered Rodabaugh:

> "Maurice Rocco, Black American jazz pianist well-known in Hollywood circles of the 1930s and 1940s, was murdered in his apartment yesterday." I rushed home. I telephoned every local radio station, and also every major TV station in northeast Ohio, also all of the major newspapers. No one had heard of the incident. I called Oxford, Ohio. No one there had heard anything about the event. In desperation, I asked the toll operator to connect me with the U.S. Ambassador to Thailand

in Bangkok. Surprisingly, in just five minutes I was talking with Ambassador Whitehead [*sic*]. He said:

"We're mighty glad you called. We're in a dither here, as to what to do with Mr. Rocco's remains. He left no next-of-kin in his folio at the Embassy. We've called his former agent in New York City, and we've called the New York City Local of the Musician's Union, but we can't find out anything. Maybe you can help us. What is your relationship to the deceased?"

"I'm just a home-town, Oxford, Ohio friend of long ago. What is going to happen, then?"

"Well, as perhaps you don't know, they don't embalm here in Thailand. If we don't locate some kin very soon, they will cremate his body and then simply dump the cremains into an unmarked hole in the ground."

"Oh, that must not happen: Maurice extracted a promise from me many years ago that I would see to it that he would be buried next to his parents in Oxford: What can I do?"

"You'll have to locate his next-of-kin, get them to send to the State Department their permission for you to supervise the burial. I'll set up a liaison desk in Washington so that you can keep in constant communication. When we get the authorizations, then you must wire $800.00 to the State Department. The Thai authorities will then cremate Rocco's body, and send the cremains, properly sealed of course, to the airport nearest you."[89]

After collecting part of the funds from friends, Rodabaugh wired $800 to the State Department, and Rocco's ashes returned to Ohio, to be buried in April 1976.

CONCLUSION
Acknowledging *thing wáy*

On a blustery afternoon in mid-March 2022, a few dozen people gathered in Woodside Cemetery for the unveiling of an Ohio Historical Marker dedicated to Maurice Rocco.[a] From the day his remains were shipped home in 1976 until the dedication ceremony forty-six years later, Rocco's grave was left unmarked. Still today he has no headstone. During the ceremony a small paper sign leaned on a vase of flowers near his resting place, listing his name and years on earth. Rocco's ashes are inside his mother's plot—in 1976 there was no money for a separate burial—near a patch of grass where the hill slides down into a nearby creek.

Friends and relatives chatted intimately before the formal part of the ceremony. Rocco's niece, now eighty, was among the crowd. The living spoke of

---

a ACKNOWLEDGMENT: I thank my longtime friend filmmaker Philip Swift for documenting the ceremony.

the dead in the present tense. There were lively and in no way somber exchanges about who rests where, the couple who raised Rodney beneath the earth a few paces that way, Leonard who arrived in the graveyard in 2011, right where we were just standing. A woman named Jayne had a fall at work, was awarded worker's compensation, and now does her genealogy full-time. Jayne knows everyone above and below. She planned to go to Richmond later that same day for research, to check in on people. Richmond is twenty-six miles north of Oxford but they're really the same place, Jayne tells me. Ruby was born in Richmond, and now she rests here. Jayne adds that there are many different surnames on these headstones, but really everyone is related. Families mingle as readily as souls between worlds.

Oxford (like kindred towns) retains a profound sense of its own Black history, in part thanks to people like Jayne. The mayor attends the dedication; in his address he points out that Oxford was once 20 percent Black. It's about 5 percent now but no less invested in that part of its heritage. Lovingly built websites map local sites along the Underground Railroad. Monuments in town recognize notable Black locals: an engraved stone for Oxford's 1964 Freedom Summer volunteers; a plaque near a tree for nineteenth-century lynching victims Simeon Garnet and Henry Corbin; a mural honoring local civil rights work. Have I toured Gennett Records in Richmond, where Louis Armstrong, Duke Ellington, Blind Lemon Jefferson, Jelly Roll Morton, and others recorded?

This was Maurice's birthplace, now his resting place. Here, his Historical Marker stands ten feet high, aptly taller than any human being, literally and figuratively larger than life. The monument exceeds the person. New myths have been made, and along with them new secrets. The towering marker is too big to speak to Rocco's totality as a person. "His 1976 murder [in Bangkok] was unsolved," declares the plaque, highlighting the unknown. Of course certain things about his murder *are* known. But most of it is left unsaid. Perhaps that is the nature of memorials. *But surely there is more to acknowledge.*

It took reflective work for me to acknowledge that Black Oxford has the right to burnish its memories as it so chooses. Academics are trained to pursue transparency as far as the evidence will take us. At the dedication, when I was called to the microphone to deliver a keynote address, a great honor, I wanted to say everything about Rocco: the good, the bad, the ambiguous. Everything. But which everything? Academics often want to acknowledge everything except ourselves.

Out in the world, history can have a gauzy quality. Sometimes that is justified. In Oxford racial backlash is never far from the surface, when it is submerged at all, in 2022 as in 1922. It bears requoting Black Oxfordian Ennis Miller: "Growing up in Oxford there was the fact that you couldn't go in the restaurant in the front, you had to go in the back in the kitchen."[1] Rev. Terriel Byrd has written about the role of Oxford's Black churches as sanctuaries: "Blacks in Oxford were offered refuge, spiritual and social meaning, and a sense of personal identity through the Black church. Though not legally enforced in Oxford, racial separation was consistent with attitudes prevalent throughout America.... Therefore it was not uncommon for blacks to form independent places of worship."[2] The stakes of Black history here are high—much higher than I stand. The need for sanctified genealogy outweighs the compulsion for transparency that can characterize academic history and ethnography, my small, peculiar worlds. Maurice Rocco, a complex and imperfect person in life, is now a character in histories that facilitate people's survival.

What's more and anyway: no one asked me. At the marker dedication I have been invited to speak, but that is not the same thing as weighing in. I am from Ohio, too, but I am also a *farang*, which I acknowledge. Sometimes shutting up is indicated, nullity nourishing.

The mayor declares March 19 "Maurice Rocco Day." We neatly fold the tent.

This book has worked to acknowledge the transnational intimacy of the Cold War relationship between the United States and Thailand, a relationship that was in many ways forged in nightlife. It has explained how that relationship produced an enduring form of *farang* privilege that not only made Euro-American visitors comfortable in the years of the war in Vietnam but continued to do so in the ensuing decades, indeed even to the present. It has explained a multiply entangled present that owes itself to a recent, if not always apparent, neocolonial past.

Maurice Rocco lived his last dozen years in the spaces of Thai-American intimacy at its apex. His story is remarkably illustrative in that regard. And yet Rocco's unmarked grave is a reminder that he returned to Ohio in anonymity, a condition that was intentional. It is a reminder that his life was not lived to be fully seen or pieced together. It is a reminder that at some point he traded notoriety for sweeter freedoms.

The phenomenon of *acknowledgment* has been theorized in the discipline of political science, among other fields, typically with reference to mass atrocities and projects of reconciliation at a national or interethnic scale.[3] Joanna Quinn argues that acknowledgments of systemic injustice and violence are necessary early steps on the path not only to forgiveness but to rebuilding both damaged physical infrastructure and trust itself.[4] Things that have occurred, especially terrible things, must be recounted aloud by perpetrators, with victims given a chance to narrativize their experiences in turn. This is the logic of truth and reconciliation commissions and the restorative justice that they claim to seek.

The work of acknowledgment in the writing of a reflexive history like this book overlaps somewhat with Quinn's ideas. The neocolonial relationship between the United States and Thailand absolutely bears acknowledgment, on behalf of the many people who were exploited, traumatized, or otherwise *thíng wáy* ("discarded"; see chapter 4) or whose lives were upended by the brutal maneuvering of the Cold War. The history of Thailand's contemporary position in a global imaginary, significantly including its reputation as a sexual paradise, also bears acknowledgment. A primary aim of this book has been to uncover and explain these colonial effects, especially as they developed within nightlife. A second, related aim has been to acknowledge the perspectives and voices of those whose lives have been shaped by these effects. A third aim has been to situate privileged living subjects—not least of all myself—within a system built on colonial effects, so that any *farang* with any connection to Thailand now, from scholar to journalist to tourist, might better understand their own status and its histories.

Yet the project of acknowledgments undertaken by this book also diverges from recent work in political science. First, a study of Maurice Rocco demonstrates the ethical limits of total transparency. Not all potentially revealable facts are equal; some are relatively neutral (a concert date), some should be disclosed (spousal abuse), while others (the inner moments of consensual intimate relationships, a month away from work, an ambiguous identification, a gruesome newspaper image) might be held at arm's length by a historian even many years later. Within war-era Thai nightlife, many things occurred that were connected on some level to a neocolonial project *and yet still* arguably private. As Saidiya Hartman incisively puts it, responding to the work of Édouard Glissant, "The right to obscurity must be respected, for the 'accumulated hurt,' the 'rasping whispers deep in the throat,' the wild notes, and the screams lodged deep within confound simple expression and, likewise, withstand the prevailing ascriptions of black enjoyment."[5] Acknowledgments may be attuned to these accumulations yet still attend to ethical claims of privacy.

Second, political scientific theories of acknowledgment tend to apply western psychoanalytic frames to the study of collective and individual emotional health. To cite one example in rejoinder, Jeffrey Dyer, Carol Kidron, and other anthropologists have argued that scholarly and political acknowledgments of the Cambodian genocide of the late 1970s (not so far from this book's focus) have relied narrowly on western theories of trauma to understand the enduring effects of mass atrocity outside the West.[6] Cambodian people consulted in Kidron's ethnography felt that collective and individual forgetting was in fact often beneficial. Her respondents "reject the pathological profile of transmitted PTSD and show a disinterest in any form of public articulation of their past." This perspective dovetails with Joshua Pilzer's recommendation that historians apply a "policy of opacity" where necessary in the aftermath of trauma.[7] The work of acknowledgment meets its limit with claims to privacy as well as with culturally distinct approaches to the management of trauma and other forms of emotional distress.

The field of acknowledgment in *Bangkok after Dark* is potentially even more richly networked. If understanding recovery in the wake of the Cambodian genocide requires some degree of relativism, as both Kidron and Dyer argue, an effective response to American neocolonialism in Thailand calls for attention not only to multiple subjectivities but also to their messy articulation in historical contact zones. Acknowledgment in this case must do more than recognize local points of view. It must also think intersectionally about, for example, a Black gay expatriate musician under whose very feet the ground of identity was shifting with every step. The researcher cannot be absent from such an analysis. An acknowledgment of someone like Rocco must incorporate the author.

Still there is value in certain disclosures, and I am moved as well as convinced by Kuan-Hsing Chen's claim, after Frantz Fanon, that "any decolonization movement cannot be completed without a corresponding deimperialization movement in the imperial center."[8] The imperial center—let's call it the realm of *farang* rather than the United States or the West—must study how its own privilege depends on historical self-erasures in order for deimperialization to proceed. After doing this reflexive work, we may no longer be able to hear bands like Phet Phin Tong as exotic mirrors of our own values. Perhaps that will be liberating.

But there are obstacles in our collective path. Just five days after Rocco's death, the Tourist Organization of Thailand (TOT) published a special supplement in the *Bangkok Post* called "Thailand's Big Plan for Developing Tourism." The supplement heralded a new "National Plan" for promoting tourism that looked forward to the 1980s and beyond, perhaps all the way to our present time. Unsurprisingly, the piece is advertorial, focusing on the economic benefits of tourism to Thailand. Above the text, a man and woman are shown in traditional Siamese clothing. The man dances as he holds a *klɔɔng yaaw* drum in front of an ancient temple and a beautiful beach. The imagery and its symbolism are immediately familiar to us as twenty-first-century viewers. No matter how well read, no matter how self-aware, we are solicited by the ad. The man and woman in the photograph are bearers of a culture that can be activated at our touristic whim. And there is always the promise of more after dark. By 1976 the TOT had already scripted many of the tropes that have continued to characterize Thai tourist promotion in the intervening decades. Sometime in the 1980s, tourism officially surpassed rice as the kingdom's primary source of foreign exchange.

What is especially striking about the supplement, given its publication in 1976, is an overt lack of reference to war or rest and recuperation (R&R) as bedrocks for tourism. Instead, the dramatic recent rise in visitors is attributed to Thailand's unmissable "natural attractions." The text of the supplement stresses the necessity of preserving these attractions (which include not only geographic features but also Siamese rituals and lifeways) in the face of a hungry modernity, that familiar custodial trope of development. In discussing all of this, "Thailand's Big Plan" goes out of its way to avoid mentioning the origins of global interest in traveling to Thailand: Cold War Orientalism spurred first by geopolitical paranoia and then by war.

The TOT/Tourist Authority of Thailand (TAT) headquarters has a free library full of agency documents dating back to the 1970s. The building is located, perhaps aptly, on New Phetchaburi Road. Like the *Post*'s tourism supplement, nothing in the TOT/TAT library refers to R&R, or to soldiers (or to Maurice Rocco, as it happens!). In the library's archived materials, graphs showing an exponential spike in tourism in the mid-1960s are presented without explanation, as if it were all a coincidence. Meanwhile, lengthy bound books printed in 1977 describe plans for developing provincial cities like Korat and Pattaya, including the placing of water pipes and waste management systems, envisioning decades of eager vacationers to come. It is never mentioned that such places had only recently been the sites of American air bases—their original touristic context. War and its attendant industries, particularly nightlife, created a template for decades of subsequent tourism. Even before the final American withdrawal in 1976, the TAT was developing and refining this template. In the process, the intimate history of Thai-American wartime entanglement was already being rendered opaque, as—too often still today—it remains.

Bygone worlds persist. To be *farang* now is to move among the ghosts of a neocolonial past, a long, dialectical encounter between souls, the one that Maurice Rocco spent twelve years mediating. These ghosts continue to haunt the present, still awaiting our acknowledgment.

Notes

INTRODUCTION: ACKNOWLEDGMENTS

1. Alex Serra, "Alex Serra's Night Spot," *Star* (Hong Kong), September 19, 1965.

2. Mongkorn Pikaew, interview with the author, March 26, 2020. Translated by the author from the original Thai; unless otherwise noted, all translations are by the author.

3. Camus, *Travels in the Americas*, 41.

4. Pitchaya, *Bangkok Wakes to Rain*, 21.

5. Chen, *Asia as Method*; Westad, *Global Cold War*.

6. Olson, "Thai Cremation Volumes." Funeral books were initially limited to Siamese elites, who in the late nineteenth century had access to printing presses, which suggested a degree of proximity to western modernity. Decades later, after funeral books had grown more accessible to common Siamese, the books became a common type of funerary gift.

7. Haraway, *Staying with the Trouble*.

8. Brooks, *Liner Notes for the Revolution*, 263.

9. Van Esterik, *Materializing Thailand*, 4.

10. Bourdaghs, Iovene, and Mason, *Sound Alignments*, is a recent collection with a similar premise at the scale of Asia more broadly.

11. Subcommittee on US Security Agreements and Commitments Abroad, *Thailand, Laos, Cambodia, and Vietnam.*

12. *Political Situation in Thailand: Hearing Before the House Subcomm. on Asian and Pacific Affairs of the Comm. on Foreign Affairs*, 93rd Cong. 55 (1973).

13. Lowe, *Intimacies of Four Continents*, 18.

14. Herzfeld, *Cultural Intimacy*.

15. Berlant, "Intimacy."

16. Wilson, *Intimate Economies of Bangkok*. See also Povinelli, *Empire of Love*.

17. Fineman, *Special Relationship*.

18. Anderson, "Withdrawal Symptoms."

19. Kurlantzick, *Ideal Man*, 46.

20. Klein, *Cold War Orientalism*.

21. This approach echoes that used in Lowe, *Intimacies of Four Continents*; Miller and Del Casino, "Spectacle, Tourism, and the Performance of Everyday Geopolitics"; Mostafanezhad and Norum, "Towards a Geopolitics of Tourism"; and Boczar, *American Brothel*. Boczar suggests, e.g., that "urban development in South Vietnam was directly linked to the rise of intercultural intimate encounters" (60).

22. "Interview with Arthur Wiknik," November 11, 2008, Vietnam Center and Archive, oh0650, Arthur Wiknik Collection, Texas Tech University, Lubbock.

23. Among these are Wilson, *Intimate Economies of Bangkok*; Phillips, *Thailand in the Cold War*, and Sudina, "Domino by Design." The journalist and fiction writer Rong Wongsawan, writing in Thai, covered similar terrain over the course of his prodigious and unique literary career. Wilson's research was conducted years after the war in Vietnam, but she takes that conflict and its effects on Thailand as a point of departure for a discussion of "intimate economies," wherein Thailand began to sell not just goods and services but intimate experiences. The marketing of intimate experience has characterized the country's tourist economy ever since. Rong, with the help of his wife, Sumalee, who conducted the interviews used in his books, wrote in a mixed journalistic-fictional style about the lives and motivations of sex workers, soldiers, and nightlife laborers during the war.

24. Pratt, "Arts of the Contact Zone."

25. On this point, e.g., see Herzfeld, "Silence, Submission, and Subversion"; and Taylor, *Archive and the Repertoire*.

26. Hanif Abdurraqib, "The Art of Disappearance," *New York Times*, August 11, 2022.

27. Brooks, *Liner Notes for the Revolution*, 266.

28. Robinson, *Hungry Listening*.

29. "Booklet—Bangkok After Dark," November 1968, Vietnam Center and Archive, box 3, folder 17, 22920317001, Larry Woodson Collection, Texas Tech University, Lubbock.

30. Larson, "Laid Open," 222.

31. Keeling, "Looking for M—," 576.

32. Larson, "Laid Open," 223.

33. Sudina, "Domino by Design," 122.

34. Wilson, *Intimate Economies of Bangkok*, 16.

35. Mao and Ahmed, *Culture, Migration, and Health Communication in a Global Context*; Maher and Lafferty, "White Migrant Masculinities in Thailand and the Paradoxes of Western Privilege."

36. Stoler, *Along the Archival Grain*.

37. Von Eschen, *Satchmo Blows Up the World*, 15.

38. The US government has committed almost no resources to reparations or acknowledgment of its actions during the war in Vietnam. Meanwhile the health effects of cancerous herbicides have been continually denied, especially through restrictions on journalism. Some American veterans have spent their lives seeking benefits from the US government to compensate for lifelong ill health or their children's birth defects, including from dioxin exposure. In many cases, widows have taken up the struggle after their partners' deaths. I wish to acknowledge Sandy from the VFW, mentioned earlier, in

this regard. Southeast Asian victims of wartime atrocities have received even less, as Viet Thanh Nguyen reminds us. And much remains unacknowledged still. Notably, the National Archives and Records Administration has not yet declassified all of its "Vietnam War" materials. Accessing certain records can entail lengthy Freedom of Information Act petitions (sometimes with multiyear waits), which may or may not be approved in the end, depending on sensitivity. Infamous as it is, and despite enormous discussion and analysis, the American war in Vietnam remains difficult to understand thoroughly.

39. Chen, *Asia as Method*, 159.

40. Janit, "(Ir)resistably Modern."

41. Ruth, *In Buddha's Company*.

42. Mignolo, "Coloniality of Power and De-colonial Thinking."

CHAPTER I. ROCCO BLUES

1. A. Kelley, "Revolution in the Atmosphere."

2. Ashe, "'Hair Drama' on the Cover of 'Vibe' Magazine."

3. Clifford-Napoleone, *Queering Kansas City Jazz*; Tucker, *Swing Shift*; Stephens, *Rocking the Closet*.

4. See Tucker, "When Did Jazz Go Straight?," for a discussion of this phenomenon.

5. McGinley, *Staging the Blues*, 19.

6. Wald, *Shout, Sister, Shout!*

7. Wald, *Shout, Sister, Shout!*, 73.

8. Walser, *Running with the Devil*, 42.

9. Southern, *Music of Black Americans*, 315.

10. On Soundies, including their recording process, see Eyman, *Speed of Sound*; MacGillivray and Okuda, *Soundies Book*; and Delson, *Soundies and the Changing Image of Black Americans on Screen*.

11. It is uncertain whether the lyrics were first adapted in this fashion by Rocco or by Maxine Sullivan, who also recorded a deathless version of "Molly Malone" in 1940. Rocco's and Sullivan's respective versions were released within a few months of each other, his on Decca and hers on Columbia Records.

12. LeBlanc and Eagle, *Blues*, 81.

13. I have found no evidence attesting to the enslavement of any members of the Rockhold family in these years, but it is possible that some were enslaved, given the inhuman conditions under slavery as an institution and its horrific treatment not only of individuals but also of families.

14. "Special Schedule—Surviving Soldiers, Sailors, and Marines, and Widows," Minor Civil Division, Oxford, Ohio, S.D. 3, E.D. 232 (1890), 2.

15. Ohmer Rockhold, "A Musical Family," *Oxford (OH) Press*, March 31, 1938.

16. Eileen Southern responds to Booker T. Washington's shock at seeing poor former slaves spend their money on organs by explaining that musical competence was an important symbol of independence for Black people in the early twentieth century. According to Southern, for this reason Black parents considered it vital to give their children a musical education. Southern, *Music of Black Americans*, 315.

17. Rodabaugh, "My Long and Rewarding Acquaintanceship with the Great Edward Kennedy." The year 1934 is based on Rodabaugh erroneously asserting that Rocco was born in 1917, rather than 1915, which is the correct year. Rocco therefore would have been nineteen, not seventeen, during the summer that Rodabaugh describes.

18. Rodabaugh, "My Long and Rewarding Acquaintanceship with the Great Edward Kennedy," 3–4. The same telegram was reported in the *Oxford Free Press* on September 26, 1935, as having been sent the previous day by Ellington himself and having offered Maurice "a position as pianist with [Ellington's] organization."

19. Trouillot, *Silencing the Past*.

20. Some among many possible examples of this point may be found in Hartman, *Wayward Lives, Beautiful Experiments*, 77–79; Goldschmitt, *Bossa Mundo*, 135–36; and Ochoa Gautier, *Aurality*, 47.

21. Ellington, *Music Is My Mistress*, 383.

22. By the early 1930s, the "RKO theater circuit" referred to theaters that showed Hollywood films rather than staging live performances. It is unclear therefore why Ellington would have invited Rocco on these terms, and Rodabaugh's memory of this detail cannot be taken at face value. An extensive search of the Duke Ellington Collection, as well as the Ruth Ellington Collection of Duke Ellington Materials, both at the Smithsonian Institution, has yielded no evidence of any financial relationship between Ellington and Rocco.

23. Ennis Miller, interview with the author, May 2, 2019.

24. "Maurice Rockhold Booked by RKO, to Make Movies," *Oxford (OH) Free Press*, December 12, 1935.

25. Many clubs featuring Black performers, including the original Cotton Club, possibly Rocco's first performing venue in the city, moved from Harlem to Midtown after the Harlem race riots of 1935.

26. *Brooklyn (NY) Daily Eagle*, August 21, 1936.

27. Musse, Gaines, and Bowser, *Oscar Micheaux and His Circle*; McGilligan, *Oscar Micheaux*; Bowser and Spence, *Writing Himself into History*.

28. Trenka, *Jumping the Color Line*, 7. Trenka analyzes the very same scene from *Vogues of 1938*, though she notes that this scene is unusually self-aware and arguably even critical of the commodification of Black performers.

29. Chauncey, *Gay New York*.

30. Heap, *Slumming*, 253.

31. Driggs and Lewine, *Black Beauty, White Heat*, 83.

32. Clifford-Napoleone, *Queering Kansas City Jazz*. Although I have found no evidence that Rocco performed in Kansas City, he did play with many musicians who were regulars there, including Mary Lou Williams.

33. Hartman, *Wayward Lives, Beautiful Experiments*, 200.

34. Chauncey, *Gay New York*, 251.

35. Garber, "Spectacle in Color."

36. Heap, *Slumming*, 254.

37. His original compositions were "Rocco's Boogie Woogie," "Rocco Blues," "Hold Me Baby" (cowriter), and "Tonky Blues," along with a number of covers or new arrangements

of existing songs, including the Broadway pieces "Donkey Serenade," "Java Jive," and "Tea for Two," jazz standards like Joe Sullivan's "Little Rock Getaway," and the novelty song "How Come You Do Me Like You Do?"

38. "Record Reviews," *Metronome*, July 1945.

39. Ramsey, *Amazing Bud Powell*, 88.

40. Driggs and Lewine, *Black Beauty, White Heat*, 197.

41. Ortner, "Is Female to Male as Nature Is to Culture?"; Amico, "Digital Voices, Other Rooms."

42. Provenzano, "Emotional Signals."

43. Feather, *Encyclopedia of Jazz*, 399. Feather does not list his criteria for ranking skill in jazz explicitly. But his language often connects gender with particular, essentialized aptitudes. For example, he describes Sister Rosetta Tharpe as having a "magnificent passion and folk quality" without mentioning her technique or ability otherwise (440). Many women musicians are said by Feather to play pop or rock rather than jazz. Male musicians Feather dislikes are dismissed with reference to femininity, such as Chet Baker, whom Feather calls "weak-voiced but appealing to feminine audiences" (109). Hazel Scott's entry begins, "Mother, multi-instrumentalist." In many moments, Feather's volume suggests a hierarchy of excellence in jazz that prioritizes improvisation, composition, and certain kinds of technical mastery, which are coded as not only male but also masculine. The kind of stagecraft at which Rocco excelled is low in Feather's hierarchy.

44. McGinley, *Staging the Blues*, 9.

45. Kerman, "How We Got Into Analysis, and How to Get Out."

46. Lewis, "Improvised Music after 1950." Lewis makes this point with regard to bebop.

47. Barg, "Queer Encounters in the Music of Billy Strayhorn."

48. *Pittsburgh (PA) Courier*, September 18, 1937.

49. *New York Post*, August 28, 1943.

50. "AFRS Jubilee," December 20, 1943. [Radio program]. Retrieved from https://archive.org/details/AfrsJubilee/1943-12-20-AFRS-Jubilee-057-Cee-Pee-Johnson-Orch-Ida-James-Maurice-Rocco-Sir-Lancelot.mp3.

51. *Pittsburgh (PA) Courier*, September 18, 1937.

52. *Oxford (OH) Free Press*, September 26, 1935.

53. "Rockhold Makes Radio Debut," *Hamilton (OH) Evening Journal*, December 12, 1932.

54. John Tennison, interview with the author, June 6, 2019.

55. "Barry Gray's Nightclub—Featuring Doris Day (and Others)," WOR (New York), February 5, 1946, Gordon Skene Sound Collection; retrieved from Past Daily: A Sound Archive of News, History, Music, https://pastdaily.com/2019/05/13/doris-day-words-and-music-1946-barry-grays-nightclub-past-daily-pop-chronicles-tribute-edition/.

56. *Star-Spangled Revue* (TV), April 9, 1955; retrieved from Internet Archive, https://archive.org/details/starspangledrevue.

57. Rafael Ortiz, interview with the author by email, May 22, 2019.

58. Aside from Rocco, the only other clear candidate is Harry "The Hipster" Gibson, a novelty pianist whose career was more or less contemporaneous with Rocco's but who

was substantially less well known and was not widely identified in the press with the technique of standing. Other boogie-woogie pianists of the 1930s, such as Gene Rodgers, sometimes stood for a few seconds at a time but not for the entire duration of their acts. Albert Ammons and Pete Johnson, electric performers though they were, did not play standing up. Hazel Scott, a Rocco contemporary, had a different remarkable talent: playing two pianos at once. But like all other boogie-woogie pianists other than Rocco, she sat when she played. Duke Ellington stands in one of his own Soundies, for the song "Hot Chocolate," released in 1941, though with little choreography or other expressive bodily movement. And by the time of Ellington's Soundie, Rocco was already firmly established as the foremost practitioner of standing at the instrument, and Ellington never made a habit of standing. I thank film critic Manohla Dargis for pointing me to the Ellington example in private conversation.

59. Steptoe, "Big Mama Thornton, Little Richard, and the Queer Roots of Rock 'n' Roll."

60. *Billboard*, February 17, 1945; quoted in Marv Goldberg, "The Loumell Morgan Trio," 2018, www.uncamarvy.com/LoumellMorganTrio/loumell.html.

61. "After Dark," *Detroit (MI) Free Press*, December 9, 1949.

62. "House Reviews," *Variety*, March 20, 1946.

63. "In Dancing Spirits, Jarrett Improvises On the Keyboard," *New York Times*, March 4, 1975.

64. Whitney Balliett, "A Quality That Lets You In," *New Yorker*, December 30, 1973.

65. Marc Myers, "Richard, the First," *Wall Street Journal*, August 10, 2010.

66. Nicholas, "Gaydar"; Rodríguez, *Sexual Futures, Queer Gestures, and Other Latina Longings*.

67. Chauncey, *Gay New York*, 54–55.

68. Chauncey, *Gay New York*, 188.

69. Graham Reid, "Maurice Rocco: Darktown Strutters Ball (1945)," Elsewhere (blog), January 23, 2013, https://www.elsewhere.co.nz/fromthevaults/5430/maurice-rocco -darktown-strutters-ball-1945/.

70. Stephens, *Rocking the Closet*, 80.

71. Marc Myers, "Richard, the First," *Wall Street Journal*, August 10, 2010.

72. Stephens, *Rocking the Closet*, 80.

73. A. Kelley, "Swing Half-Breed."

74. Robin Rodabaugh, interview with the author, June 10, 2019.

75. Mahon, *Black Diamond Queens*. Mahon's sweeping history of the structures of influence/marginalization of Black women artists in the American music industry is instructive for understanding Lewis's reliance on the innovations of Rocco and other Black performers.

76. Louis Rodabaugh helpfully notes one distinction between Rocco and Lewis: Rocco's sweeping runs "were not simple glissandos (a la the much later Jerry Lee Lewis), but were actually complex broken chords"; L. Rodabaugh, "My Long and Rewarding Acquaintanceship with the Great Edward Kennedy," 3. The pieces Rocco played were significantly more complex than Lewis's, and onstage Rocco complemented this musical complexity with difficult physical maneuvers, including tap dancing and other tightly choreographed dance steps, spins, and percussive uses of the body of the piano.

Lewis never approached this level of craft or complexity in either his pianism or his choreography.

77. Hartman, *Wayward Lives, Beautiful Experiments*, 299.

78. "Mama Didn't Object, so Rocco Went to Town," *Afro-American* (Baltimore), January 29, 1944.

79. "Mama Didn't Object, so Rocco Went to Town," *Afro-American* (Baltimore), January 29, 1944.

80. "Vaudeville Reviews," *Billboard*, January 15, 1944.

81. *It's Time to Smile* (radio), June 7, 1944. See "The War Episode 204: It's Time to Smile with Maurice Rocco," YouTube, https://www.youtube.com/watch?v=7LtieUJ9zLM&list=PLDFIOdWlnzL-F4BZrernrX_bX33KtwAXt&index=1.

82. "Rocco Stomped Her, Says Wife in Separation Suit," *Afro-American* (Baltimore), October 26, 1946; "'Maurice Beat Me—I Screamed for Mercy' Says Mrs. Rocco," *People's Voice* (New York), May 10, 1947.

83. "'Maurice Beat Me—I Screamed for Mercy' Says Mrs. Rocco."

84. Treitler, *Ethnic Project*.

85. "Chi Lounges Slow Booking; Await Better Conditions," *Billboard*, February 3, 1945.

86. "Top 'Name' Talent Nudging Out the Lesser Knowns in Loew 1-Nighters," *Variety*, July 3, 1946.

87. Birnbaum, *Before Elvis*, 122.

88. "Broadway Newsreel," *Film Bulletin*, October 11, 1946.

89. Ramsey, *Amazing Bud Powell*.

90. Ramsey, *Amazing Bud Powell*, 18.

91. Szwed, "Musical Style and Racial Conflict."

92. Gioia, *History of Jazz*, 235.

93. "Racial Discrimination Suits vs Panama Clubs Block Use of U.S. Negro Acts," *Variety*, December 26, 1945.

CHAPTER 2. HEART OF NIGHTLIFE, ARTERY OF WAR

1. Fineman, *Special Relationship*, 32.

2. Thak, *Thailand*, 150.

3. For further detail on the silk trade under a global gaze, see Dalferro, "Shimmering Surfaces."

4. For exemplary works that deal with state-level engagements during this period, see Fineman, *Special Relationship*; Thak, *Thailand*; Wiwat and Ramsay, *U.S.-Thailand Relations*; Charnvit, ประวัติการเมืองไทย-สยาม พ.ศ. *2475–2500* [Political history of Thailand-Siam, 1932–1957]; and Baker and Pasuk, *History of Thailand*.

5. Massey, *Spatial Divisions of Labour*, offers one general theory of the social reproduction of space. In Thai studies, Askew, *Bangkok*, uses a human geographical approach to analyze space in Bangkok specifically.

6. Askew, *Bangkok*, 25. Thailand (Siam) experienced a number of cosmopolitan phases in the prior decades and centuries, although for the most part the kingdom had

previously looked to China as a regional center of political and economic gravity, while relying on immigrant Chinese labor for its own internal development. But by the mid-nineteenth century, particularly under the modernizing programs of King Rama IV, Siam moved out of China's orbit and into that of England, France, and other western nations. The sway of these nations over Siam/Thailand since the 1800s has been widely described by historians as neocolonial or semicolonial, even without formal colonization. The American era of the mid-twentieth century was in many ways the culmination—as well as the final chapter—of a century-long historical phase during which Chinese influence became less decisive than Euro-American influence.

7. Jim Thompson is far better known today than Krull. Especially because the silk business he founded remains globally successful and because his ornate home in Bangkok is now a popular tourist site, his life has been the subject of multiple biographies. Thompson disappeared in the Malaysian jungle in 1967. To this day rumors persist about his covert role as a spy, as well as the possibility that he absconded with a lover. Thompson is not extensively discussed in this book because he had little known connection to the Bamboo Bar, or to music and nightlife otherwise.

8. The year 1946 was also when the film *Anna and the King of Siam* was released. This film, as well as the subsequent Broadway play (1951) and film version (1956) titled *The King and I*, point toward an emerging awareness of Thailand among American bourgeois consumers at the same moment that the US government and private entrepreneurs were also investing in the country. Phillips, *Thailand in the Cold War*, describes the role of both play and film in the growing American vogue for all things Thai around 1950.

9. Krull and Melchers, *Bangkok*, 21.

10. Krull and Melchers, *Bangkok*, 11.

11. Phillips argues that in the early part of the Cold War there were a number of American and European expatriate developers operating in Thailand according to a similar ethic. He writes that "Jim Thompson's house sat squarely at the center of a narrative in which Thai traditions needed to be protected, despite the incorporation of Western lifestyle needs and economic systems; a story that resonated with the idea that a successful, and indeed authentic, Thai modernity could be achieved only under US guidance." Phillips, *Thailand in the Cold War*, 46–48.

12. Krull, *Tales from Siam*, 11.

13. Lair, *Armed with Abundance*, 105.

14. Bishop and Robinson, *Night Market*. The authors find an especially active rhetoric of this kind in eighteenth-century France, including in the writings of Denis Diderot.

15. Loos, "Respectability's Edge."

16. Loos, "Respectability's Edge," 154.

17. Janit, "(Ir)resistably Modern," 130.

18. Phillips, *Thailand in the Cold War*, 156.

19. Bollen, *Touring Variety in the Asia Pacific Region, 1946–1975*, 27.

20. Krull and Melchers, *Bangkok*, 105.

21. "Audio Letter from Major Thomas Sheppard to His Wife," no date, Vietnam Center and Archive, 1705AU1717, Dr. I. Thomas Sheppard Collection, Texas Tech University, Lubbock.

22. Dr. Charles Henn, interview with the author, July 9, 2019. Dr. Henn, who now owns the Atlanta, is the son of the late Max Henn and his wife, who is Thai.

23. Krull and Melchers, *Bangkok*, 138–39.

24. Clarion, *Behind the Glittering Lights of Bordellos and Brothels*, 191.

25. รงค์ [Rong], สัตหีบ [Sattahip], 82.

26. Bernard Trink, "Nite Owl," *Bangkok World*, December 19, 1968.

27. กรมที่ดิน [Bangkok Department of Lands], ระบบค้นหารูปแปลงที่ดิน [System for searching information about areas], accessed July 30, 2019, http://dolwms.dol.go.th /tvwebp/.

28. Michael Montesano, interview with the author, June 15, 2019.

29. Joslin, *Pattaya Beach and Thailand*.

30. Sopranzetti, *Owners of the Map*, also refers to the palimpsestic character of Bangkok's development—an apt metaphor.

31. Porphant, "Vietnam War and Tourism in Bangkok's Development, 1960–70."

32. Ahamed-Broadhurst, "Understanding Canals in Bangkok Using Historic Maps and GIS."

33. USOM was later housed under the US Agency for International Development (USAID).

34. US Operations Mission Thailand, *Thai-American Economic and Technical Cooperation*, January 1961, p. 2, Thailand Information Center, Chulalongkorn University, Bangkok.

35. Randolph, *United States and Thailand Alliance Dynamics, 1950–1985*, 22.

36. International Cooperation Administration, Office of Finance, Budgets, and Accounts, *USOM Thailand Financial Report*, p. 4, Thailand Information Center, Chulalongkorn University, Bangkok.

37. US Operations Mission Thailand, *Thai-American Economic and Technical Cooperation*, p. 3.

38. "Lomsak-Saraburi Highway," American Embassy, Bangkok, telegram to US Secretary of State, January 20, 1967, National Archives and Records Administration, College Park, Maryland.

39. "Ghost Town, but Roads Are Real," *Bangkok Post*, January 31, 1971.

40. Surachat, "United States Foreign Policy and Thai Military Rule, 1947–77," 139.

41. International Cooperation Administration, Office of Finance, Budgets, and Accounts, *USOM Thailand Financial Report*, p. 7, Thailand Information Center, Chulalongkorn University, Bangkok.

42. รงค์ [Rong], สัตหีบ [Sattahip], 32.

43. The demographics of that area were not well documented at that time. But William Skinner, drawing on census records, notes that Bangkok's central business area (then the area along Charoenkrung Road near the river) was majority ethnic Chinese (almost 80 percent), with a lower but still significant presence of ethnic Chinese in nearby areas (about 45 percent), which likely would have included the area of the New Phetchaburi extension. Skinner, *Chinese Society in Thailand*, 206.

44. Skinner, *Chinese Society in Thailand*, 164.

45. Chua, "City and the City."

46. Wasana, *Crown and the Capitalists*, 140.

47. Fineman, *Special Relationship*, 254–55.

48. Fineman, *Special Relationship*, 76. The Thai government had opposed communism since at least the early 1930s, when strikes by Chinese laborers were met with state violence and repression of political collectivism. In other words, communism and Chineseness were to some degree linked in the minds of conservative Thai nationalists. Still, by the 1950s the Thai state's suspicion of ethnic Chinese was wrapped up in all manner of racist ideas, frequently expressed in ways that overtly paralleled historical anti-Semitism, while fear of communism remained the primary engine of American policy.

49. "Monthly Report," International Cooperation Administration, November 1958: 20.

50. Petipong Pungbun Na Ayudhya, interview with the author, July 9, 2019.

51. Fineman, *Special Relationship*, 99.

52. "Letter from Dr. Thomas E. Naughton," March 11, 1960, Thai Govt Comments Mar 1960, folder Transportation-Highways 7-1-59 to 6-30-60, RG 469 Entry UD 1383, Thailand box 162, National Archives and Records Administration, College Park, Maryland.

53. Klein, *Cold War Orientalism*, 13.

54. Radom, "Street Administration in the Bangkok Metropolitan Area," 28.

55. Radom, "Street Administration in the Bangkok Metropolitan Area," 61.

56. Klein, *Cold War Orientalism*, 13.

57. Litchfield, Whiting, Bowne, and Associates, *Greater Bangkok Plan, 2533*.

58. Askew, *Bangkok*, 52; US Operations Mission Program Office, Bangkok, *Summary of US Aid to Thailand and Related Statistical Data*, October 13, 1965, Thailand Information Center, Chulalongkorn University, Bangkok.

59. Sopranzetti, *Owners of the Map*, 36; Askew, *Bangkok*.

60. Sopranzetti, *Owners of the Map*, 30.

61. Chua, *Bangkok Utopia*, 192.

62. Phimmasone, "Thai Hearts and Minds," 75.

63. Porphant, "Vietnam War and Tourism in Bangkok's Development, 1960–70."

64. "Thailand's Big Plan for Developing Tourism," *Bangkok Post*, March 29, 1976.

65. I close this chapter with a brief professional acknowledgment. The new spaces created amid Sarit's reforms afforded more than tourism, more than music, and more than war. *Farang* privilege in conducting intellectual labor—the privilege that underwrites this book—was formed in these spaces as well. As Michael Herzfeld notes, "The discipline of social and cultural anthropology emerged from the ferment of Western European world domination as instrument and expression of the colonial project" (Herzfeld, "Absent Presence," 899). For Herzfeld, anthropological scholarship still bears the imprint of its own "cryptocolonial" origins. Anthropologies and musical studies of Southeast Asia took hold in the same years that the Bamboo Bar was designed and New Phetchaburi Road was built. Anthropologist Clifford Geertz first arrived in Indonesia in 1952, on a grant from the Ford Foundation (Geertz, *Development of the Javanese Economy*). Ethnomusicologist Mantle Hood created the first Indonesian gamelan ensemble in the United States in 1958. Benedict Anderson began studying Indonesian culture in 1958 at the Southeast Asia Program at Cornell, which itself was established in 1950. Wisconsin's Center for Southeast Asian Studies dates to the early 1950s. Michigan State University

not only housed Southeast Asian studies on its own campus but also had a significant hand in the development of the Thai education system. ("Letter to Secretary of State Dean Rusk from Michigan State University president John A. Hannah," March 29, 1968, National Archives and Records Administration, College Park, Maryland). In other words, it was not only the military and CIA that benefited from the American presence in Southeast Asia. University scholars likewise availed themselves of the money and infrastructure that appeared in the region in the 1950s. Just as the experience of GIs in Thailand was essentially touristic, *farang* ethnographers and journalists from the West have moved along tracks of opportunity that preceded their arrival. Imperialism and scholarship have often moved in parallel.

CHAPTER 3. "WHAT EVER HAPPENED TO MAURICE ROCCO?"

1. Mahon, *Black Diamond Queens*, 55.

2. Ed Sullivan, "O'Dwyerville on the Subway," *Citizen-News* (Hollywood, CA), April 13, 1950.

3. "Pianist Cleared on Check Charge," *Daily News* (NY), July 28, 1950.

4. *St. Louis Post-Dispatch*, March 22, 1956.

5. *Cincinnati Enquirer*, July 24, 1951.

6. Rodabaugh, "My Long and Rewarding Acquaintanceship with the Great Edward Kennedy," 13.

7. Ted Hallock, "Timid Op, Too Busy WGN Merge to Oust Burkhart," *DownBeat*, May 19, 1948.

8. "Unique U.S. Revue to Open in Sydney," *Sydney Morning Herald*, June 12, 1955.

9. Betty Frazier, interview with the author, July 5, 2021.

10. "Rocco Wants a Ranch," *Sydney Morning Herald*, July 3, 1955.

11. "What a Wonderful Town for Piano Tuners," *Cue: The Weekly Magazine of New York Life*, 1955.

12. Betty Frazier, interview with the author, July 5, 2021.

13. James Baldwin, "This Morning, This Evening, So Soon," *Atlantic*, September 1, 1960.

14. George Cole, "Miles Davis: A Love Affair with Paris," *Guardian*, December 10, 2009.

15. Fleming, *Resurrecting Slavery*. Baldwin made a similar point during a National Press Club speech in 1986.

16. Driggs and Lewine, *Black Beauty, White Heat*, 242.

17. Jones, *Yellow Music*.

18. Wright, *Color Curtain*, 438.

19. Wright, *Color Curtain*, 439.

20. Izzy Rowe, "Izzy Rowe's Notebook," *Pittsburgh Courier*, October 29, 1955.

21. Izzy Rowe, "Izzy Rowe's Notebook," *Pittsburgh Courier*, March 23, 1957.

22. "Pianist Maurice Rocco Jailed on Check Charge," *Jet*, January 9, 1958.

23. "The Night Spots," *St. Louis Post-Dispatch*, June 22, 1958.

24. "Beauty Not Enough to Keep Spouse," *Dayton (OH) Daily News*, July 6, 1958.

25. "เอกสารถูกปลวกทำลาย" [Document regarding termite damage], 2530 [1987], Office of the Prime Minister of Thailand, accessed June 17, 2021, http://www.oic.go .th/FILEWEB/CABINFOCENTEROPM/DRAWER01/GENERAL/DATA0002 /00002592.PDF.

26. Bille, Hastrup, and Sørensen, *Anthropology of Absence*, 4.

27. Taylor, *Archive and the Repertoire*, 34.

28. Haberkorn, *In Plain Sight*.

29. Davorn, "US Secret War in Laos."

30. Stoler, *Along the Archival Grain*, 24.

31. Hartman, *Lose Your Mother*; Hartman, *Wayward Lives, Beautiful Experiments*.

32. Herzfeld, "Silence, Submission, and Subversion," 82.

33. Larson, "Laid Open," 229.

34. Simpson, "Ethnographic Refusal." See also Simpson, *Mohawk Interruptus*.

35. "Louis Rodabaugh on Jazz Musician Maurice Rocco," February 1980, audio tape, Miami University Oral History Collection, Oxford, OH.

36. "Louis Rodabaugh on Jazz Musician Maurice Rocco."

37. "Louis Rodabaugh on Jazz Musician Maurice Rocco."

38. Hartman, *Wayward Lives, Beautiful Experiments*, 46.

39. Charles Govey, "Bill Kenny's Rich Singing," *New Musical Express*, May 8, 1959.

40. "Reizvoller Heiri-Ball," *Die Tat (Switzerland)*, December 7, 1959.

41. The office of the Swiss banking ombudsman will not permit searches for dormant assets in Swiss banks except on behalf of relatives or legal representatives of the deceased. Rocco has neither, so information regarding any assets he might have held will remain private until sixty years after their abandonment, perhaps by 2025. Future readers might check this. Rocco's associate from Oxford, Ohio, Dr. Charles Teckman told me in 2019 that he tried to find information about Rocco's home ownership or other records when he went to Switzerland in person in the 1980s but to no avail.

42. "Jazz-pianist Maurice Rocco STAAT achter zijn piano," *De Telegraaf* (Amsterdam), May 14, 1960. Translated by Dr. Meredith Schweig, Emory University.

CHAPTER 4. INTIMATE NEOCOLONIAL NIGHTLIFE

1. Pattana, "Ambiguous Intimacy."

2. Pitchaya, *Bangkok Wakes to Rain*, 22.

3. "Reciprocal Club Focus: Royal Varuna Yacht Club," *Rag* (newsletter of the US Army and Navy), Winter 2018.

4. Baker and Pasuk, *History of Thailand*, 90.

5. Pattana, "Ambiguous Intimacy," 58.

6. Chakrabarty, "Foreword," xii.

7. "Interview with Bill McCollum," December 11, 2002, Vietnam Center and Archive, oho248, Mr. Bill McCollum Collection, Texas Tech University, Lubbock.

8. "Interview with Sandra McRainey," June 13, 2001, Vietnam Center and Archive, oho181, Sandra McRainey Collection, Texas Tech University, Lubbock.

9. Phillips, *Thailand in the Cold War*, 151.

10. "Protect the Tourist," *Bangkok Post*, December 17, 1964.

11. Brock and Thistlethwaite, *Casting Stones*, 116.

12. Tourist Authority of Thailand, *Status Report on the Tourism Industry of Thailand: Policy, Budget, and Plans*, 1978, Tourist Authority of Thailand Library, Bangkok.

13. Porphant, "Vietnam War and Tourism in Bangkok's Development, 1960–70."

14. Kislenko, "Not So Silent Partner."

15. Surachat, "United States Foreign Policy and Thai Military Rule, 1947–77," 153.

16. รงค์ [Rong], สัตหีบ [Sattahip], 34.

17. Surachat, "United States Foreign Policy and Thai Military Rule, 1947–77," 155.

18. "Thailand: The New Center of Gravity in Southeast Asia," *Air Force*, April 1973.

19. "Interview with LT COL Jerry A. Singleton" (US Air Force Academy), October 30, 1992, Vietnam Center and Archive, box 1, folder 26, 0050126001, Air Force POW Oral History Collection, Texas Tech University, Lubbock.

20. Lair, *Armed with Abundance*, 20.

21. "Entertainment Places Act, B.E. 2509."

22. Horn et al., *Americans in Thailand*, 195.

23. "Entertainment Places Act, B.E. 2509."

24. K. Kelley, "Patriarchy, Empire, and Ping Pong Shows."

25. Janit, "(Ir)resistably Modern," 104.

26. Horn et al., *Americans in Thailand*, 185. The act also had a protectionist element; even as it allowed Americans to own businesses, it restricted their right to own land.

27. The 1967 Joint Use and Air Defense Operations Agreement simultaneously gave the United States joint-use rights over air bases.

28. *Hearings Before US Senate Subcomm. on US Security Agreements and Commitments Abroad of the Comm. on Foreign Relations*, 91st Cong. (1969) (statement of Hon. Leonard Unger, Ambassador of the United States to Thailand, United States Security Agreements and Commitments Abroad, Kingdom of Thailand).

29. Randolph, *United States and Thailand Alliance Dynamics, 1950–1985*, 62.

30. "Interview with James Marvin Montgomery," August 12, 1996, The Foreign Affairs Oral History Collection of the Association for Diplomatic Studies and Training, Library of Congress. https://www.loc.gov/item/mfdipbib000826/. Surachat Bamrungsuk ("United States Foreign Policy and Thai Military Rule, 1947–77," 124) similarly notes that "agreements on base rights, in-country personnel, and other matters of a legal nature were reached through a process of 'informal consultation,' generally on a case-by-case basis. Thus there was no piece of paper existing as a legal sanction for the massive US military presence in Thailand, nor was there subsequently any documentary evidence for the deal."

31. Levan, "Curtailing Thailand's Child Prostitution through an International Conscience."

32. The name *Tommie's* is frequently spelled *Tommy's* in secondary sources. However, materials such as booklets and advertisements almost always render the name as *Tommie's*.

33. *Hearings Before US Senate Subcomm. on US Security Agreements and Commitments Abroad of the Comm. on Foreign Relations*, 91st Cong. (1969) (statement of Hon. Leonard

Unger, Ambassador of the United States to Thailand, United States Security Agreements and Commitments Abroad, Kingdom of Thailand).

34. Dawee had prior experience overseeing a wartime public/private monopoly in the form of the Express Transport Organization, an agency that helped the American military move materials around Thailand at low costs beginning in the 1950s.

35. Baker and Pasuk, *History of Thailand*, 169.

36. Broman, *Risk Taker, Spy Maker*, 69–70.

37. Surachat, "United States Foreign Policy and Thai Military Rule, 1947–77," 155.

38. "สงครามเวียดนาม สู่ตำนานเมียเช่า เมียฝรั่ง และลูกครึ่งในสังคมไทย" [The Vietnam War and the struggles of *mia chao*, *mia farang*, and half children in Thai society].

39. Harry Rolnick, interview with the author, March 8, 2019.

40. William Warren, "City on the Chao Phya," *Orientations*, March 1972.

41. "Interview with Theodore Acheson," April 28, 2003, Vietnam Center and Archive, oho291, Ted Acheson Collection, Texas Tech University, Lubbock.

42. "Interview with James Marvin Montgomery."

43. Although it is largely outside the scope of this book's focus, widespread violence against Asian and Asian-presenting women persists in the United States, among other places. In cases such as the murder of four massage parlor workers by a male patron in Atlanta in 2021, the presumption of Asian female sexual availability has figured in many instances of anti-Asian violence.

44. Pahole, "Bangkok Is Burning."

45. Saranphon, "Stereotypical Depiction of Women in Thai Films."

46. Van Esterik, *Materializing Thailand*, 6.

47. Dalferro, "Shimmering Surfaces."

48. Pahole, "Bangkok Is Burning," 143.

49. See, e.g., Pilzer, *Hearts of Pine*.

50. Klein, *Cold War Orientalism*.

51. Kislenko, "Not So Silent Partner."

52. Bollen, *Touring Variety in the Asia Pacific Region, 1946–1975*.

53. Thongchai, *Siam Mapped*.

54. The same phenomenon also occurred in the art world. See, e.g., Kowal, *Dancing the World Smaller*.

55. Klein, *Cold War Orientalism*, 23.

56. Bollen, *Touring Variety in the Asia Pacific Region, 1946–1975*, 11.

57. hooks, "Eating the Other."

58. "Interview with Timothy Eby," August 28, 2008, Vietnam Center and Archive, oho630, Timothy Eby Collection, Texas Tech University, Lubbock.

59. Keppy, *Tales of Southeast Asia's Jazz Age*, 33.

60. Sykes, *Musical Gift*.

61. Jaji, *Africa in Stereo*, 90–91.

62. *Bangkok Post*, July 23, 1964.

63. David Streckfuss, "Good Daughters of Isaan," *Isaan Record*, August 23, 2020.

64. See, e.g., Pasuk, *From Peasant Girls to Bangkok Masseuses*; Truong, *Sex, Money, and Morality*; and Enloe, *Bananas, Beaches, and Bases*. Notably, and as Ryan Bishop and Lil-

lian Robinson point out, some scholarship on the Thai economy has ignored sex work as an economic engine. But especially since the 1990s, sex work has become a major topic in scholarship on the Thai economy, as it has long been a major topic in popular literature.

65. Kislenko, "Not So Silent Partner."

66. *Political Situation in Thailand: Hearing Before the House Subcomm. on Asian and Pacific Affairs of the Comm. on Foreign Affairs*, 93rd Cong. 55 (1973).

67. Wilson, *Intimate Economies of Bangkok*, 9.

68. White, *Comforts of Home*.

69. Engels, *Socialism*.

70. On the subject of *mia chao*, see also Bishop and Robinson, *Night Market*; and Mills, *Thai Women in the Global Labor Force*.

71. Patcharin, *Love, Money and Obligation*.

72. Any tape of the show that originally featured the song has been lost.

73. Sudina, "Domino by Design," 109.

74. Streckfuss, "Good Daughters of Isaan," part 7.

75. Karuna Chuangchan, interview with the author and Peter Doolan, July 15, 2019. The conversation has been lightly edited for clarity.

76. Patcharin and Thompson, "Masculinity, Matrilineality and Transnational Marriage."

77. Streckfuss, "Good Daughters of Isaan," part 3.

78. Pahole, "Bangkok Is Burning," 117.

79. "Interview with Sandra McRainey."

80. "Interview with Larry Henry," March 18, 2009, Vietnam Center and Archive, oho681, Mr. Larry Henry Collection, Texas Tech University, Lubbock.

81. "Interview with Charles Lloyd," May 28, 2023, Vietnam Center and Archive, oho305, Charles Lloyd Collection, Texas Tech University, Lubbock.

82. Ochoa Gautier, *Aurality*.

83. "Diary of President Lyndon B. Johnson's Visit to Thailand," October 1966, Vietnam Center and Archive, box 14, folder 7, 0241407009, Larry Berman Collection (Presidential Archives Research), Texas Tech University, Lubbock.

84. "Personal Narrative—Remember When," no date, Vietnam Center and Archive, box 7, folder 63, 23850763001, 35th Infantry Regiment Association Collection, Texas Tech University, Lubbock.

85. A comparable story in American popular music involves the band Butthole Surfers sampling a Thai *luk thung* song originally recorded by the artist Phloen Phromdaen. In the song Phloen repeats the word *khan*, meaning "itch," which the Butthole Surfers heard as a cognate of the misogynist English word *cunt*. The band sampled the word from the original recording, using it to sophomoric effect in their 1987 song "Kuntz."

86. "Personal Narrative—Marine Helo: War Years in U.S. Marine Corps Aviation (Chapters 20–23)—October 1966–January 1967," 1990, Vietnam Center and Archive, box 1, folder 20, 14060120001, David Petteys Collection, Texas Tech University, Lubbock.

87. Klein, *Cold War Orientalism*, 203.

88. "ของฝรั่ง (มะริกัน)," *Siam Rath (Bangkok)*, April 4, 1967.

89. Sudina, "Domino by Design," 24.

90. Notably, the phrase *thai kham angkrit kham* reads grammatically more like English than Thai. In the latter language, the adjectival modifier *thai* would be placed after the noun that it describes. The mixture of Thai words with English grammatical structure further underscores the cultural amalgamation at work in the phenomenon itself.

91. A number of other songs mixed Thai and English even earlier than "Love letter." The Pong Mukda band's "ทีนเอจรำลึก" (Teenage memories), released in 1942, uses the English loanword *teenage* in its Thai title. The earliest example in popular music may be "Jan jem" (Bright moon), recorded by Pratum Nangek Kanasilapasamreng with backing by a group called Khrน̀eang Sน̀aay Farang (the Farang String Band) sometime between the two world wars. "Jan jem" was a government-supported recording meant to demonstrate Siam's ascendant modernity.

92. A 2013 linguistics study drew on 146 code-mixed songs released in a four-year period, attesting to the ubiquity of the phenomenon. Teeratorn and Pattama, "Study of English Code-Mixing and Code-Switching in Thai Pop Songs."

93. See also Thompson, Pattana, and Smutkupt, "Transnational Relationships, Farang-Isaan Couples, and Rural Transformation"; and Sirijit and Angeles, "From Rural Life to Transnational Wife."

94. Asaree Thaitrakulpanich, *Khao Sod (Bangkok),* November 30, 2017.

95. See ทินวัฒน์ [Thinnawat], "'ดิฉัน (เมียฝรั่ง)ไม่ใช่โสเภณี'" ["I (a *farang* wife) am not a whore"]. For the novel, see ผกามาศ [Pakamas], *ดิฉันไม่ใช่โสเภณี* (I am not a whore).

96. Baker and Pasuk, *History of Thailand,* 113. The authors locate one historical instance of language-mixing panic as early as the late 1920s.

97. Ross, *Listen to This.*

98. Parkorn, "Sounding Civilization." Parkorn provides detailed evidence of aural and phonographic encounters between Siamese and European elites in the early twentieth century.

99. "Siam Radio Goes Yankee Style," *Broadcasting,* October 21, 1957.

100. "Proposed Village Radio Plan for Thailand," September 13, 1965, Chief Public Safety Division, US Operations Mission Thailand, National Archives and Records Administration, College Park, Maryland.

101. นพดล ดวงพร [Noppadon Duangporn], 19.

102. Randolph, *United States and Thailand Alliance Dynamics, 1950–1985,* 114.

103. นพดล ดวงพร [Noppadon Duangporn], 28.

104. Garzoli, "Mawlam and Jazz in Intercultural Musical Synthesis," 10.

105. Talusan, *Instruments of Empire.*

106. Schenker, "Empire of Syncopation," 115.

107. "Interview with Theodore Acheson."

108. "Interview with Larry Henry."

109. See, e.g., Kang, "Surfing the Korean Wave"; and De Kosnik, "Perfect Covers."

110. Bollen, *Touring Variety in the Asia Pacific Region, 1946–1975,* 6. The regional migration of artists from the Philippine archipelago and other areas in fact dates back to hundreds of years earlier. Colonialism and imperialism established new routes, but they were not the first historical triggers of Asian musical migration.

111. Talusan, *Instruments of Empire*.

112. Nagel, "Democracy for Whom?"

113. Talusan, *Instruments of Empire*, 54.

114. Schenker, "Circuit Tour of the Globe."

115. Keppy, *Tales of Southeast Asia's Jazz Age*.

116. Jess Jocson, interview with the author, March 12, 2019.

117. Sudina, "Domino by Design," 25.

118. Boczar, *American Brothel*.

119. "สมัยสงครามเวียดนาม อเมริกันมาตั้งฐาน+สร้างสนามบิน อะไรทิ้งไว้ที่อีสานบ้างครับ" (In the Vietnam War era, Americans built bases and airports; What did they leave behind in Isaan?), thread at Pantip, topicstock.pantip.com/wahkor/topicstock/2009/12/X8645769/X8645769.html.

120. Devine, *Decomposed*. Devine's treatment of musical materiality and its waste products, while oriented somewhat differently from this chapter, bears mention as kindred to this discussion.

121. For a discussion of the role of "world music" intermediaries, see Goldschmitt, *Bossa Mundo*, chap. 4 ("Brazilian Music as World Music in the Late 1980s").

122. For two examples of this argument related to case studies in Burma, see Ferguson, "Yesterday Once More"; and MacLachlan, *Burma's Pop Music Industry*.

123. Harry Rolnick, interview with the author, July 8, 2021.

124. Rafael Ortiz, interview with the author, June 1, 2019.

125. Charles Teckman, interview with the author, February 2, 2019.

126. Teckman interview.

CHAPTER 5. RICE OUTSIDE THE FIELD

1. Janit, "(Ir)resistably Modern," 117.

2. สีฟ้า [Si Fa], ข้าวนอกนา (Rice outside the field).

3. hooks, "Eating the Other," 367.

4. Weisman, "Rice outside the Paddy," 52.

5. Napat, "Thailand."

6. Johnson, *Mekong Dreaming*.

7. Weisman, "Rice outside the Paddy," 59.

8. สีฟ้า [Si Fa], ข้าวนอกนา (Rice outside the field).

9. Gerald F. Goodwin, "Black and White in Vietnam," *New York Times*, July 18, 2017.

10. Bradley and Werner, *We Gotta Get Out of This Place*, 202.

11. Goodwin, "Race in the Crucible of War," 106.

12. Terry, *Bloods*, 39.

13. Terry, *Bloods*, 25.

14. Terry, *Bloods*, 164.

15. Malcolm W. Browne, "Sensors Attune U.S. Base in Thailand to Movements on Ho Chi Minh Trail," *New York Times*, October 23, 1972.

16. Mii, interview with the author, July 12, 2019.

17. Chepesiuk, *Sergeant Smack*, 89.

18. กมลธรรม [Kamontam], "ดนตรีแจ๊สในสังคมไทยในยุคเริ่มต้น" [Birth of jazz music in Thai society].

19. Barmé, *Woman, Man, Bangkok*, 37.

20. Chua, "City and the City."

21. Weisman, "Rice outside the Paddy," 59.

22. โบตั๋น [Botan], *ผู้หญิงคนนั้นชื่อบุญรอด* [That woman is called Bunrot], 6.

23. Weisman, "Rice outside the Paddy," 66.

24. Weisman, "Rice outside the Paddy," 68.

25. Newley Purnell, "Images Spark Racism Debate in Thailand," *New Yorker*, October 31, 2013.

26. Stephan Turner, interview with the author, March 15, 2022.

27. "Black Experience in Thailand: Is There Racism in Thailand?" *Minority Nomad* (blog), accessed October 11, 2024, minoritynomad.com/black-experience-thailand-racism-thailand/.

28. Jackson, "Explosion of Thai Identities."

29. Käng, "Conceptualizing Thai Genderscapes." The tension between vernacular and cosmopolitan frameworks for explaining gender and sex can be seen for example in the word *phet* (เพศ), which refers to both gender identity and sexuality without distinguishing clearly between the two concepts. The collapsing of sex and gender into a single word, which has no English equivalent, typifies the difficult fit between conventional Thai and Euro-American structures of identification. This is one of many ambiguities that has characterized intimate neocolonial relationships in Thailand. See, e.g., Nattapol, "Spicy," 26.

30. Tinsley, "Black Atlantic, Queer Atlantic," 211.

31. Bérubé, *My Desire for History*, 128.

32. "Girls Who Like Girls," *Bangkok Post*, April 11, 1976.

33. *Bangkok Post*, April 15, 1976.

34. *Bangkok Post,* March 19, 1976.

35. *Statistical Yearbook Thailand 1965*, 1966, National Statistical Office, Office of the Prime Minister of Thailand.

36. Jackson, "American Death in Bangkok."

37. ฮิมวัง [Himwang], "พระยาอนิรุทธเทวา มหาดเล็ก 'คนโปรด' ในรัชกาลที่ 6 ที่ 'งามเหมือนเทวามาจากสวรรค์' " [Major General Phraya Anirutthewa, royal page: The "pet" of King Rama VI who was "beautiful as an angel from heaven"], *Silpa-Mag*, December 11, 2021, www.silpa-mag.com/history/article_34767.

38. Jackson, "Non-normative Sex/Gender Categories in the Theravada Buddhist Scriptures."

39. Loos, *Subject Siam*.

40. Morris, "Three Sexes and Four Sexualities."

41. Brad the Impala, reply to "Bangkok Scene 25+ Years Ago," Sawatdee Gay Thailand forum, Sawatdee Network, August 18, 2009, 6:37 a.m., sawatdeenetwork.com/v4/showthread.php?9992-Bangkok-scene-25-years-ago/page4.

42. Jackson, *First Queer Voices from Thailand*.

43. Käng, "Conceptualizing Thai Genderscapes."

44. Kanjana, "Dressing Thai," 7; Phillips, *Thailand in the Cold War*, 70–71.

45. Sonthaya Kalasin, interview with the author, June 22, 2022.

46. Morris, "Three Sexes and Four Sexualities," 23.

47. Visisya, "Performing Alterity of Desire," 104.

48. Amporn, Arunrat, and Arratee, "Masculinity for Sale."

49. Jackson, "American Death in Bangkok." Nattapol ("Spicy," 22) similarly offers that in Thailand "what brings an individual's sexual morality into question is deviance from the heteronormative."

50. Jackson, "American Death in Bangkok."

51. Sanders, "Some Say Thailand Is a Gay Paradise."

52. Harry Rolnick, interview with the author, July 8, 2021.

53. Rafael Ortiz, interview with the author, June 1, 2019.

54. Mongkorn Pikaew, interview with the author, March 26, 2020.

55. Pitchaya, *Bangkok Wakes to Rain*, 36.

56. "Business: The Pain of Yankee Going Home," *Time*, January 11, 1971.

57. Quoted in "Thailand in a Changing World," *Indochina Chronicle*, May–June 1975.

58. Surachat, "United States Foreign Policy and Thai Military Rule, 1947–77," 153.

59. "Ghost Town, but Roads Are Real," *Bangkok Post*, January 31, 1971.

60. Darling, "Student Protest and Political Change in Thailand," 7. The author quotes estimates that there were fifteen thousand students at a total of five Thai universities in 1961, which rose to 100,000 students at seventeen universities by 1972. See also Anderson, "Withdrawal Symptoms," 16.

61. Thongchai, *Moments of Silence*.

62. Janit, "(Ir)resistably Modern," 124. Ta Tha-It's given name was Chusak Rasijan.

63. ต๊ะ [Ta], ตะลุยเกย์คลับ [Heading into a gay club].

64. Janit, "(Ir)resistably Modern," 125.

65. Notably, the editor of the magazine that originally ran the "Gay Club" stories was none other than Ajin Banjaporn, the songwriter who composed the classic *thai kham angkrit kham* song จดหมายรักจากเมียเช่า (Love letter from a rented wife), discussed in chapter 4. The exact circulation figures of the magazine are unknown, but it is thought to have been popular with an educated, mainly middle-class readership.

66. Phillips, *Thailand in the Cold War*, 162–63. Phillips notes that the Tourism Organization of Thailand was similarly engaged in the marketing of remote Thai places to middle-class Thais themselves, a decade or so earlier than Ta's stories.

67. Chua, *Bangkok Utopia*, 188.

68. ต๊ะ [Ta], ตะลุยเกย์คลับ [Heading into a gay club].

69. Ortiz, interview, June 1, 2019.

70. Mongkorn, interview, March 26, 2020.

71. Rolnick, interview, July 8, 2021.

72. Charnvit Kasetsiri, interview with the author, July 15, 2019.

73. ต๊ะ [Ta], ตะลุยเกย์คลับ [Heading into a gay club].

74. Rolnick interview.

75. ต๊ะ [Ta], ตะลุยเกย์คลับ [Heading into a gay club].

76. Rolnick interview.

77. "Rocco's Murder: Hunt Continues," *Bangkok Post*, April 9, 1976.

78. *Thai Rath (Bangkok)*, March 26, 1976.

79. Mongkorn interview.

80. Harry Rolnick, interview, July 8, 2021.

81. Harry Rolnick, interview, July 8, 2021.

82. Harry Rolnick, interview, July 8, 2021.

83. The front page of *Thai Rath* on Friday, March 26, 1976, the day Rocco's murder made the papers, showed images of Rocco and the murder investigation in the bottom left-hand corner of the front page, while the banner at the top announced the story. The largest headline on the cover reported that a large bomb had killed nine and injured twenty-six elsewhere in Bangkok the same day, underscoring the widespread violence of the time.

84. *Thai Rath*, March 26, 1976.

85. Klima, *Funeral Casino*.

86. Morris, "Educating Desire," 53.

87. "Rocco's Murder: Hunt Continues."

88. To my knowledge this is the only historical link between Henry Kissinger and jazz.

89. "Louis Rodabaugh on Jazz Musician Maurice Rocco," February 1980, audio tape, Miami University Oral History Collection, Oxford, OH.

"Whitehead" is a misstating of the last name of Charles S. Whitehouse, US ambassador to Thailand at the time of Rocco's murder. I communicated with US senator from Rhode Island Sheldon Whitehouse, Charles's son, who was twenty years old when Rocco died, but he told me that he has no memory of the incident.

CONCLUSION: ACKNOWLEDGING *THÍNG WÁY*

1. Ennis Miller, interview with the author, May 2, 2019.

2. Byrd, "Black Church in Oxford, Ohio."

3. Govier, *Taking Wrongs Seriously*.

4. Quinn, *Politics of Acknowledgement*.

5. Hartman, *Scenes of Subjection*, 36. Glissant. *Caribbean Discourse*.

6. Kidron, "Alterity and the Particular Limits of Universalism"; Dyer, "Sounding the Dead in Cambodia."

7. Pilzer, *Hearts of Pine*, 138.

8. Chen, *Asia as Method*, 200.

Bibliography

ARCHIVES

Foreign Affairs Oral History Collection of the Association for Diplomatic Studies and Training, Library of Congress.

Miami University Oral History Collection, Oxford, Ohio.

National Archives of Thailand, National Library of Thailand, Fine Arts Department, Ministry of Culture, Bangkok.

National Statistics Office, Office of the Prime Minister of Thailand, Bangkok.

Office of the Prime Minister of Thailand, Bangkok.

Thailand Information Center, Chulalongkorn University, Bangkok.

Tourist Authority of Thailand Library, Bangkok.

U.S. National Archives and Records Administration (NARA), College Park, Maryland.

Vietnam Center and Archive, Texas Tech University, Lubbock.

    35th Infantry Regiment Association Collection

    Ted Acheson Collection

    Air Force POW Oral History Collection

    Larry Berman Collection

    Timothy Eby Collection

    Mr. Larry Henry Collection

    Charles Lloyd Collection

    Mr. Bill McCollum Collection

    Sandra McRainey Collection

    David Petteys Collection

    Dr. I. Thomas Shepphard Collection

    Arthur Wiknik Collection

    Larry Woodson Collection

BOOKS, ARTICLES, AND OTHER SOURCES

Ahamed-Broadhurst, Kathleen E. "Understanding Canals in Bangkok Using Historic Maps and GIS." Master's thesis, Harvard University, 2017.

Amico, Stephen. "Digital Voices, Other Rooms: Pussy Riot's Recalcitrant (In)Corporeality." *Popular Music and Society* 39, no. 4 (2016): 423–47.

Amporn Jirattikorn, Arunrat Tangmunkongvorakul, and Arratee Ayuttacorn. "Masculinity for Sale: Shan Migrant Sex Worker Men in Thailand and Questions of Identity." *Men and Masculinities* 25, no. 5 (2022): 782–801.

Anderson, Benedict. "Withdrawal Symptoms: Social and Cultural Aspects of the October 6 Coup." *Bulletin of Concerned Asian Scholars* 9, no. 3 (1977): 13–30.

Ashe, Bertram D. "'Hair Drama' on the Cover of 'Vibe' Magazine." *Race, Gender and Class Journal* 8, no. 3 (2001): 64–77.

Askew, Marc. *Bangkok: Place, Practice and Representation*. New York: Routledge, 2002.

Baker, Chris, and Pasuk Pongpaichat. *A History of Thailand*. Cambridge: Cambridge University Press, 2005.

Barg, Lisa. "Queer Encounters in the Music of Billy Strayhorn." *Journal of the American Musicological Society* 66, no. 3 (2013): 771–824.

Barmé, Scot. *Woman, Man, Bangkok: Love, Sex, and Popular Culture in Thailand*. Bangkok: Silkworm Books, 2006.

Berlant, Lauren. "Intimacy: A Special Issue." *Critical Inquiry* 24, no. 2 (1988): 281–88.

Bérubé, Allan. *My Desire for History: Essays in Gay, Community, and Labor History*. Chapel Hill: University of North Carolina Press, 2011.

Bille, Mikkel, Frida Hastrup, and Tim Flohr Sørensen, eds. *An Anthropology of Absence: Materializations of Transcendence and Loss*. New York: Springer, 2010.

Birnbaum, Larry. *Before Elvis: The Prehistory of Rock 'n' Roll*. Lanham, MD: Scarecrow, 2013.

Bishop, Ryan, and Lillian Robinson. *Night Market: Sexual Cultures and the Thai Economic Miracle*. New York: Routledge, 1998.

Boczar, Amanda. *An American Brothel: Sex and Diplomacy during the Vietnam War*. Ithaca, NY: Cornell University Press, 2022.

Bollen, Joshua. *Touring Variety in the Asia Pacific Region, 1946–1975*. London: Palgrave Macmillan, 2020.

โบตั๋น [Botan]. *ผู้หญิงคนนั้นชื่อบุญรอด* [That woman is called Bunrot]. Bangkok: ชมรมเด็ก, 2524 [1981].

Bourdaghs, Michael K., Paola Iovene, and Kelsey Mason. *Sound Alignments: Popular Music in Asia's Cold Wars*. Durham, NC: Duke University Press, 2021.

Bowser, Pearl, and Louise Spence. *Writing Himself into History: Oscar Micheaux, His Silent Films, and His Audiences*. New Brunswick, NJ: Rutgers University Press, 2000.

Bradley, Doug, and Craig Werner. *We Gotta Get Out of This Place: The Soundtrack of the Vietnam War*. Amherst: University of Massachusetts Press, 2015.

Brock, Rita Nakashima, and Susan Brooks Thistlethwaite. *Casting Stones: Prostitution and Liberation in Asia and the United States*. Minneapolis, MN: Fortress, 1996.

Broman, Barry Michael. *Risk Taker, Spy Maker: Tales of a C.I.A. Case Officer*. Havertown, PA: Casemate, 2020.

Brooks, Daphne. *Liner Notes for the Revolution*. Cambridge, MA: Belknap Press of Harvard University Press, 2021.

Byrd, Terriel. "The Black Church in Oxford, Ohio." Bachelor of Philosophy thesis, Miami University, 1986.

Camus, Albert. *Travels in the Americas: Notes and Impressions of a New World*. Edited by
    Alice Kaplan. Translated by Ryan Bloom. Chicago: University of Chicago Press, 2023.
Chakrabarty, Dipesh. "Foreword: The Names and Repetitions of Postcolonial History." In
    The Ambiguous Allure of the West: Traces of the Colonial in Thailand, edited by Rachel V.
    Harrison and Peter A. Jackson, vii–xviii. Hong Kong: Hong Kong University Press, 2010.
Charnvit Kasetsiri. ประวัติการเมืองไทย-สยาม พ.ศ. *2475–2500* [A political history of
    Thailand-Siam, 1932–1957]. Bangkok: Foundation for the Promotion of Social Sci-
    ences and Humanities Textbooks Projects, 2007.
Chauncey, George. *Gay New York: Gender, Urban Culture, and the Making of the Gay
    World, 1890–1940*. New York: Basic Books, 1994.
Chen, Kuan-Hsing. *Asia as Method: Toward Deimperialization*. Durham, NC: Duke
    University Press, 2010.
Chepesiuk, Ron. *Sergeant Smack: The Legendary Lives and Times of Ike Atkinson, King-
    pin, and His Band of Brothers*. Rock Hill, SC: Strategic Media, 2010.
Chua, Lawrence. *Bangkok Utopia: Modern Architecture and Buddhist Felicities*. Hono-
    lulu: University of Hawaii Press, 2021.
Chua, Lawrence. "The City and the City: Race, Nationalism, and Architecture in Early
    Twentieth-Century Bangkok." *Journal of Urban History* 40, no. 5 (2014): 933–58.
Clarion, Thomas. *Behind the Glittering Lights of Bordellos and Brothels: Thailand*. Vol 1.
    Oklahoma City, OK: Smashwords Editions, 2011.
Clifford-Napoleone, Amber R. *Queering Kansas City Jazz: Gender, Performance, and the
    History of a Scene*. Lincoln: University of Nebraska Press, 2018.
Dalferro, Alexandra Grace. "Shimmering Surfaces: An Ethnography of Silk Production
    in Surin, Thailand." PhD diss., Cornell University, 2021.
Darling, Frank C. "Student Protest and Political Change in Thailand." *Pacific Affairs* 47,
    no. 1 (1974): 5–19.
Davorn Sisavath. "The US Secret War in Laos: Constructing an Archive from Military
    Waste." *Radical History Review*, no. 133 (2019): 103–16.
De Kosnik, Abigail. "Perfect Covers: Filipino Musical Mimicry and Transmedia
    Performance." *Verge: Studies in Global Asias* 3, no. 1 (2017): 137–61.
Delson, Susan. *Soundies and the Changing Image of Black Americans on Screen One Dime
    at a Time*. Bloomington: Indiana University Press, 2021.
Devine, Kyle Ross. *Decomposed: The Political Ecology of Music*. Cambridge, MA: MIT
    Press, 2019.
Driggs, Frank, and Harris Lewine. *Black Beauty, White Heat: A Pictorial History of Clas-
    sic Jazz, 1920–1950*. New York: Da Capo, 1995.
Dyer, Jeffrey Michael. "Sounding the Dead in Cambodia: Cultivating Ethics, Generating
    Wellbeing, and Living with History through Music and Sound." PhD diss., Boston
    University, 2022.
Ellington, Duke. *Music Is My Mistress*. Boston: Da Capo, 1976.
Engels, Friedrich. *Socialism: Utopic and Scientific*. Translated by Edward Aveling (1892).
    In *Selected Works*, by Karl Marx and Friedrich Engels, vol. 3. Moscow: Progress, 1970.
Enloe, Cynthia. *Bananas, Beaches, and Bases: Making Feminist Sense of International
    Politics*. Berkeley: University of California Press, 1989.

"Entertainment Places Act, B.E. 2509." *Government Gazette* 83, no. 88 (October 4, 1966): 626.

Eyman, Scott. *The Speed of Sound: Hollywood and the Talkie Revolution*. New York: Simon and Schuster, 2015.

Feather, Leonard. *The Encyclopedia of Jazz*. New York: Da Capo, 1984.

Ferguson, Jane M. "Yesterday Once More: Tracking (Un)Popular Music in Contemporary Myanmar." *Journal of Burma Studies* 20, no. 2 (2016): 229–57.

Fineman, Daniel. *A Special Relationship: The United States and Military Government in Thailand, 1947–1958*. Honolulu: University of Hawaii Press, 1997.

Fleming, Crystal Marie. *Resurrecting Slavery: Racial Legacies and White Supremacy in France*. Philadelphia, PA: Temple University Press, 2017.

Garber, Eric. "A Spectacle in Color: The Lesbian and Gay Subculture of Jazz Age Harlem." In *Hidden from History: Reclaiming the Gay and Lesbian Past*, edited by Martin Duberman, Martha Vincus, and George Chauncey Jr., 318–31. New York: New American Library, 1989.

Garzoli, John. "Mawlam and Jazz in Intercultural Musical Synthesis." *Rian Thai: International Journal of Thai Studies* 11, no. 1 (2018): 1–18.

Geertz, Clifford. *The Development of the Javanese Economy: A Socio-Cultural Approach*. Cambridge, MA: Center for International Studies, Massachusetts Institute of Technology, 1956.

Gioia, Ted. *The History of Jazz*. New York: Oxford University Press, 1998.

Glissant, Édouard. *Caribbean Discourse: Selected Essays*. Translated by J. Michael Dash. Charlottesville, VA: Caraf Books, 1989.

Goldschmitt, Kaleb. *Bossa Mundo: Brazilian Music in Transnational Music Industries*. New York: Oxford University Press, 2020.

Goodwin, Gerald F. "Race in the Crucible of War: African American Soldiers and Race Relations in the 'Nam.'" PhD diss., Ohio University, 2014.

Govier, Trudy. *Taking Wrongs Seriously: Acknowledgement, Reconciliation, and the Politics of Sustainable Peace*. Amherst, NY: Humanity Books, 2006.

Haberkorn, Tyrell. *In Plain Sight: Impunity and Human Rights in Thailand*. Madison: University of Wisconsin Press, 2018.

Haraway, Donna. *Staying with the Trouble: Making Kin in the Chthulucene*. Durham, NC: Duke University Press, 2016.

Hartman, Saidiya. *Lose Your Mother: A Journey along the Atlantic Slave Route*. New York: Farrar, Straus and Giroux, 2007.

Hartman, Saidiya. *Scenes of Subjection: Terror, Slavery, and Self-Making in Nineteenth-Century America*. New York: Oxford University Press, 1997.

Hartman, Saidiya. *Wayward Lives, Beautiful Experiments: Intimate Histories of Riotous Black Girls, Troublesome Women, and Queer Radicals*. New York: W. W. Norton, 2019.

Heap, Chad. *Slumming: Sexual and Racial Encounters in American Nightlife, 1885–1940*. Chicago: University of Chicago Press, 2008.

Herzfeld, Michael. "The Absent Presence: Discourses of Cryptocolonialism." *South Atlantic Quarterly* 101, no. 4 (2002): 899–926.

Herzfeld, Michael. *Cultural Intimacy: Social Poetics in the Nation-State*. New York: Routledge, 2005.

Herzfeld, Michael. "Silence, Submission, and Subversion: Towards a Poetics of Womanhood." In *Contested Identities: Gender and Kinship in Modern Greece*, edited by Peter Loizos and Evthymios Papataxiarchis, 79–97. Princeton, NJ: Princeton University Press, 1991.

hooks, bell. "Eating the Other: Desire and Resistance." In *Black Looks: Race and Representation*, 21–40. Boston: South End, 1992.

Horn, Robert, Denis Grey, Nicholas Grossman, Jim Algie, Jeff Hodson, and Wesley Hsu. *Americans in Thailand*. Kuala Lumpur: Éditions Didier Millet, 2015.

Jackson, Peter. "An American Death in Bangkok: The Murder of Darrell Berrigan and the Hybrid Origins of Gay Identity in 1960s Thailand." *GLQ: A Journal of Lesbian and Gay Studies* 5, no. 3 (1999): 361–411.

Jackson, Peter. "An Explosion of Thai Identities: Global Queering and Re-imagining Queer Theory." *Culture, Health, and Sexuality* 2, no. 4 (2000): 405–24.

Jackson, Peter. *First Queer Voices from Thailand: Uncle Go's Advice Columns for Gays, Lesbians and Kathoeys*. Hong Kong: Hong Kong University Press, 2016.

Jackson, Peter. "Non-normative Sex/Gender Categories in the Theravada Buddhist Scriptures." *Australian Humanities Review*, no. 1 (April 1996). https://web.archive.org/web/20120224134527/http://rspas.anu.edu.au/papers/pah/theravada.html.

Jaji, Tsitsi Ella. *Africa in Stereo: Modernism, Music, and Pan-African Solidarity*. New York: Oxford University Press, 2014.

Janit Feangfu. "(Ir)resistably Modern: The Construction of Modern Thai Identities in Thai Literature during the Cold War Era, 1958–1976." PhD diss., University of London, School of Oriental and African Studies, 2011.

Johnson, Andrew. *Mekong Dreaming: Life and Death along a Changing River*. Durham, NC: Duke University Press, 2020.

Jones, Andrew. *Yellow Music: Media Culture and Colonial Modernity in the Chinese Jazz Age*. Durham, NC: Duke University Press, 2001.

Joslin, Les. *Pattaya Beach and Thailand: Liberty Information Guide, Overseas Diplomacy Program*. N.p.: USS Kitty Hawk Overseas Diplomacy Council, 1978.

กมลธรรม เกื้อบุตร [Kamontam Kuabutr]. "ดนตรีแจ๊สในสังคมไทยในยุคเริ่มต้น" [The birth of jazz music in Thai society]. นเรศวรวิจัย [nárêeswɔɔnwíʔcay], no. 12 (2016): 1995–2006.

Käng, Dredge Byung'chu. "Conceptualizing Thai Genderscapes: Transformation and Continuity in the Thai Sex/Gender System." In *Contemporary Socio-cultural and Political Perspectives in Thailand*, edited by Pranee Liamputtong, 409–429. Dordrecht: Springer, 2014.

Käng, Dredge Byung'chu. "Surfing the Korean Wave: Wonder Gays and the Crisis of Thai Masculinity." *Visual Anthropology* 31, nos. 1–2 (2018): 45–65.

Kanjana Hubik Thepboriruk. "Dressing Thai: Fashion, Nation, and the Construction of Thainess, 19th Century–Present." *Journal of Applied History*, 2, no. 1–2 (September 2020): 1–17.

Keeling, Kara. "Looking for M—: Queer Temporality, Black Political Possibility, and Poetry from the Future." *GLQ: A Journal of Lesbian and Gay Studies* 15, no. 4 (2009): 565–82.

Kelley, Andrea. "'A Revolution in the Atmosphere': The Dynamics of Site and Screen in 1940s Soundies." *Cinema Journal* 54, no. 2 (2015): 72–93.

Kelley, Andrea. "A Swing Half-Breed." In *Soundies, Jukebox Films, and the Shift to Small-Screen Culture*, edited by Andrea J. Kelley, 89–113. New Brunswick, NJ: Rutgers University Press, 2018.

Kelley, Kristen. "Patriarchy, Empire, and Ping Pong Shows: The Political Economy of Sex Tourism in Thailand." PhD diss., Columbia College Chicago, 2015.

Keppy, Peter. *Tales of Southeast Asia's Jazz Age: Filipinos, Indonesians and Popular Culture, 1920–1936*. Singapore: National University of Singapore Press, 2019.

Kerman, Joseph. "How We Got into Analysis, and How to Get Out." *Critical Inquiry* 7, no. 2 (1980): 311–31.

Kidron, Carol. "Alterity and the Particular Limits of Universalism: Comparing Jewish-Israeli Holocaust and Canadian-Cambodian Genocide Legacies." *Current Anthropology* 53, no. 6 (2012): 723–54.

Kislenko, Arne. "A Not So Silent Partner: Thailand's Role in Covert Operations, Counter-Insurgency, and the Wars in Indochina." *Journal of Conflict Studies* 24, no. 1 (2004): 65–96.

Klein, Christina. *Cold War Orientalism: Asia in the Middlebrow Imagination, 1940–1961*. Berkeley: University of California Press, 2003.

Klima, Alan. *The Funeral Casino: Meditation, Massacre, and Exchange with the Dead in Thailand*. Princeton, NJ: Princeton University Press, 2002.

Kowal, Rebekah. *Dancing the World Smaller: Staging Globalism in Mid-century America*. New York: Oxford University Press, 2019.

Krull, Germaine. *Tales from Siam*. New York: Adventurers Club, 1966.

Krull, Germaine, and Dorothea Melchers. *Bangkok: Siam's City of Angels*. London: Robert Hale, 1964.

Kurlantzick, Joshua. *The Ideal Man: The Tragedy of Jim Thompson and the American Way of War*. Hoboken, NJ: Wiley, 2010.

Lair, Meredith. *Armed with Abundance: Consumerism and Soldiering in the Vietnam War*. Chapel Hill: University of North Carolina Press, 2011.

Larson, Scott. "Laid Open: Examining Genders in Early America." In *Trans Historical: Gender Plurality before the Modern*, edited by Greta LaFleur, Masha Raskolnikov, and Anna Klosowska, 350–365. Ithaca, NY: Cornell University Press, 2021.

LeBlanc, Eric S., and Bob Eagle. *Blues: A Regional Exploration*. Santa Barbara, CA: ABC-CLIO, 2013.

Levan, Patricia D. "Curtailing Thailand's Child Prostitution through an International Conscience." *American University International Law Review* 9, no. 3 (1994): 869–912.

Lewis, George. "Improvised Music after 1950: Afrological and Eurological Perspectives." *Black Music Research Journal* 16, no. 1 (1996): 91–122.

Litchfield, Whiting, Bowne, and Associates. *Greater Bangkok Plan, 2533: Final Report of Litchfield Whiting Bowne and Associates to the Minister of Interior*. Bangkok: Ministry of Interior, 1960.

Loos, Tamara. "Respectability's Edge: Transnational Sex Radical René Guyon." *Sexualities* 23, nos. 1–2 (2020): 146–69.

Loos, Tamara. *Subject Siam: Family, Law, and Colonial Modernity in Thailand*. Ithaca, NY: Cornell University Press, 2006.

Lowe, Lisa. *The Intimacies of Four Continents*. Durham, NC: Duke University Press, 2015.

MacGillivray, Scott, and Ted Okuda. *The Soundies Book: A Revised and Expanded Guide*. Bloomington, IN: iUniverse Books, 2007.

MacLachlan, Heather. *Burma's Pop Music Industry: Creators, Distributors, Censors*. Rochester, NY: Rochester University Press, 2011.

Maher, Kristen Hill, and Megan Lafferty. "White Migrant Masculinities in Thailand and the Paradoxes of Western Privilege." *Social and Cultural Geography* 15, no. 4 (2014): 427–48.

Mahon, Maureen. *Black Diamond Queens: African American Women and Rock and Roll*. Durham, NC: Duke University Press, 2020.

Mao, Yuping, and Rukhsana Ahmed. *Culture, Migration, and Health Communication in a Global Context*. New York: Routledge, 2017.

Massey, Doreen. *Spatial Divisions of Labour: Social Structures and the Geography of Production*. London: Red Globe, 1995.

McGilligan, Patrick. *Oscar Micheaux: The Great and Only; The Life of America's First Black Filmmaker*. New York: Harper Perennial, 2008.

McGinley, Paige. *Staging the Blues: From Tent Shows to Tourism*. Durham, NC: Duke University Press, 2014.

Mignolo, Walter D. "Coloniality of Power and De-colonial Thinking." *Cultural Studies* 21, nos. 2–3 (2007): 155–67.

Miller, Jacob, and Vincent Del Casino Jr. "Spectacle, Tourism and the Performance of Everyday Geopolitics." *Politics and Space* 38, nos. 7–8 (2020): 1412–28.

Mills, Mary Beth. *Thai Women in the Global Labor Force: Consuming Desires, Contested Selves*. New Brunswick, NJ: Rutgers University Press, 1999.

Morris, Rosalind. "Educating Desire: Thailand, Transnationalism, and Transgression." *Social Text*, no. 52/53 (1997): 53–79.

Morris, Rosalind. "Three Sexes and Four Sexualities: Redressing the Discourses on Gender and Sexuality in Contemporary Thailand." *positions* 2, no. 1 (1994): 15–43.

Mostafanezhad, Mary, and Roger Norum. "Towards a Geopolitics of Tourism." *Annals of Tourism Research* 61, no. C (2016): 226–28.

Musse, Charles, Jane Marie Gaines, and Pearl Bowser, eds. *Oscar Micheaux and His Circle: African-American Filmmaking and Race Cinema of the Silent Era*. Bloomington: Indiana University Press, 2001.

Nagel, Amanda. "Democracy for Whom? The Spanish-American War, the Philippine-American War, World War I, and the NAACP." PhD diss., University of Mississippi, 2014.

Napat Chaipraditkul. "Thailand: Beauty and Globalized Self-Identity through Cosmetic Therapy and Skin Lightening." *Ethics in Science and Environmental Politics* 13, no. 1 (2013): 23–37.

Nattapol Wisuttipat. "Spicy: Gendered Practices of Queer Men in Thai Classical String Music." PhD diss., University of California, Riverside, 2022.

Nicholas, Cheryl L. "Gaydar: Eye-Gaze as Identity Recognition among Gay Men and Lesbians." *Sexuality and Culture* 8, no. 1 (2004): 60–86.

นพดล ดวงพร (ณรงค์ พงษ์ภาพ): พ.ศ. 2484–2562 [Noppadon Duangporn (Narong Pongpap): 1941–2019]. Funeral book/cremation volume.

Ochoa Gautier, Ana María. *Aurality: Listening and Knowledge in Nineteenth-Century Colombia.* Durham, NC: Duke University Press, 2014.

Olson, Grant A. "Thai Cremation Volumes: A Brief History of a Unique Genre of Literature." *Asian Folklore Studies* 51, no. 2 (1992), 279–94.

Ortner, Sherry B. "Is Female to Male as Nature Is to Culture?" In *Woman, Culture, and Society*, edited by M. Z. Rosaldo and L. Lamphere, 68–87. Stanford, CA: Stanford University Press, 1974.

Pahole Sookkasikon. "Bangkok Is Burning: Queer Cultural Productions of Thainess in Diaspora." PhD diss., University of Hawaii at Manoa, 2018.

ผกามาศ ปรีชา [Pakamas Pricha]. *ดิฉันไม่ใช่โสเภณี* (I am not a whore). Bangkok: สำนัก พิมพ์ บางหลวง, 2537 [1994].

Parkorn Wangpaiboonkit. "Sounding Civilization: Race and Sovereignty in the Imperial Music of Siam." PhD diss., University of California, Berkeley, 2023.

Pasuk Phongpaichit. *From Peasant Girls to Bangkok Masseuses.* Geneva: International Labour Office, 1982.

Patcharin Lapanun. *Love, Money and Obligation: Transnational Marriage in a Northeastern Thai Village.* Singapore: National University of Singapore Press, 2019.

Patcharin Lapanun and Eric C. Thompson. "Masculinity, Matrilineality and Transnational Marriage." *Journal of Mekong Societies* 14, no. 2 (2018): 1–19.

Pattana Kitiarsa. "An Ambiguous Intimacy: *Farang* as Siamese Occidentalism." In *The Ambiguous Allure of the West: Traces of the Colonial in Thailand*, edited by Rachel V. Harrison and Peter A. Jackson, 57–74. Hong Kong: Hong Kong University Press, 2010.

Phillips, Matthew. *Thailand in the Cold War.* New York: Routledge, 2015.

Phimmasone M. Rattanasengchanh. "Thai Hearts and Minds: The Public Diplomacy and Public Relations Programs of the United States Information Service and Thai Ministry of Interior, 1957–1979." PhD diss., Ohio University, 2019.

Pilzer, Joshua. *Hearts of Pine: Songs in the Lives of Three Korean Survivors of the Japanese "Comfort Women."* New York: Oxford University Press, 2012.

Pitchaya Sudbanthad. *Bangkok Wakes to Rain.* New York: Riverhead, 2019.

Porphant Ouyyanont. "The Vietnam War and Tourism in Bangkok's Development, 1960–70." *Southeast Asian Studies* 39, no. 2. (2001): 157–87.

Povinelli, Elizabeth. *The Empire of Love: Toward a Theory of Intimacy, Genealogy, and Carnality.* Durham, NC: Duke University Press, 2006.

Pratt, Mary Louise. "Arts of the Contact Zone." *Profession* (1991): 33–40.

Provenzano, Catherine. "Emotional Signals: Digital Tuning Software and the Meanings of Pop Music Voices." PhD diss., New York University, 2019.

Quinn, Joanna. *The Politics of Acknowledgement: Truth Commissions in Uganda and Haiti.* Vancouver: University of British Columbia Press, 2010.

Radom Setteeton. "Street Administration in the Bangkok Metropolitan Area." Master's thesis, Thammasat University, 2503 [1960].

Ramsey, Guthrie. *The Amazing Bud Powell: Black Genius, Jazz History, and the Challenge of Bebop*. Berkeley: University of California Press, 2013.

Randolph, R. Sean. *The United States and Thailand Alliance Dynamics, 1950–1985*. Berkeley: Institute of East Asian Studies, University of California, 1986.

Robinson, Dylan. *Hungry Listening: Resonant Theory for Indigenous Studies*. Minneapolis: University of Minnesota Press, 2020.

Rodabaugh, Louis D. "My Long and Rewarding Acquaintanceship with the Great Edward Kennedy." Unpublished manuscript, 1994. PDF.

Rodríguez, Juana María. *Sexual Futures, Queer Gestures, and Other Latina Longings*. New York: New York University Press, 2014.

รงค์ วงษ์สวรรค์ [Rong Wongsawan]. สัตหีบ: ยังไม่มีลาก่อน [Sattahip: There's no goodbye yet]. Bangkok: สามัญชน [Samanchon Books], 2009.

Ross, Alex. *Listen to This*. New York: Picador, 2011.

Ruth, Richard A. *In Buddha's Company: Thai Soldiers in the Vietnam War*. Honolulu: University of Hawaii Press, 2010.

Sanders, Doug. "Some Say Thailand Is a Gay Paradise." In *Gay Tourism: Culture, Identity and Sex*, edited by Carry Callister, Michael Luongo, and Stephen Clift, 42–62. London: Continuum Books, 2002.

Saranphon Poltecha. "Stereotypical Depiction of Women in Thai Films." Master's thesis, Thammasat University, 2017.

Schenker, Fritz. "Circuit Tour of the Globe." *Journal of the Society for American Music* 13, no. 1 (2019): 1–26.

Schenker, Fritz. "Empire of Syncopation: Music, Race, and Labor in Colonial Asia's Jazz Age." PhD diss., University of Wisconsin–Madison, 2016.

สีฟ้า [Si Fa]. ข้าวนอกนา (Rice outside the field). Bangkok: บำรุงสาส์น, 2516 [1973].

Simpson, Audra. "Ethnographic Refusal: Indigeneity, 'Voice' and Colonial Citizenship." *Junctures: The Journal for Thematic Dialogue*, no. 9 (2007): 67–80.

Simpson, Audra. *Mohawk Interruptus: Political Life across the Borders of Settler States*. Durham, NC: Duke University Press, 2014.

Sirijit Sunanta and Leonora C. Angeles. "From Rural Life to Transnational Wife: Agrarian Transition, Gender Mobility, and Intimate Globalization in Transnational Marriages in Northeast Thailand." *Gender, Place and Culture* 20, no. 6 (2013): 699–717.

Skinner, William G. *Chinese Society in Thailand: An Analytical History*. Ithaca, NY: Cornell University Press, 1957.

Sopranzetti, Claudio. *Owners of the Map: Motorcycle Taxi Drivers, Mobility, and Politics in Bangkok*. Berkeley: University of California Press, 2018.

Southern, Eileen. *The Music of Black Americans: A History*. New York: W. W. Norton, 1971.

Stephens, Vincent Lamar. *Rocking the Closet: How Little Richard, Johnnie Ray, Liberace, and Johnny Mathis Queered Pop Music*. Urbana: University of Illinois Press, 2019.

Steptoe, Tyina. "Big Mama Thornton, Little Richard, and the Queer Roots of Rock 'n' Roll." *American Quarterly* 70, no. 1 (2018): 55–77.

Stoler, Ann Laura. *Along the Archival Grain: Epistemic Anxieties and Colonial Common Sense*. Princeton, NJ: Princeton University Press, 2010.

"สงครามเวียดนาม สู่ตำนานเมียเช่า เมียฝรั่ง และลูกครึ่งในสังคมไทย" [The Vietnam
    War and the struggles of *mia chao, mia farang,* and half children in Thai society].
    ประวัติศาสตร์นอกตำรา [Untold history], episode 129, February 11, 2022. https://www
    .youtube.com/watch?v=Rs5yNX5N9ho.
Subcommittee on US Security Agreements and Commitments Abroad. *Thailand, Laos,
    Cambodia, and Vietnam: April 1973.* Washington, DC: Government Printing Office,
    1973. https://li.proquest.com/elhpdf/histcontext/CMP-1973-FOR-0017.pdf.
Sudina Paungpetch. "Domino by Design: Thai-U.S. Relations during the Vietnam War."
    PhD diss., Texas A&M University, 2011.
Surachat Bamrungsuk. "United States Foreign Policy and Thai Military Rule, 1947–77."
    PhD diss., Cornell University, 1988.
Sykes, Jim. *The Musical Gift: Sonic Generosity in Post-war Sri Lanka.* New York: Oxford
    University Press, 2018.
Symington Subcommittee Hearings. October 30, 1969. In *Foreign Relations of the United
    States, 1969–1976.* Vol. 20, *Southeast Asia, 1969–1972,* edited by Daniel J. Lawler,
    196–97. Washington, DC: Department of State, 2006.
Szwed, John F. "Musical Style and Racial Conflict." *Phylon* 27, no. 4 (1966): 358–66.
ต๊ะ ท่าอิฐ [Ta Tha-It]. ตะลุยเกย์คลับ (ไก๊ด์บางกอกชุด7) [Heading into a gay club (Bang-
    kok guide number 7)]. Bangkok: Baankit, 1976.
Talusan, Mary. *Instruments of Empire: Filipino Musicians, Black Soldiers, and Military
    Band Music during US Colonization of the Philippines.* Jackson: University of Missis-
    sippi Press, 2021.
Taylor, Diana. *The Archive and the Repertoire.* Durham, NC: Duke University Press, 2003.
Teeratorn Likhitphongsathorn and Pattama Sappapan. "A Study of English Code-Mixing
    and Code-Switching in Thai Pop Songs." PhD diss., Language Institute, Thammasat
    University, 2013.
Terry, Wallace. *Bloods: An Oral History of the Vietnam War.* New York: Random House,
    1984.
Thak Chaloemtiarana. *Thailand: The Politics of Despotic Paternalism.* Cornell, NY: Cor-
    nell Southeast Asia Program Publications, 2007.
ทินวัฒน์ สร้อยกุดเรือ [Thinnawat Sroikudrua]. "'ดิฉัน (เมียฝรั่ง)ไม่ใช่โสเภณี': ภาษากับ
    อัตลักษณ์ ในวาทกรรมสาธารณะ" ["I (a *farang* wife) am not a whore": Language and
    identity in public discourse]. *Journal of Graduate Study in Humanities and Social Sci-
    ences* 5, no. 1 (2016): 37–58.
Thompson, Eric C., Pattana Kitiarsa, and Suriya Smutkupt. "Transnational Relationships,
    Farang-Isaan Couples, and Rural Transformation." *Journal of Sociology and Anthropol-
    ogy* 37, no. 1 (2018): 95–126.
Thongchai Winichakul. *Moments of Silence: The Unforgetting of the October 6, 1976, Mas-
    sacre in Bangkok.* Honolulu: University of Hawaii Press, 2020.
Thongchai Winichakul. *Siam Mapped: A History of the Geo-body of a Nation.* Honolulu:
    University of Hawaii Press, 1997.
Tinsley, Omise'eke Natasha. "Black Atlantic, Queer Atlantic: Queer Imaginings of the
    Middle Passage." *GLQ: A Journal of Lesbian and Gay Studies* 14, nos. 2–3 (2008):
    191–215.

Treitler, Vilna Bashi. *The Ethnic Project: Transforming Racial Fiction into Ethnic Factions.* Chicago: University of Chicago Press, 2013.

Trenka, Susie. *Jumping the Color Line: Vernacular Jazz Dance in American Film, 1929–1945.* Bloomington: Indiana University Press, 2021.

Trouillot, Michel-Rolph. *Silencing the Past: Power and the Production of History.* Boston: Beacon, 1995.

Truong, Thanh-Đam. *Sex, Money, and Morality: Prostitution and Tourism in Southeast Asia.* London: Zed, 1990.

Tucker, Sherrie. *Swing Shift: "All-Girl" Bands of the 1940s.* Durham, NC: Duke University Press, 2001.

Tucker, Sherrie. "When Did Jazz Go Straight? A Queer Question for Jazz Studies." *Critical Studies in Improvisation* 4, no. 2 (2008): 1–16.

Van Esterik, Penny. *Materializing Thailand.* New York: Routledge, 2000.

Visisya Pinthongvijayakul. "Performing Alterity of Desire: Bodiliness and Sexuality in Spirit Mediumship in Northeast Thailand." *American Anthropologist* 121, no. 1 (2019): 101–12.

Von Eschen, Penny. *Satchmo Blows Up the World: Jazz Ambassadors Play the Cold War.* Cambridge, MA: Harvard University Press, 2004.

Wald, Gayle F. *Shout, Sister, Shout! The Untold Story of Rock-and-Roll Trailblazer Sister Rosetta Tharpe.* Boston: Beacon, 2008.

Walser, Robert. *Running with the Devil: Power, Gender, and Madness in Heavy Metal Music.* Hanover, NH: University Press of New England, 1993.

Wasana Wongsurawat. *The Crown and the Capitalists: The Ethnic Chinese and the Founding of the Thai Nation.* Seattle: University of Washington Press, 2019.

Weisman, Jan R., "Rice outside the Paddy: The Form and Function of Hybridity in a Thai Novel." *Crossroads: An Interdisciplinary Journal of Southeast Asian Studies* 11, no. 1 (1997): 51–78.

Westad, Odd Arne. *The Global Cold War: Third World Interventions and the Making of Our Times.* Cambridge: Cambridge University Press, 2017.

White, Luise. *The Comforts of Home: Prostitution in Colonial Nairobi.* Chicago: University of Chicago Press, 1990.

Wilson, Ara. *Intimate Economies of Bangkok: Tomboys, Tycoons, and Avon Ladies in the Global City.* Berkeley: University of California Press, 2004.

Wiwat Mungkandi and Ansil Ramsay. *U.S.-Thailand Relations: Changing Political, Strategic, and Economic Factors.* Berkeley: University of California, Institute of East Asian Studies, 1988.

Wright, Richard. *The Color Curtain.* In *Black Power: Three Books from Exile.* New York: HarperCollins, 2008.

Index

Page references in *italics* indicate illustrations.

performance and performativity: Black performativity, 54–55; of excess, 33

Petteys, David, 143

Phetchaburi Road (Bangkok), 70, 71, 77, 154. *See also* New Phetchaburi Road

"Phetchaburi Tat Mai" (Jittima), 189–90

Phet Phin Tong (musical group), 153, 155–56, 157, 160, 168, 205

Phibun Songkhram, 82, 184

Philippine Constabulary Band, 158

Philippines, 98, 158, 159–60, 222n110

Phillips, Matthew, 214n11, 225n66

phin (musical instrument), 152, 153, 155, 156

phleeng phůa chiiwít (songs for life), 190

phleeng såakon (international music), 150

Phloen Phromden, 172, 221n85

phûu chaay, 183, 186

piano playing: left hand (Rocco's), 33, 58, 60, 93; in ragtime, 34; stride piano, 31

Pilzer, Joshua, 205

Pitchaya Sudbanthad, 5, 6, 8, 113, 188–89

policing, 122–23, 195–99

Pong Prida, *179*

pop music, 139, 149, 158

Por Chalat Noi, 141, 152

Pote Sarasin, 71

Powell, Bud, 64

Pratunam (intersection, Bangkok), 78

President Hotel (Bangkok), 115

Presley, Elvis, 92, 94

primitivism, 73

privatization: of economy, 119–21, 122; nightlife and, 119–20

privilege: *farang* privilege, 17, 19, 117, 118, 122, 123, 127, 130–31, 138, 169, 203, 216n65; tourism and, 19

progressive politics, 190

propaganda, Bhumibol's representation in, 132

protests, 139–40, 190, 191, 225n60

psychedelic music, 58, 150, 153, 155, 156

psychoanalysis, 198, 204

"Pua negro" (Pong), *179*

public space, 32

Punyisa Silparassamee, 24

queer experience: exclusion from military, 181; for lesbians, 45, 182, 185; nightlife for, 181, 182, 186, 192; queer Blackness, 181; queer-

phobia, 181, 186, 193, 197; Rocco's, 15, 54, 61, 107, 183, 188, 194–95, 198–99; in Thailand, 17, 187. *See also* homophobia

queerness: death connected to, 183; eyes as signifying, 53–54; *farang* and, 183; gay relations, 183; gay venues, 182, 186–88; in jazz venues, 31; shame and, 182; Thai reception of, 182

queer performance, 45, 53–54

queer studies, gaps in, 15

race: hierarchy of, 17, 62, 176; music performance through lens of, 40, 47; telling history of, 202–3. *See also* Blackness

racism: anti-Black racism, 196; blackface, 179; essentialism and, 96; extraction (of labor) and, 159–60; Jim Crow laws, 64; mythmaking and, 39; nightlife and, 175; racial capitalism, 176; segregation, 164–65; stereotypes in advertisements, 133–34; structural racism, 174–75; wildness as descriptor, 48; yellowface, 159

radio, 143, 150, 151, 153

Radom Setteeton, 84–85, 87

Rajdamnoen Road (Bangkok), 159

Ramsey, Guthrie, 47, 64

Randolph, A. Philip, 59

Randolph, Sean, 79, 154

records (media format), 151, 153

Redman, Don, 59

refusal, ethnographic (Simpson), 104–5

reparations, 208n38

rest and recuperation program (R&R), 9, 77; economics behind, 121; as empowering troops, 122; Filipino music and, 157, 159; global imaginary and, 133; limits on, 125–26; live music and, 161; New Phetchaburi Road and, 70, 126–27, 151–52; R&R memorandum of understanding (MoU), 123, 124, 126, 127, 131; venues for, 159; visitors from Vietnam for, 76. *See also* Americans in Thailand

rhythm, syncopation, 153, 155, 159

rice farming, 163

Rice outside the field (*Khâaw nɔ̀ɔk naa*), 172–73, 174, 176–78

Richard, Cliff, 150, 160

Richard, Little, 33, 34, 49, 50, 51, 52–54, 58, 92

Turner, Ike, 91, 92
Turner, Stephan, 180
"Turn On That Red Hot Heat (Burn Your Blues Away)" (Berigan), 43
Twilight (gay bar, Bangkok), 186

Ubon Musicians Legend (UML) (Facebook page), *162*, 162–63, *164*
Ubon Ratchathani (Thailand), 121, 152
Udon Thani (Thailand), 121, 140, 145, 148
ugliness, 94–95
United Service Organizations (USO), 5
United States: Blackness in, 173; Joint US Military Advisory Group Thailand (JUS-MAGTHAI), 102, 126, 154; military support in Thailand, 11; nightlife in, 23; patronage of Thailand, 67; Philippines (occupation of), 158; violence against Asian and Asian-presenting women, 220n43. *See also* Thai-US relations
US Operations Mission (USOM), 79–80, 82, 84, 86, 151, 154

Vajiravudh (king), 81
Van Esterik, Penny, 8, 128
vaudeville, 158
veterans, trauma triggers for, 12
Veterans of Foreign Wars (VFW) Post, 12
Vietnam War. *See* American war in Vietnam
Vinaya (clerical code), 184
violence, state, 102
V.I.P. Band, 161, *162*, 163, 165, 166
visibility and invisibility, 107. *See also* Rocco, Maurice—life: disappearance
Visisya Pinthongvijayakul, 181, 185
Vogues of 1938 (Wanger), 43–44, 45

Wachtveitl, Kurt, 197
Wanger, Walter, 43–44, 45

war. *See* American war in Vietnam; World War II
Washington, Dinah, 4
waterways, 77–78, 82, 85, 86
Weerawat Somnuek, 140
Weisman, Jan, 173, 174, 176
western music, 143, 150, 151
Whiskey Jazz (soul bar, Bangkok), 175
white audiences, 44, 45, 56
white supremacy, 96
"Whole Lot of Shakin' Going On" (Lewis), 55, 56
wildness, 48, 54, 56
Williams, Robert Franklin, 98
Williams, Tennessee, 167
Wilson, Ara, 9, 19, 73, 137
Wilson, John S., 52
Winchell, Walter, 59
Windsor Coffee House (Bangkok), 115, *116*
withdrawal from Thailand (US), 23, 24, 189–90, 191, 206
women: as attraction for tourism, 182; *farang* and, *163*; gendered expectations, 155; instrumentalization by wartime development, 128; labor of, 136–37, 138–41, 148; *mia farang* (*farang* wife), 138, 147, 148; musical experiences, 47; policing of, 122, 123; protests by, 139–40; Thainess signified by, 128
worldliness, 114
World War II, 21–22, 23, 63
Wren, Harry, 110
Wright, Billy, 52
Wright, Richard, 99, 158

yellowface, 159
Yodh Warong, 152, 163

"Zombie" (The Cranberries), 150
ZuDrangMa (record label), 166

www.ingramcontent.com/pod-product-compliance
Lightning Source LLC
Chambersburg PA
CBHW032347280326
41935CB00008B/476